SPECIAL FORCES COMMANDER

For Peter

Happy the Man, and happy he alone,
He who can call today his own:
He who, secure within, can say,
Tomorrow do thy worst, for I have lived today.

Horace

By the same author

The Royal Rifle Volunteers: On Operations
(The Royal Rifle Volunteers, 2005)

SPECIAL FORCES COMMANDER

The Life and Wars of Peter Wand-Tetley OBE MC
Commando, SAS, SOE and Paratrooper

Mike Scott

by

Michael Scott

Foreword by
General Sir David Richards GCB CBE DSO ADC Gen

Pen & Sword
MILITARY

First published in Great Britain in 2011 by
PEN & SWORD MILITARY
An imprint of
Pen & Sword Books Ltd
47 Church Street
Barnsley
South Yorkshire
S70 2AS

ISBN 978-1-84884-673-9

A CIP catalogue record for this book is
available from the British Library

Typeset in 10.5/12.5pt Palatino by
Concept, Huddersfield, West Yorkshire

Printed and bound in England by CPI

Pen & Sword Books Ltd incorporates the Imprints of Pen & Sword
Aviation, Pen & Sword Family History, Pen & Sword Maritime, Pen &
Sword Military, Pen & Sword Discovery, Wharncliffe Local History,
Wharncliffe True Crime, Wharncliffe Transport, Pen & Sword Select,
Pen & Sword Military Classics, Leo Cooper, The Praetorian Press,
Remember When, Seaforth Publishing and Frontline Publishing

For a complete list of Pen & Sword titles please contact
PEN & SWORD BOOKS LIMITED
47 Church Street, Barnsley, South Yorkshire, S70 2AS, England
E-mail: enquiries@pen-and-sword.co.uk
Website: www.pen-and-sword.co.uk

Contents

Acknowledgements

The year 2010 was the seventieth anniversary of the formation, in 1940, of the Special Operations Executive, the Army Commandos and the Parachute Regiment, with the Special Air Service Regiment formed from the Commandos the following year. All owe their existence in large part to Churchill's vision and determination to hit back at Hitler's Germany by unconventional as well as conventional means. I should therefore like to thank Pen and Sword, and its staff, especially Henry Wilson, Richard Doherty, Jon Wilkinson, Emma Howe and Matt Jones for publishing this book to mark this special anniversary and Peter Wand-Tetley's odyssey through these four unique organizations.

I should like to thank General Sir David Richards, Chief of the Defence Staff, for writing the Foreword to this book. This is the second of my books for which he has considerately taken the time to pen a kind word or two, and his wholehearted support is very much appreciated.

My gratitude also goes to Philip Best who has spent countless hours checking the typescript. This is the second occasion upon which he has gallantly 'volunteered for the guardroom' in this respect. I should like to thank him for his considerable care and patience, for the book is undoubtedly a great deal better for his numerous suggestions, corrections and wise counsel. Nonetheless any mistakes made, which given the sweep of history is a distinct possibility, are entirely mine.

Charles Owen of *The Daily Telegraph* is warmly thanked for drafting Peter Wand-Tetley's obituary. My gratitude also goes to Ron Youngman, General Secretary of the Commando Association, who was most helpful in my early research enquiries at the time of Peter Wand-Tetley's death, and to Jim Condon at the Army Medal Office, who was so helpful in sorting out the matter of Peter Wand-Tetley's missing medals.

Many thanks to Terry Rogers, Archivist to Marlborough College, for his hospitality and assistance, and I am also most grateful to him and Marlborough College for allowing me to reproduce the photograph of the College's victorious 'Shooting VIII' of 1935. Thanks also to Kate

Thompson, Archivist to Downing College, Cambridge University, who was more than helpful, and to Justine Taylor, Archivist to the Honourable Artillery Company, who was similarly obliging. I am indebted to the staff at the National Archives, and to the Trustees of the Imperial War Museum, who kindly permitted me to make use of a number of photographs from their collection.

My thanks go to Michael Cornwell, Curator of the Rifles Museum, Salisbury, for allowing me access to the Wiltshire Regiment archives. My gratitude goes to Bob Kelly, Curator of the Royal Army Physical Training Corps Museum, Aldershot, for his kind assistance, and also to Ted Molyneux, Curator of the National Rifle Association Museum, Bisley. Thank you to Chris Dodkin and Grenville Bint at the SAS Regimental Association for their assistance. I am also very grateful to Jon Baker and Becks Skinner at the Airborne Assault Museum, Duxford, and to John Greenacre for related Parachute Regiment research advice. I also wish to thank John Skliros for rising to the challenge of producing a prototype dust jacket for the book at very short notice.

The family have been unstintingly supportive, particularly Peter Wand-Tetley's widow, Felicia, his son, Charles, and his cousin, Angela Carter, all of whom helped me with the first and last chapters of the book and allowed me to reproduce family photographs. My wife, Debby, did sterling work in producing the maps for the book, for which I owe her a debt of gratitude, and thanks also go to the remainder of my family for their support and encouragement throughout.

Mike Scott
Khartoum
January 2011

Foreword

By General Sir David Richards GCB CBE DSO ADC Gen
Chief of the Defence Staff

As both Chief of the Defence Staff and as an Army commando myself, it gives me tremendous pleasure to write the Foreword to this book on Peter Wand-Tetley and his exceptional service during the Second World War, especially since I know the author Mike Scott very well. The publication of this meticulously researched book is particularly timely. Not only in terms of marking the Seventieth Anniversary of the formation of the unique organizations in which Peter Wand-Tetley served, and because it is appropriate that we remember the service and sacrifice of our officers and soldiers of yesteryear, but also because many of the themes within the narrative have a resonance and relevance for us today.

For many in this country the Second World War may seem like ancient history. However, today's generation of British Army senior officers and warrant officers were born closer to that conflict than they were to the beginning of the decade-long war on terror, in the aftermath of the 2001 attack on New York's World Trade Centre, in which they now find themselves engaged. Peter Wand-Tetley was self-evidently an exemplar of professional soldiering at its best: selfless, brave and devoted to duty. Sadly as the years pass fewer of those, like him, who fought in the Second World War survive to tell their tale. Yet, in setting such a fine example for us, their legacy most assuredly lives on.

I am certain that Peter Wand-Tetley would instantly recognize in today's generation of soldiers, as they serve their country in the inhospitable and challenging environments of Afghanistan, Iraq, Africa and elsewhere, the same professionalism and commitment to others he displayed. I sense he would draw much reassuring comfort from this and that he would agree that these men and women are worthy successors to those, like him, who served their country so gallantly during the Second World War. It is also interesting to note that many of his old stamping grounds – the Balkans and the Middle East – have also been recent operational theatres for today's generation of British soldiers.

Peter Wand-Tetley's achievements and those of his wartime comrades-in-arms have been recorded for posterity in this book, as has the formative history of the unique organizations in which they served. All who have been associated with or taken an interest in such history owe a debt of gratitude to the author who has so eruditely and painstakingly written this absorbing narrative. With this book – a work of real and enduring importance – he has made a significant contribution to a unique element of Second World War history; in particular the part played by the SOE in Greece, which still lacks an official history. I hope that this book may prove to be a catalyst in this respect.

A great deal of credit must therefore go to Mike Scott for seizing the moment and recording for posterity the remarkable story of Peter Wand-Tetley, whose wartime service is an example of British soldiering at its best and whose legacy is a very fine one indeed. His tale has been vividly brought to life in this important and engrossing book. I wholeheartedly commend it to all who take a justifiable pride in the British Army.

London
January 2011

Preface

Peter Wand-Tetley died on 16 March 2003. His widow, Felicia, found amongst his personal papers a 'Narrative Account of a Mission to Peloponnese' which he penned upon returning from a fourteen-month SOE mission behind enemy lines in Greece. Felicia had not previously been aware of the report's existence, but it was evident that here was a compelling tale. So I contacted Charles Owen of *The Daily Telegraph*, who expressed an enthusiastic interest which resulted in the obituary that appeared in the newspaper on 22 May 2003. In the course of researching for the obituary I also contacted Jim Condon at the Army Medal Office, for I suspected that Peter Wand-Tetley's existing medal group was not fully representative of his wartime service. This was indeed found to be the case, and in due course he was posthumously awarded two further wartime medals which, on behalf of Felicia, I arranged to have mounted with his medal group.

In the course of addressing the matter of the obituary and medals I was encouraged by the family to take my research further and write a small booklet covering Wand-Tetley's wartime service. However, any such project was delayed while I wrote a regimental history during the time that I was Commanding Officer of the Royal Rifle Volunteers. Thereafter, an assignment to the Middle East further postponed me from applying myself to any such project. However, upon returning from the deserts of Iraq, and before my next assignment, this time to the deserts of Sudan, a posting in Wiltshire finally provided me with the necessary breathing space to put pen to paper and bring the project to fruition. Although initially intended as a short narrative for family and friends, the scope of the work developed over time and I was persuaded to have it published on account of its potentially wider appeal.

Peter Wand-Tetley had himself been encouraged by the family to draft a wartime memoir. However, his inherent modesty tended to militate against this, and he also expressed a view that, having only been a junior officer in the war, much of the material he might have recounted would no doubt have already been covered in the memoirs of officers more senior than him. However, everyone has a tale to tell and, given that very few served in quite as many special service units as he did, his is of more than average interest. Besides, as time passes there is always a fresh audience keen to read about the exploits of those, like Peter Wand-Tetley, who served their country so selflessly and gallantly during the darkest hours of the Nazi threat.

Peter Wand-Tetley never kept a journal. I wish he had, for my task would have been a good deal simpler. His Peloponnese Narrative represents a rich seam of gold from which I have drawn heavily for the SOE chapter, but he left few other written records. Indeed, for security reasons he was positively discouraged from doing so, given his secret line of work. Inevitably historical records are often not as comprehensive as we would wish them to be, and this is often the case with respect to secret or clandestine organizations.

It is estimated that eighty-five per cent of SOE records have been lost. Those abroad were always subject to destruction in the face of the enemy, as with 'The Flap' in Cairo when GHQ Middle East burnt its documents. Weeding exercises and a fire at SOE Headquarters at Baker Street after the end of the war accounted for further losses. No doubt there are treasures yet to be discovered in the archives, and it is of note that I unearthed a second copy of Peter Wand-Tetley's Peloponnese Narrative – of which initially I believed that I was in sole possession – buried in the National Archive files some time after I had commenced drafting this book. Similarly, wartime SAS records are scant and those that exist tend to focus on those operations in which David Stirling and other 'Originals' took part. Yet by late 1942 there were dozens of SAS officers, Peter Wand-Tetley included, as well as hundreds of other ranks, the majority of whose exploits have presumably been lost to posterity. Similarly frustrating is that although there is a comprehensive report covering 5 Parachute Brigade's activities in Semarang from January to May 1946, I have been unable to track down the corresponding war diaries for the brigade's component battalions: 7th (Light Infantry) Parachute Battalion, 12th (Yorkshire) Parachute Battalion and 13th (Lancashire) Parachute Battalion.

This book does not therefore purport to be pure 'biography' as such, for there is insufficient of Peter Wand-Tetley's personal record for it to be so. Rather, as the sub-title suggests, this is a 'life and times' narrative that focuses as much upon his wartime comrades-in-arms as well as providing a synopsis of the early history of the special service organizations of which he was an officer, with the final chapter providing a glimpse into a bygone era and the life of a colonial officer during the breakup of Empire.

Given the sensitive nature of special forces operations and the imperative to maintain security, no attempt is made to link or compare any of the Second World War special forces organizations with their modern day equivalent and, for similar reasons, all the information in this book is derived from open source references in the public domain, all of which are listed in the bibliography.

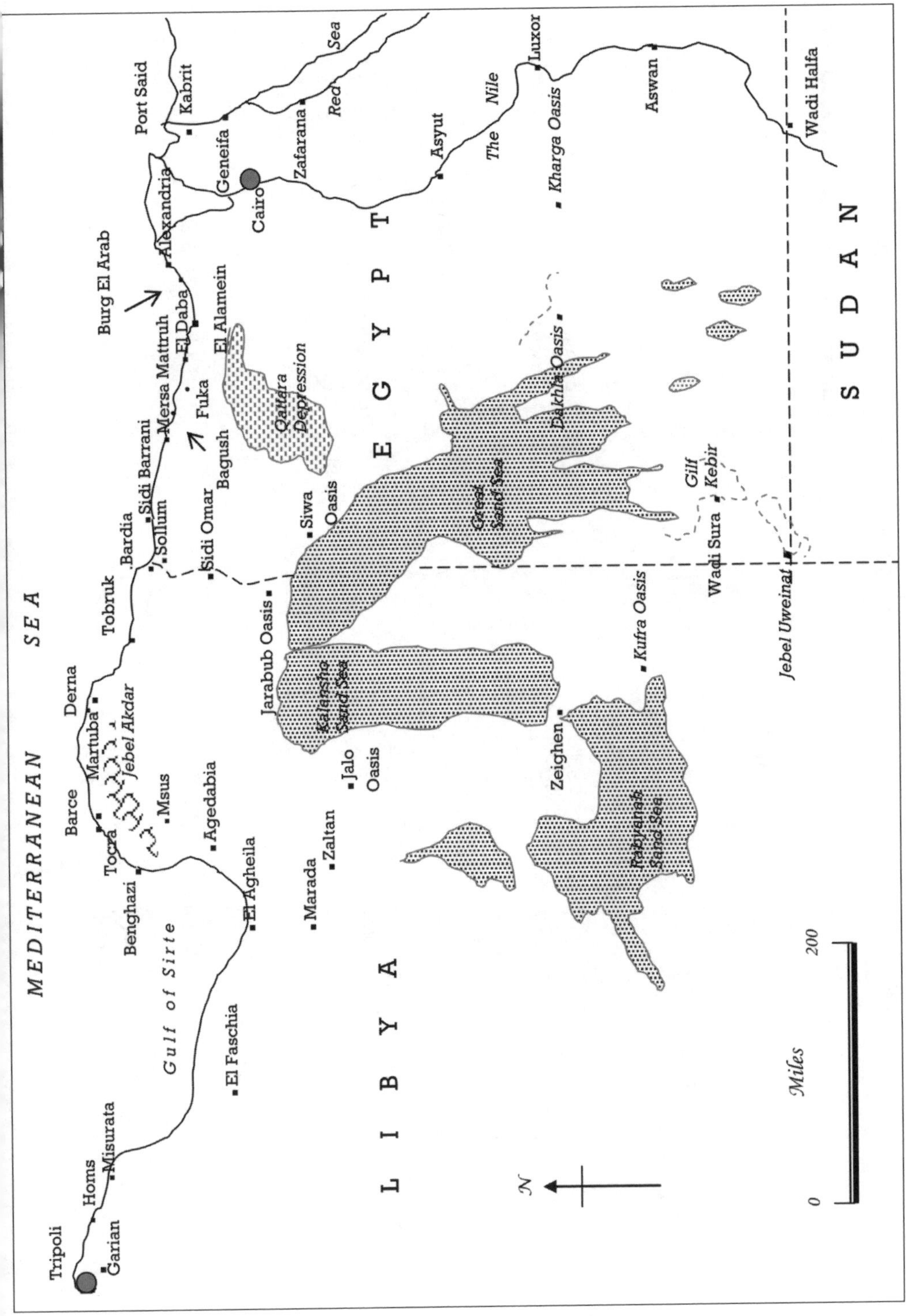

Map 1. The Western Desert

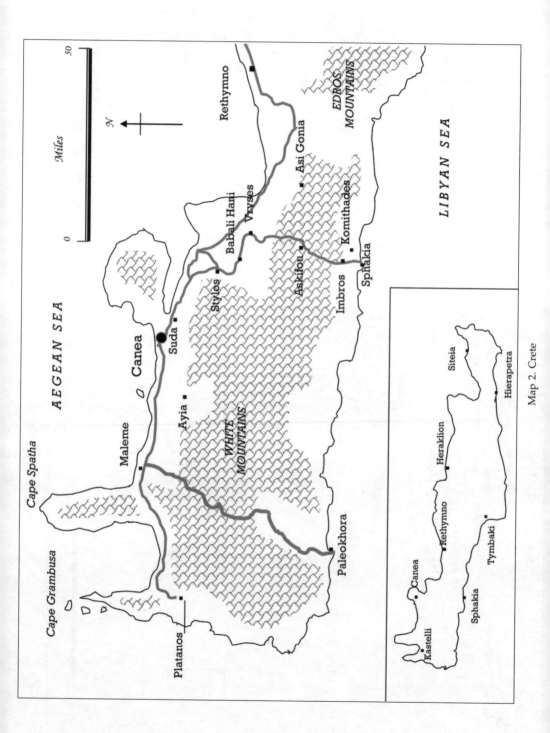

AEGEAN SEA

Cape Spatha

Cape Grambusa

Maleme

Canea

Suda

Ayia

Stylos

WHITE
MOUNTAINS

Babali Hani

Vryses

Rethymno

Asi Gonia

EDROS
MOUNTAINS

Askifou

Imbros

Komithades

Sphakia

Paleokhora

Platanos

LIBYAN SEA

N

Miles

0   50

Canea

Kastelli

Sphakia

Rethymno

Heraklion

Tymbaki

Siteia

Hierapetra

Map 2. Crete

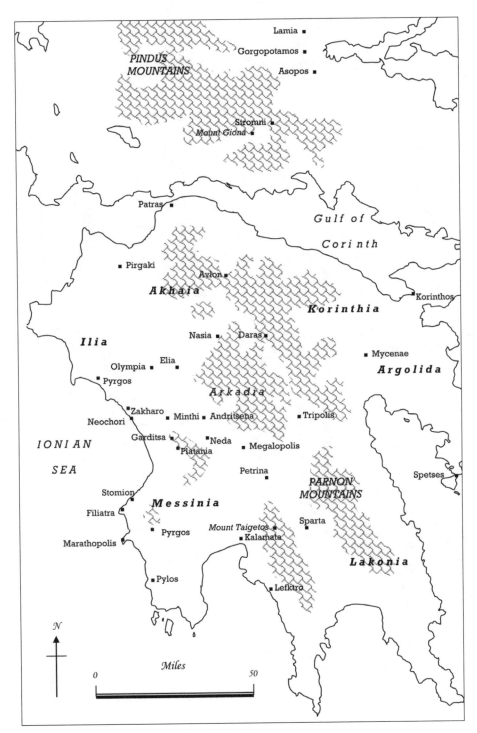

Map 3. The Peloponnese

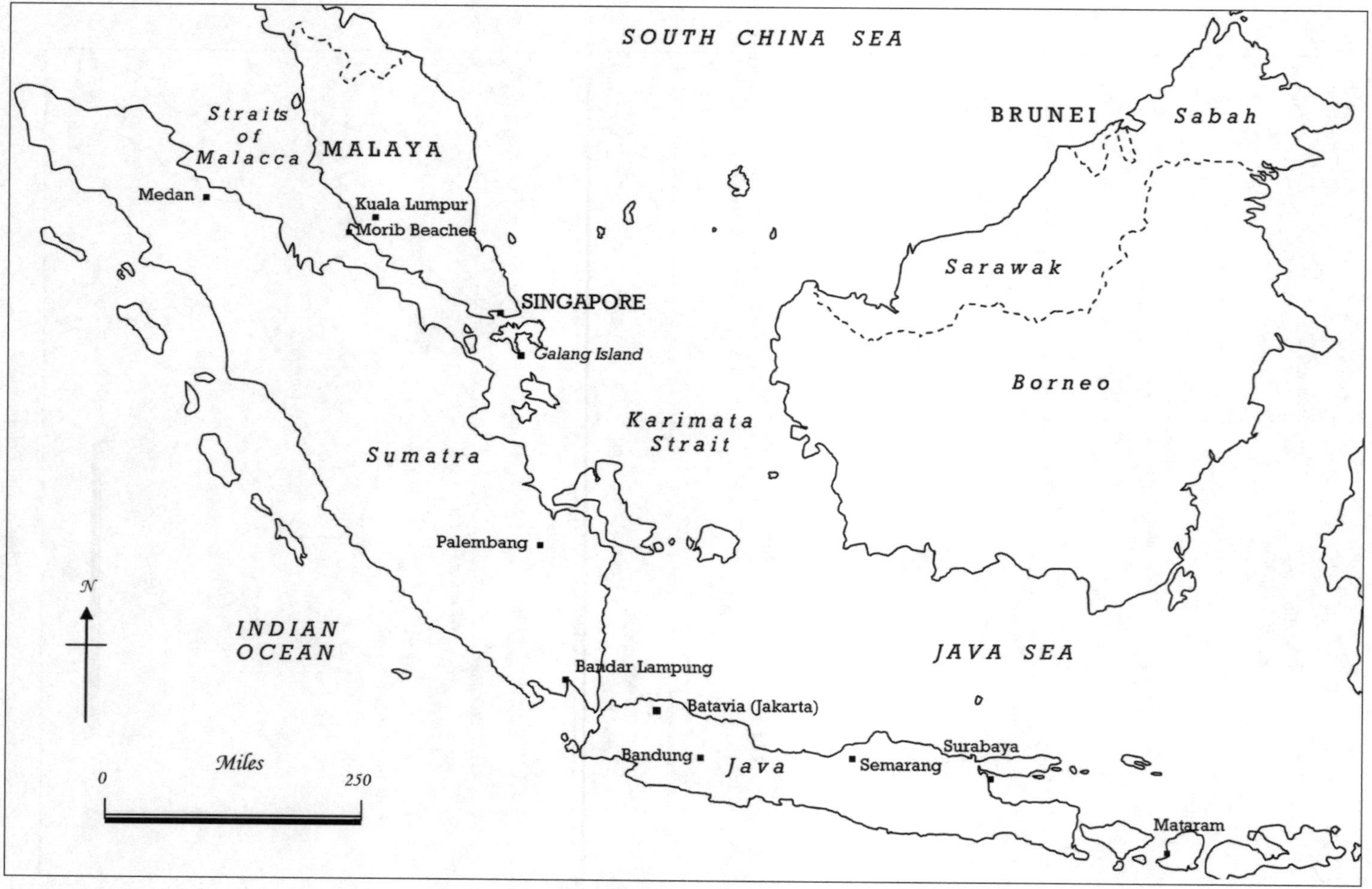

SOUTH CHINA SEA

BRUNEI

Sabah

Sarawak

Borneo

JAVA SEA

Mataram

Surabaya

Semarang

Batavia (Jakarta)

Bandung

Java

Karimata Strait

Bandar Lampung

Palembang

Sumatra

SINGAPORE

Galang Island

MALAYA

Kuala Lumpur

Morib Beaches

Medan

Straits of Malacca

INDIAN OCEAN

N

Miles

0   250

Map 4. Malaya and the Dutch East Indies

xvi

Prologue

Behind Enemy Lines

It was an early evening in late April 1943. Take-off was scheduled for 2030 hours, and it was likely to be a four-hour journey. The three SOE agents walked slowly across the airfield to the plane, a large four-engined Halifax Mk II heavy bomber. Major Bill Reid, Lieutenant Peter Wand-Tetley and Lieutenant 'Yannis' Yannopoulos, the team's wireless operator, were all perspiring freely in their thick battledress, which would keep them warm in the mountains of Greece but was ill-suited to the balmy North African evening. They were all wearing parachute harnesses, crash helmets, and gauntlets, and were further weighed down with the personal equipment with which each of them would jump; a haversack, a pistol and ammunition, a commando knife and a water bottle. Their haversacks contained sundry emergency and survival items including a tin of hard rations, a mess-tin, a miniature compass, a silk map, coloured flares, a torch, a field-dressing, benzedrine pills, RAF badges of rank so that they could assume the identity of aircrew if shot down, and a poison pill (as a last resort, under torture). Under their clothing, next to their skin, they all wore leather money belts containing gold sovereigns and drachmae. The men knew that the gold was a two-edged sword, and that other agents operating in the Balkans had been murdered for it. The rest of their equipment had already been loaded on the bomber. As they neared the plane its engines roared into life. They stopped and stood a moment until all four Rolls-Royce Merlin engines were running smoothly.[1] Spurts of flame from the exhausts were clearly visible against the gloom of the early evening. The RAF despatcher beckoned them to advance once again to board the plane.

They climbed the ladder and followed one another into the bomber. Once inside they checked that their equipment and supplies in the long cylindrical metal containers had all been loaded, and then settled themselves down for the take-off. Having taxied to the end of the main runway, the pilot, Wing Commander Blackburn, tested the brakes and each of the four engines. He then opened the throttles and, with the

1

engines roaring, the bomber quickly gathered speed and raced towards the end of the runway. Lifting slowly off the ground over the airfield boundary the plane gained altitude, and the navigator set a course for Greece. The despatcher spoke to the pilot over his helmet intercom, and then the men took off their parachutes and relaxed as best they could. It was difficult to talk against the deafening noise of the powerful engines, so the three men sat silently, each immersed in his own thoughts, eating sandwiches and drinking from thermos flasks of hot coffee. Heading north, the plane soon left the coastline behind and flew out over the Mediterranean Sea, climbing to 9,000 feet. It was now growing dark and the moon was up, casting a silvery light on the sea below, as the bomber thundered through the night. Approaching Crete, Blackburn took the Halifax around the island and higher to 12,000 feet, flying off the coast to better avoid flak from anti-aircraft guns and *Luftwaffe* nightfighters. At this height it was now quite cold in the plane, and the three men were thankful for the warmth of their battledress as they dozed fitfully.

After what seemed only a short while the despatcher shook them alert and warned them that they were approaching the target area. The men stared briefly out of the side windows to where, illuminated by the silver moonlight, they could clearly see the contrast between the Mediterranean and the coastline of southern Greece. It was now after midnight. They would be over the drop zone shortly, an area dominated by Mount Taigetos in the central prong of the Peloponnesian trident. The three of them pulled on their parachutes, and with a torch the despatcher checked their harness buckles were secure and that their static lines were anchored firmly to the strongpoint on the inside of the fuselage. Before they knew it they had reached the drop zone, a point high over the village of Nasia. The Halifax banked slowly, and Blackburn brought it down to a height of 3,000 feet while the navigator kept up a steady stream of instructions. Then, pulling back on the throttles, Blackburn put down the plane's flaps to reduce his speed and the bomber shuddered as it slowed down. There were no bonfire signals on the ground below to guide them and no reception party arranged by local resistance fighters to secure their drop zone and receive them. The three men were going to jump 'blind' into enemy-held Greece.

If caught, then torture and summary execution at the hands of the *Gestapo* and *Sicherheitsdienst* (SD) would be their fate. Adolf Hitler had made this crystal clear the previous autumn in his infamous *Kommandobefehl* of 18 October 1942:

> From now on all enemies on so-called Commando missions in Europe or Africa ... are to be slaughtered to the last man ... Even if these individuals, on discovery, make obvious their intention to give themselves up as prisoners, no pardon is on any account to be

given. ... If individual members of such Commandos, such as agents, saboteurs, et cetera, fall into the hands of the military forces by some other means ... they are to be handed over immediately to the SD. To hold them in military custody ... even if only as a temporary measure is strictly forbidden. [In a supplementary order Hitler stressed:] ... all sabotage troops will be exterminated, without exception, to the last man.

The three men watched intently as the despatcher opened the trapdoor. A gust of cold air rushed in and the noise of the powerful engines filled the fuselage of the plane. The parachutists felt the familiar hollow feeling in the pit of their stomachs. On the first pass the containers with their equipment were rolled out. The plane circled around once again to the same point. Now it was the turn of the men. Wand-Tetley moved to the trapdoor and sat down, firmly gripping the edge, his legs hanging into the empty space beneath him. He watched the small red stand-by light in front of him. It went out and the green light flashed on. The despatcher tapped him on his shoulder and at the signal he pushed himself forward, dropped down into the abyss below, and was immediately swept away in the slipstream of the powerful engines. After a few feet the static line started to pull the parachute out of his pack. The string attached to both the static line and the top of the parachute then broke, and his canopy filled with air. Wand-Tetley looked up and with relief saw that his parachute had opened perfectly above him and that there were no twists in his rigging lines. After a moment, and having caught his breath, he looked about him and could see the white blur of the other parachutes supporting Bill, Yannis and the containers, illuminated in the moonlight and floating down in the cool night air. He could also still hear the Halifax, but the sound of its four mighty engines was now starting to fade into the distance, and he recalled the somewhat disquieting farewell of one of the ground crew prior to take-off: 'Good luck, it'll be a Wooden Cross or a Military Cross for you.'

Note
1. The Special Liberator (X) Flight/No. 148 Squadron used HP Halifax Mk II aircraft, which had Rolls-Royce Merlin engines.

Chapter 1

A Martial Upbringing

Family

Peter Michael Wand-Tetley was born in Farnham, Surrey, on 2 February 1920, the first of three sons born to Cécile Florence (née Tatham). His two younger brothers would follow at two-yearly intervals, John arriving on the scene in 1922 and Nigel in 1924. His father, Thomas (Tommy) Harrison Wand-Tetley, at the time an Army captain, was stationed in the neighbouring military town of Aldershot. Tommy had been born in September 1890 at Paignton, South Devon. He was the second son of Emily Jane (née Harrison) and Ernest Wand, his elder brother, Clarence, having been born a year earlier. Tommy's mother and father divorced and his mother remarried, in 1909, Joseph Tetley of the tea dynasty; the family name was changed to Wand-Tetley in recognition of their stepfather.

Tommy's father, Ernest Wand, was a hotel proprietor and in 1891 was running the Esplanade Hotel, Paignton. Born in Grantham, Lincolnshire in 1866, he was the youngest of five children born to Mary (née James) and Charles Wand. Ernest arrived on the scene somewhat to the surprise of his mother who was forty-six at the time. Charles Wand, who was born in Newark in 1821, was a year younger than his wife and together they ran a family business in Castlegate, Grantham.[1]

Cécile had been born in Natal, South Africa, on 20 September 1894 and educated at Priorsfield, in England. She was descended from the branch of the Tathams that established itself in County Durham during the sixteenth century, and directly from William Tatham of Sunderland, Salt Officer and merchant, and his wife Alice (née Raisbeck); the Raisbeck family was the principal Stockton family during the eighteenth century. Their eldest son Ralph Tatham, 1732–1779, established himself as a successful merchant, took to horse-breeding, and in later life was private secretary to Captain (later Lord) Rodney. He and his wife, Elizabeth (née Bloxham), the daughter and heiress of a hosier in Cateaton

4

Street with considerable property in the neighbourhood of St Paul's and Westminster, had five sons.[2]

Ralph and Elizabeth Tatham's fifth son, and Cécile's great-grandfather, was Charles Heathcote Tatham, 1772–1842, the notable British architect who, while working for Henry Holland, the Prince of Wales's architect, designed the ornamental decorations for Drury Lane Theatre and, with Samual Wyatt, designed Dropmore House in Buckinghamshire for the Prime Minister, Lord Grenville. He first exhibited at the Royal Academy in 1797 and regularly continued to do so, contributing a total of fifty-three designs, until 1836. His wife, Harriet (née Williams), was equally energetic and bore him four sons and six daughters.[3]

The two youngest sons, Edmund and Robert, born in 1822 and 1824 respectively, both emigrated to South Africa in 1850. Robert, Cécile's grandfather, who was first Surveyor-General of the Transvaal and also tried his luck, somewhat unsuccessfully, at the Kimberley diamond fields, married Susan (née Noon) in 1861. Their second son, Frederick (Fred) Tatham, who had been born in 1865, married Ada (Lolly) (née Molyneux) and they had seven children. Cécile, the eldest of the three daughters would grow into an attractive young lady and would keep her figure and looks throughout her life, although future daughters-in-law would find that she was not always the easiest of ladies to get along with.[4]

Fred Tatham grew to eminence in law and politics and as a soldier. He finally retired as acting Judge-President in 1931. When the Basuto War broke out in November 1880 he enlisted at the age of fifteen in Willoughby's Horse as a trooper and reached the rank of sergeant before the war's end the following year. In the Boer War of 1899–1902 he successively served on the staff of Sir George White during the siege of Ladysmith, as Brigade Major of the Natal Volunteer Brigade under General Sir J. G. Dartnell, and as Divisional Intelligence Officer to General Locke Elliot. During the conflict he ranged far across the country and, besides Ladysmith and the battles of Wagon Hill and Caesar's Camp, he was present at the engagements at Elandslaagte, Intinta Inyoni, Lombaard's Kop, Biggarsberg and Laing's Nek, ending the war with six clasps to his campaign medal and being twice Mentioned in Despatches. In the First World War he served once more despite his advancing age and, between 1915 and 1918, saw service in Egypt and the Western Front in the rank of lieutenant colonel, was present at the battles of the Somme, Messines, and the third battle of Ypres, and was awarded the DSO and twice Mentioned in Despatches.[5]

By the time Cécile's first son, Peter, had been born, Tommy had already made a good start in carving out for himself the beginnings of a long and distinguished military career that would eventually span both world wars. Educated at Eastbourne College and Sandhurst, he was commissioned into the Wiltshire Regiment in 1910. On leaving the Royal Military College he passed his first two months in Portobello Barracks, Dublin, with 2nd Battalion The Wiltshire Regiment, which had been stationed there since 1908, before setting sail in June on the SS *Durham Castle* for South Africa. Disembarking the following month, he joined 1st Battalion The Wiltshire Regiment at Fort Napier in Pietermaritzburg, where it had moved in 1909 following a fourteen-year stint in India. This was a garrison posting, but the Boer War was still a very recent memory and the commanding officer, Lieutenant Colonel Louis Warden, a large distinctive character with impressive moustaches, ensured that military exercises, besides sport and fitness, were very much the order of the day. Here Tommy served for two-and-a-half years, in which time he met and courted his future wife, Cécile, before returning, in March 1913, with 1st Wiltshires to Jellalabad Barracks in Tidworth, where the CO found his battalion posted a hundred yards on the wrong side, as he perceived it, of the Wiltshire County border with Hampshire.[6]

At the outbreak of the First World War Tommy, a lieutenant at the time, was in Aldershot attending the Assistant Instructors Course at the Army School of Physical and Bayonet Training. The course was terminated and he returned immediately to Tidworth to resume his battalion appointment as commander of the Regimental Scouts. He embarked at Southampton with 1st Wiltshires, just over 1,000-strong, in mid-August 1914, as an 'Old Contemptible' of the highly professional but relatively small 120,000 strong British Expeditionary Force (BEF), bound for France. By the end of the month the battalion, under the command of Lieutenant Colonel A. W. Hasted, was digging in just south of Mons, in Belgium. On 23 August, 1st Wiltshires fought in the First Battle of Mons. The initial German onslaught was beaten off, but the weight of German numbers soon told and the BEF was slowly pushed back.[7]

Three days later 1st Wiltshires were in action again, during the Battle of le Cateau. In early October Tommy was Mentioned in the Despatches of Field Marshal Sir John French for his work in the Regimental Scouts. In the First Battle of Ypres 1st Wiltshires were at Neuve Chapelle, west of Lille. Here they engaged in heavy fighting for the best part of a fortnight, twice restoring the British line after it had been penetrated by the enemy. With battalion casualties rising, Tommy was placed in command of A Company on 25 October. Two days later, in heavy fighting around Neuve Chapelle, much of it with the bayonet, he was shot in the neck and leg and captured by the Germans. By the end of October, just ten weeks after leaving England, 1st Wiltshires, although heavily reinforced, had lost twenty-six officers and 1,000 men, the equivalent of an entire battalion.[8]

6

Tommy remained a prisoner of war throughout the remainder of the conflict, first in Germany and then, from February 1918, in Holland, where he remained until the Armistice. Even in captivity he had made his mark, for in 1919 he was Mentioned in Despatches for valuable war services rendered as a prisoner of war, and again in 1920 for gallant conduct and determination displayed in attempting to escape from captivity.[9]

However, Tommy's elder brother Clarence did not survive the war. He was killed in Turkey in 1915 while serving as a lieutenant with the Lancashire Fusiliers, the regiment immortalized for its 'Lancashire Landing' at W Beach, Gallipoli. The battalion successfully fought its way ashore in the face of a withering barrage of enemy machine-gun fire, sustaining heavy casualties – 'mown down as by a scythe', as the Allied Commander General Sir Ian Hamilton stated – but winning in the process 'six VCs before breakfast'. He was to die four months after the beach landing. His name is remembered with honour at the Cape Helles Memorial.

At the end of the First World War Tommy took up where he had left off. As the war drew to a close he was released from captivity in Holland and Cécile travelled to The Hague where, in August, they were married at the English Church. Their reception was held at the British Legation at the invitation of Sir Walter and Lady Susan Townley. Tommy returned to England a week after the Armistice and, in February 1919, he moved to Aldershot to take up the appointment of Officer Instructor at the Army School of Physical and Bayonet Training. Fifteen months later, three months after Peter had been born, he was appointed Superintendent and Chief Instructor at the school, a post he would hold until February 1923. Thus began a long career in the specialist field of Army physical training, one in which he would alternate with regimental postings to 1st Wiltshires.

It was no accident that Tommy had gravitated towards Army physical training appointments, for he was himself an outstanding athlete. In June 1920, four months after the birth of Peter, he learnt from the Secretary of the Amateur Fencing Association that he had been selected to represent Great Britain at the Olympic Games in Antwerp. Besides fencing, in which he would fight with foil and épée, he was also selected to represent his country in the modern pentathlon. Nor did his sporting talents stop with fencing and modern pentathlon, for throughout the 1920s he would also box for the Army at welterweight, and play hockey for the Army and his country.[10]

In March 1923 Tommy returned for six months to 1st Wiltshires at Lucknow Barracks in Tidworth, where this time the battalion was twenty yards on the right side of the Wiltshire County border with Hampshire, before he set sail from Southampton in September on the

SS *Kilronan Castle*, bound for South Africa. Cécile accompanied him with their two very young sons, Peter and John; Nigel would be born within six months. While at Robert's Heights, near Pretoria, as Instructor of Physical and Recreational Training, he earned substantial plaudits for establishing a sound basis for physical training in the South African Army, Air Force and Police. He returned to Tidworth a year later, now with three sons, and remained with 1st Wiltshires for a further year before, in November 1925, returning to Aldershot as Superintendent of Physical Training, in which post he remained for four years. He was promoted to major in 1927, represented the British Fencing Team once more, with foil, at the 1928 Olympic Games in Amsterdam, and was appointed OBE in the King's Birthday Honours List of 1929.[11]

Having rejoined 1st Wiltshires in December 1929, now based at Crownhill Fort, Plymouth, Tommy embarked with them, on HMT *Somersetshire*, for Egypt in the spring of 1930. Arriving in April, having called in at Gibraltar and Malta en route, the battalion took up residence in the Mustapha Barracks in Alexandria. Initially in command of Headquarters Company, Tommy took over command of C Company halfway through his tour there. As part of the Canal Brigade, regular training exercises would take place at Sidi Bishr. However, an otherwise happy tour was blighted by the death of the CO, Lieutenant Colonel Percy ('Jerry') Rowan DSO, in a flying accident, when an RAF Armstrong Whitworth Atlas, in which he was a passenger, sustained engine failure soon after take-off at Ismailia airfield. When the battalion returned to England in March 1931, Tommy departed to take up a two-year appointment with Eastern Command, as its General Staff Officer for Physical Training.[12]

In May 1933 Tommy moved his family to Le Marchant Barracks, Devizes, and assumed command of the Wiltshire Regimental Depot from Major Hugh Segrave, with whom he had earlier served in South Africa in 1st Wiltshires. The Depot was an impressive Victorian barracks, completed in 1878 and guarded by the castellated Keep's massive tower at its main entrance. It was named after the colourful character Sir John Gaspard le Marchant who had commanded an antecedent regiment of the Wiltshires. Between the wars a regimental depot was a major's independent command and a pleasant place to be, its role being to enlist and train recruits for the regular battalions, and it acted as home and heart of the regiment so its small permanent staff were very carefully selected.

On his arrival, the *Journal of The Wiltshire Regiment* records: 'We are lucky to have in our new Commanding Officer one who is so keen and proficient in physical training, boxing and fencing, and we look forward to reaping the benefit.' The Depot soldiers were not to be disappointed, for he immediately set about making his mark and putting sport on the map, instigating a regular Inter-Depot Sports Competition, consisting of cross-country running, shooting and boxing, with a series of home and away matches.[13]

Engagement with the local Wiltshire community was an important role, not least in terms of recruitment, and in this regard Cécile would be in her element in ensuring a lively social programme. Always guaranteed to be an exciting occasion, the Avon Vale Hunt would regularly meet at the Depot with anything up to 150 guests, including many of the local farmers. When Tommy came to the end of his tour at the Depot in June 1935, he handed over command to Major 'Oily' Oliphant MC who, in the First World War, had been captured during the fighting at Neuve Chapelle on the same day as he had been and, like him, had spent the remainder of the war in German captivity.[14]

After two years in command at Devizes Tommy moved to Aldershot in June 1935, on promotion to lieutenant colonel, and was appointed Commandant, Army School of Physical Training; during his time in this post he drew up plans for a new and up-to-date gymnasium at Aldershot, which still bears his name.

In February 1939 he was promoted to colonel, moved to Horse Guards, and assumed the appointment of Inspector of Physical Training at the War Office. He would oversee the expansion of the physical training staff from its pre-war strength of 280 to some 3,000 by the final year of the war. During the war he would open three Army Physical Development Centres; through this initiative many thousands of sub-standard recruits, who would otherwise have been lost to the Army, were able to be enlisted. This was, perhaps, his most valuable endeavour for the Army. As Inspector he would also be responsible for converting the old Army Physical Training Staff into the Army Physical Training Corps, and would thus be acknowledged as the founder of the APTC; on retirement from the Army as an honorary Brigadier in January 1945, he would be recognized for his services with the CBE.[15]

Thus, Peter Wand-Tetley had as a role model a father whose service to King and Country would be hard to match, and he had spent a good deal of his early boyhood in and around Aldershot, 'The Home of the British Army'.

Marlborough College

Wand-Tetley joined Marlborough College at the start of the Michaelmas Term in September 1933, in the year that his father assumed command of the Wiltshire Regimental Depot down the road at Devizes. Founded in August 1843, the College was relatively young compared to some of the more established English boarding schools, but had already forged an enviable reputation. Located on the Bath Road at the western end of the ancient market town of Marlborough, the school was established,

9

with the support of the Archbishop of Canterbury, by a group of Church of England clergymen, on the site of the Castle Inn, a fashionable coaching inn and previously the family home of Lord Hertford.[16]

Wand-Tetley was placed in Wykeham House, otherwise known as '50, The High Street', which was a small junior boarding house for first-year boys whose housemaster was William Cheeseman. In September the following year he moved to C2, one of the six senior in-College boarding houses run during his time there by the Housemasters Bernard Newman and, later, Reginald Jennings. He would remain in C2 until he left the College at the end of the Summer Term in July 1937. Academically, Wand-Tetley did not draw undue attention to himself, although by the time he left school at the age of seventeen he had managed to work his way up to a respectable enough position in the middle of his class. In his early College years he played for his house in all the main team games, but soon came to focus on the martial skills of fencing and shooting. By his final year he had become Captain of the College Fencing Team and fought successfully with both foil and épée. Private tutelage from his father no doubt stood him in good stead in this respect, and on occasion his father would travel to Marlborough and provide Olympian master classes to the entire Fencing Team. However, it was for rifle-shooting that he developed a real passion and prowess.[17]

The shooting team, known as the Shooting VIII, came under the auspices of the Officer Training Corps, which was run under the watchful eye of the College Regimental Sergeant Major, G. H. Lawrence, Royal Scots Fusiliers, a First World War veteran who had been captured at Mons and had been treated very poorly by the Germans – a subject he was most reluctant to discuss. An active and tireless soldier, Lawrence was a much respected man who could be seen striding energetically about the College grounds in his glengarry. He remained at Marlborough from 1924 to 1938, and was a first class rifle-shot, county champion on numerous occasions, and several times in the Bisley King's Hundred. Importantly, he was also a patient and skilled rifle-shooting coach and was able to pass on his skill. Wand-Tetley enjoyed the OTC, and he served in it alongside some 300 of his fellow cadets throughout his time at Marlborough. Although there had been a change in nomenclature to 'OTC' at the time of the Haldane Reforms of 1908, Marlborough College's Cadet Corps dated back to 1860, and had come into existence in parallel with the establishment of the Volunteer Force of 1859. Indeed, the College was one of the four 'founder schools' of the cadet movement, and in 1861 had adopted its own Marlborough College Rifle Corps cap-badge and a light grey uniform which earned the cadets the nickname of 'The Millers'. By happy coincidence military assistance was provided by instructors from the Wiltshire Regimental Depot at Devizes. Before leaving the College Wand-Tetley gained his 'Certificate A', a demanding series of OTC written and practical examinations in a range of leadership and military skills that qualified the officer cadet in question for a Territorial Army commission.[18]

During Wand-Tetley's time at the College, the Shooting VIII's finest hour came in the summer of 1935 in a closely-fought contest for the annual inter-school competition at Bisley, in which they beat Winchester and Wellington, and secured for the School the Ashburton Shield and the Country Life Trophy. On returning to Marlborough the VIII was received by the Mayor of Marlborough, Alderman V. Head. The reception given by the Mayor and townspeople, as the band played 'See the Conquering Hero Comes', was particularly memorable for those involved. For the Shooting VIII it had been an excellent day, but for Wand-Tetley it had been an outstanding one for he had excelled himself by achieving an individual score of 68, with 34 points apiece gained at 200 yards and 500 yards, thereby securing the highest individual score and establishing himself as the best shot in the school at the age of just fifteen. Thus began a life-long interest in shooting, a sport that he would enjoy competing in even after he had finished his Army service.[19]

Another highlight during his Marlborough College days was a visit to the 1936 Berlin Olympics, as Wand-Tetley recalled many years later in a letter to his young great-niece concerning a school project she was undertaking:[20]

I went to the 1936 Olympic Games at the age of sixteen as a guest of the German government, which had invited each competing nation to send thirty boys to represent its youth. I had been nominated by my father, who had competed in the fencing and modern pentathlon in 1920 [and fencing in 1928] and was going in 1936 as a judge of fencing. I felt bound to spend time at the fencing, although it is not one of the world's most exciting sports to watch, because my father was judging and because I was captain of fencing at school.

The 'royal' box, that is to say Hitler's, was in the middle of one side of the stadium, above the dais on which the winners stood to receive their medals. On one occasion when Hitler was there I decided to see how near I could get to him and asked the guards in my school certificate German to let me through so that I could see *Der Führer* up close. They seemed very interested in the badge of crossed rifles on my blazer and asked what it meant. When I explained that I was a member of my school's rifle shooting team, and boasted that we had won the annual trophy for schools the previous year, they broke into broad grins and let me through, so I got right up to the section where Hitler was sitting a few feet away.

Little could Wand-Tetley have guessed at the time that within three years he would be fighting Hitler's *Wehrmacht*, but for now, with the end of his school days in sight, he had the more immediate business of considering what he would do afterwards. Initially, it had been intended that he would follow a career in the Army, and his father had been instrumental in mapping out such a course. However, Wand-Tetley was not convinced that this was necessarily for him and felt more inclined towards a career in writing. Accordingly, the course of his academic studies was changed to become more literary in content. He left school having passed the London Matriculation Examination (in Latin, Maths, French, English and European History). With a view to a career in journalism, his housemaster and tutor, Reginald Jennings, wrote of him by way of a reference:

> His cast of mind is essentially independent and unconventional: he thinks hard for himself and the results of his thought are honestly got and part of himself. I am quite confident that one day he will write what will be both pleasing to read, and profitable as well. He enjoys – and with considerable discrimination – poetry and all good literature, music, and some philosophy. At any rate he has wide interests, independence, a capacity for hard work and sets himself a high standard.[21]

South Africa

Wand-Tetley left Marlborough College at the age of seventeen after the summer term of 1937 and travelled to Natal, South Africa, for a 'gap year', as it would now be called. Here he made the most of his mother's family connections and worked as a cub reporter on *The Natal Witness* until the following year. While in Pietermaritzburg he stayed with cousins at the Parkside house that Fred and Lolly Tatham had lived in until Fred's death in 1934. Lolly was still living there, but the house was now run by one of her daughters, Joan, and her husband Phil Davis, who in the First World War had served as a captain with the Natal Carbineers in the German South Africa campaign, and in 2 Mounted Brigade in the East Africa campaign. It had been Phil's father, Peter Davis, who had founded *The Natal Witness*, and Phil now also had a position on the paper as the Managing Director. He and his wife Joan had two young daughters, Priscilla and Betty. Wand-Tetley was given work on, among other things, court reporting and cinema reviews. He found this stimulating and he also thoroughly enjoyed the lively social life in Natal.

The Tathams were a large family, so Wand-Tetley had many cousins in and around Pietermaritzburg. In particular he struck up a good friendship with his cousin, Frederick (Bobs) Tatham and his two sisters Pam and Angela, the children of Cécile's surviving brother, Tyrone, and his wife Nicola. Both Bobs and Pam were a couple of years older than Wand-Tetley, but he was perceived as mature for his age and his sense of fun and good humour meant that he settled easily into their large circle of friends. Tennis parties were frequent, a lot of billiards was played, and dance parties were the usual Saturday night entertainment. Besides his work with *The Natal Witness*, Wand-Tetley also did a spell working on the farm of other relatives, George and Marie-Leone Tatham, at Berville, north of Pietermaritzburg and close to the Drakensburg Mountains. He enjoyed the open air way of life on the farm and was sad to leave. All too soon his interlude in South Africa passed and it was time for him to catch a ship for the return voyage home.[22]

Cambridge University

Having returned to England, Wand-Tetley set his sights upon Downing College, Cambridge, to study English. With a few months in hand before the academic year commenced, and by way of preparation, he undertook a short course in English Studies in London during the early summer. The intention had initially been that this might also prepare him to take an entrance Scholarship or Exhibition in English. However, the decision to go up to Cambridge in 1938, rather than wait until the following year, meant that he missed the boat in terms of taking an entrance Scholarship for that year. Nonetheless the extra study stood him in good stead and his English tutor, T. H. Thompson, wrote of him by way of a testimonial:

I have always found him a keen and intelligent pupil, and have been struck by his genuine appreciation of literature and by his insight into its values. I feel confident that he will do well in the English Tripos at Cambridge.[23]

The new Michaelmas Term commenced on 7 October, but Wand-Tetley arrived in Cambridge somewhat late, for having finished his English course he took a two-month trip on a cargo steamer which did not dock at Liverpool until 10 October. He went up to Cambridge the following day and there met his College tutor, William Cuttle, and the Director of English Studies, Dr Frank Leavis, who brought him up to speed with the work he had missed over the last few days and explained the curriculum. While he had been away at sea his father had arranged lodgings for him just to the south of the College grounds at 15 Hills Road – rooms which were popular with undergraduates – as the College rooms were at that time all full. These he found to be more than comfortable and he quickly settled in to College as one of the freshmen.[24]

The College had been founded by Sir George Downing, third baronet, who died in 1749, with an inheritance left to him by his grandfather who had built No. 10 Downing Street, the Prime Minister's residence, and had served both Cromwell and Charles II. Built to the design of William Wilkins and inspired by the classic buildings that had so impressed him in Greece, the handsome range of buildings set around the quadrangle, built of Portland and Ketton stone, provided an inspirational and grand setting in which to study. Besides his academic pursuits, Wand-Tetley readily immersed himself in the University's busy social life and activities. Not surprisingly, perhaps, he represented Downing College at fencing, during which time the team enjoyed a winning streak. He also played bridge for the College, being described as one of the two most promising freshmen, and played some squash for the College.[25]

Despite the relatively care-free existence at University, Wand-Tetley was impatient to move on and start his chosen career and spoke on the matter with his father. Accordingly, in the final term of his first year at Cambridge, his father wrote to Downing College with the intention of withdrawing his son from the University at the end of that academic year in order that he could embark immediately upon a career in journalism. However, he also took the precaution of enquiring as to whether his son might complete the remaining two years of his degree at a later stage.[26]

In the event such considerations proved to be relatively academic, because war broke out during that long summer vacation of 1939 and Wand-Tetley's studies would, regardless, have been interrupted on that account alone. On 1 September Hitler invaded Poland. In response Britain and France presented him with an ultimatum to halt the German advance and, when this was ignored, declared war on Germany on 3 September. Like many across the country, Wand-Tetley listened intently to Neville Chamberlain's somewhat weary announcement, that Sunday morning on the wireless, that the country was now at war.

The Second World War had commenced, and for a generation of young men and women the regular pattern of life was interrupted. Wand-Tetley decided to enlist in the Army and seek a commission in his father's regiment. To him the infantry represented the quintessential essence of soldiering, and it was where he knew that he would experience the greatest leadership and physical challenges. Pursuing a commission in the Wiltshires seemed an obvious choice, not least because it was a regiment with which he had grown up, and his father could provide him with the all-important introduction. However, in some respects enlistment was not quite as straightforward as he had expected.

The Army recruiting offices were overwhelmed with enquiries from similarly-minded young men, all of them eager to volunteer their services to King and Country. It appeared to Wand-Tetley that there

14

might be a very real danger that it would take months to get his foot in the door. However his father, now at Horse Guards, was able to make a few enquiries on his behalf to sound out where openings might exist. It appeared that one of the quickest ways for him to get ahead of the game might be to enlist first with the Honourable Artillery Company (HAC). Although the HAC was a Territorial Army unit, since the declaration of war it had, like other such units across Britain, adopted a war-footing and thus a full-time stance. With the HAC he could conduct basic training before proceeding on to officer training and subsequently a commission in the Wiltshires. Importantly, he learnt that he could be signed up with the HAC the following month.

The Honourable Artillery Company and Officer Training

Accordingly Wand-Tetley travelled to Armoury House, the HAC headquarters, for an interview with the CO, Lieutenant Colonel Guy Heseltine MC, who had been in command for just a month. The interview was polite and friendly although relatively short, and during its course Wand-Tetley confirmed to the CO his desire to secure a commission in the Wiltshires. To some it may seem somewhat strange that he would have expressed quite so openly his desire for a commission in a unit other than the one in which he was being enlisted. However, this did not faze the CO in the slightest, for the HAC had a long custom of supplying officers and non-commissioned officers to units throughout the British Army. Because Wand-Tetley was enlisted under the National Service Act and intended for subsequent officer training and a commission in the Wiltshires, he never technically became a member of the HAC; instead he was merely attached for training purposes, a situation not uncommon during the war.

Upon leaving the CO's office Wand-Tetley learnt from the Adjutant, Captain Harold Armstrong, that its infantry battalion, the oldest unit of the HAC, had been converted at the outbreak of war into an Officer Cadet Training Unit (OCTU). Additionally, the HAC had formed National Defence Companies to guard the London docks, a Special Constabulary unit whose beat was in the East End, and a Heavy Anti-Aircraft Regiment. The artillery element was still in the process of expansion and would eventually send three Royal Horse Artillery (RHA) regiments overseas, including North Africa, Sicily, Italy and Europe. The pre-war artillery headquarters and its two batteries, A and B, had become 11th (HAC) Regiment RHA and in May, following the decision by the War Office to duplicate the Territorial Army, this unit had provided the basis for 12th (HAC) Regiment RHA, consisting of C and D batteries. In due course each regiment would form a third battery, E and F, respectively, and the following year a third regiment, 13th (HAC) Regiment RHA, was destined to follow.[27]

15

After a brief discussion covering various administrative matters, the Adjutant told Wand-Tetley to report for duty with 12th (HAC) Regiment RHA on 19 October and bade him farewell. By the time he returned the unit had left its permanent base at Artillery Gardens and moved to billets at Boreham Wood, near Elstree. Wand-Tetley was placed in the Depot Troop with some 100 other recruits. Here he was given his first Army number to memorize, 6463867, and put through initial training under the watchful eye of the Depot Troop commander, Captain Norman Radford DSO MC. His initial individual training went smoothly, and he found that his prior experience in the OTC at Marlborough College stood him in very good stead and not surprisingly he excelled at rifle-shooting. At the end of November he and his intake passed out and were absorbed into C and D Batteries. Thereafter duties consisted primarily of guarding various Vulnerable Points (VPs) around London, including various docks, railway and underground stations, and road and rail tunnels. Standing guard over VPs during that bitterly cold winter of 1939–40 was an often thankless and far from glamorous task.

In March 1940, following a Board of Officers, it was confirmed to Wand-Tetley that he would indeed go forward to officer training. Up to this point it was entirely possible that, had he not been up to standard, he would not have progressed to an OCTU, so it was with a degree of relief that he heard the good news. His six months with the HAC was now rapidly drawing to a close, but amidst the routine of the VP guard tasks there was one memorable moment of light relief before he departed for pastures new. In the middle of April a sizeable party from 12th (HAC) Regiment RHA went along to Elstree railway station to give a good send-off to their colleagues in 11th (HAC) Regiment RHA who were moving to a new camp at Swanage. Under the watchful eye of the CO, the Guard of Honour, of some thirty men and trumpeters under Second Lieutenant Lewis Burtt, duly formed up at the end of the train opposite its engine. However, instead of rolling forward, the train backed out of the station, leaving the CO and the well-rehearsed Honour Guard in the lurch. Fortunately, after half-a-mile the train stopped and then returned. As it passed, the Honour Guard finally got its opportunity to present arms and Guy Heseltine his chance to give the military compliment of 'Regimental Fire' – an ancient HAC custom, equivalent to 'Three Cheers'.[28]

Towards the end of April, as 12th (HAC) Regiment RHA prepared to depart from Boreham for a new war station at Skegness, and a full six months after he had enlisted with them, Wand-Tetley prepared to take his leave of the HAC and the friends he had made there. Having travelled down to Aldershot from London he joined 168th Infantry OCTU on 26 April 1940 for four months training.

With his fellow officer cadets Wand-Tetley underwent a thorough military syllabus of leadership training and theoretical and practical military exercises. There were lectures on Military Law and disciplinary procedures, the use of I Groups (Information Groups), O Groups (Order Groups), and 'appreciations' conducted on various military scenarios, including offensive and defensive operations. There were numerous field exercises, with cadets taking it in turns to assume the role of commander; there were also TEWTS (Tactical Exercises Without Troops). The importance of logistics supply was stressed, with drills on handling of fuel, ammunition and rations to ensure prompt arrival at the front line. Emphasis was placed upon physical fitness, with early morning runs every day, or route marches carrying full kit against the clock. There was a good deal of map and compass work, all placed within a competitive context. And considerable time was spent honing their skills on the rifle range.

Nor was Army 'bullshit' overlooked. In the evenings Wand-Tetley and his fellow cadets would spend hours on 'spit and polish', cleaning their boots, blancoing their equipment and polishing any brass on their kit, as well as cleaning their rooms in preparation for the daily inspection the following morning. All deadly dull, but important in instilling cleanliness, smartness and discipline, and invariably not without its humorous side. To reinforce the discipline there were regular periods of square-bashing, with the cadets being 'beasted' about the parade ground to the tune of the fierce, oath-ridden commands of the OCTU Regimental Sergeant Major, for whom everyone had a healthy respect.

During his training Wand-Tetley had followed the course of the war with great interest. At the commencement of hostilities the British and French had adopted a largely defensive posture along the Franco-German border behind the heavily defended Maginot Line. With Hitler engaged in Denmark and Norway, invasion of the Low Countries was postponed. This long period of inactivity, the 'phoney war', from 3 September 1939 to 10 May 1940, badly affected Allied morale. When the Germans did make their move, they swept Allied resistance aside in a blitzkrieg that drove the Allies back westwards and forced most of the BEF to evacuate from Dunkirk in late May and early June.

There then followed a defensive period, one of German air raids, RAF fighters and the Home Guard. Britain's coastline was mined, surrounded with wire, and defended by battalions strung out along stretches of the coast. Anti-invasion measures were clearly evident. Road signs and railway station signs were taken down, and maps could not be bought. Anti-glider poles were erected in fields and other open spaces. Key installations were protected with barrage balloons, and concrete pillboxes sprang up across the countryside on anticipated enemy routes from the south coast to London and other important cities. The nightly 'blackout' was strictly observed, and notices and posters warned citizens that 'Careless talk costs lives'; to 'Be suspicious of strangers'; and to 'Keep Mum'. For following victory in France, Hitler prepared for the invasion of Britain, codenamed Operation SEALION. To be successful he first needed to achieve air superiority over the English Channel, and the Battle of Britain commenced.

Having completed his training in the summer of 1940, Wand-Tetley was commissioned into the Wiltshires on 17 August, given an officer's Army number to memorize, 143484, and joined 2nd Wiltshires a few days later. The Battle of Britain was then at its very height. In a desperate struggle for mastery of the skies the RAF was, however, able to better the *Luftwaffe*. Failing to achieve air superiority, Hitler was forced in mid-September to call off SEALION and the invasion of England. The Blitz against London and England's other industrial centres, such as Coventry, now commenced in earnest.

The Wiltshire Regiment (Duke of Edinburgh's)

When Wand-Tetley joined 2nd Wiltshires on 20 August 1940 the battalion was encamped at Muthill, in the Strathearn area of Perthshire, under command of Lieutenant Colonel George Thompson DSO MC, although he would depart at the end of that month on promotion. The battalion spent the summer on various anti-invasion exercises around Scotland and then, in October, now under command of Lieutenant Colonel George Oldfield, it moved to new quarters at Aintree Race-course, Liverpool. This made for novel accommodation and one entire platoon was able to be billeted in Lord Derby's private box! Here the battalion continued with similar training to that experienced in Scotland.[29]

Wand-Tetley learnt that 2nd Wiltshires had already been through the mill. The previous year, on the eve of war, the battalion had been based at Catterick Camp, Yorkshire, under command of Lieutenant Colonel 'Oily' Oliphant MC. The battalion had deployed, as part of 13 Infantry Brigade of the 5th Division, with the BEF to France in mid-September 1939. During the period of the 'phoney war' it had adopted a defensive posture, initially based around Nantes and St Nazaire on the river Loire, before moving to the Lille area at the end of the year. Early in the morning of 10 May 1940, the Germans launched their blitzkrieg attack, sweeping the Allies aside. Second Wiltshires, now under command of Lieutenant Colonel Eric Moore DSO, fought a series of rearguard actions while withdrawing back to the coast and eventually embarking with the remnants of the BEF from the beaches of Dunkirk on the night of 31 May 1940. The battalion arrived back in England, only 270 strong, in a variety of ships and small boats, and had moved to Scotland with the rest of 5th Division to recuperate.[30]

Of course, when Wand-Tetley reported for duty he knew far more about the Wiltshires than his fellow newly-arrived subalterns. For him it was really a home from home, and very much a case of a family regiment with which he had become familiar from his earliest of years. This intimate sense of belonging to the regiment that proudly wore the cap-badge of the 'Maltese Cross and Duke of Edinburgh's Coronet and Cipher' had been reinforced by considerable exposure to the Wiltshires over the years, particularly during his impressionable time as a young teenager when he had been in the Marlborough College OTC and when his father had commanded the Regimental Depot at Devizes. On walking into the Officers' Mess of 2nd Wiltshires early memories, such as mess curry lunches enjoyed with his father and mother at the Regimental Depot, and riding out with the hounds of the Avon Vale Hunt, came flooding back to him. His father had, of course, also set up the Regimental Museum at the Depot, and on many occasions he had strolled around it during school holidays, taking in the stories of battles fought over the best part of 200 years.

The ancient oil paintings on the mess walls and the regimental silver of 2nd Wiltshires told of its living history. Of how the regiment could trace its history back to the raising of the 4th Regiment of Foot in 1756 and how two years later the 2/4th Regiment of Foot was re-designated as the 62nd Regiment of Foot. Of campaigns fought in North America, in the Napoleonic Wars and in the Crimea, and of involvement in campaigns from the West Indies to India upon which the British Empire had been founded. Of how the 99th Regiment of Foot, with which the 62nd Regiment of Foot would be linked under the Childers Reforms, was founded in 1824 and of the numerous campaigns in which it too had fought with great distinction in far-flung corners of the world, from New Zealand, to China, and to South Africa against first the Zulu and then the Boer. Of the gallant deeds done and also of the regiment's style – for it was from the 99th that the expression 'Dressed up to the Nines' was derived, for even among the very many smart regiments of the British Army the 99th had a reputation for sartorial elegance second to none. And of how, under the Childers Reforms of 1881 and the 'localization scheme', the 62nd and 99th were linked, lost their old regimental numbers, and were thereafter known by their county title of Wiltshire, with their Headquarters and Regimental Depot at Le Marchant Barracks, Devizes.[31]

In the First World War the Wiltshires fought in all theatres and in doing so won an enviable reputation. Wand-Tetley was not destined to fight with the regiment in the Second World War, during which they would achieve similar laurels to those of the First. When he joined 2nd Wiltshires the first Commando recruiting signals, despatched towards the end of June 1940, had already been received by the chain of command. Wand-Tetley read in Battalion Part One Orders that volunteers were needed for 'special service of a hazardous nature' in special force 'mobile operations'. With Britain on the back-foot for the previous year, Wand-Tetley felt intensely frustrated by the pounding that the country was receiving in the Blitz, and welcomed this opportunity to take the fight back to the enemy. He knew that this was just the thing for him and so applied, through the Adjutant, to his CO, George Oldfield, to be considered, despite not knowing exactly what it was likely to entail.[32]

However, his father, still very influential within the regiment, initially opposed his son's desire to volunteer. He made his views clear to Oldfield, a contemporary of his, who did not need much encouragement to turn a blind eye to Wand-Tetley's application, for no CO would wish to lose his young officers and the best of his men to such a scheme. Besides, the Commando concept was at that stage untried and infantry regiments are by nature fiercely proud of their own record, believing that they are the best, second to none. The Wiltshires were no exception. When eventually the Adjutant informed Wand-Tetley that his applications for special service were going straight in the wastepaper basket he had it out with his father, remonstrating that he had no right to hold him back. After this showdown his father capitulated and the CO processed Wand-Tetley's application for special service.[33]

Notes

1. Census notes, compiled by Philip Best.
2. Curtis, *A Pedigree of The Tathams of Co. Durham*.
3. Ibid.
4. Notes and discussion, Angela Carter (née Tatham), niece of Cécile Wand-Tetley, with author.
5. Tatham, *A Memoire*.
6. Kenrick, *The Story of The Wiltshire Regiment*. Ch. 12.
7. NA Kew, WO 95/1415, WO 95/2243 & WO 95/2165. War Diary, 1 Wiltshire Regiment, 4 Aug 1914–29 May 1919.
8. Ibid.
9. T. H. Wand-Tetley, Army Service Record.
10. Ibid.
11. The Wiltshire Regiment Archives (at The Rifles Museum), Salisbury has in its possession two Olympic Gold Medals attributed to T. H. Wand-Tetley: one for the London Olympics of 1908 and one for the Amsterdam Olympics of 1928. Although he competed at the 1928 Games he is not recorded as a medal winner, and there is no record of him having competed at the 1908 Games, in which year he would have been eighteen and had not yet joined the Army. This, for now, remains inconclusive.
12. *The Journal of The Wiltshire Regiment, 1930–1931*.
13. *The Journal of The Wiltshire Regiment, 1933–1935*.
14. Ibid.

15. Oldfield, *History of the Army Physical Training Corps*. Chs 3 & 4. The year 2010 marked the seventieth anniversary of the modern APTC. Tracing its origins back to 1860 in the Crimean War, in 2010 the Corps celebrated 150 years since its inception, and in November of that year was granted the title prefix 'Royal', thus becoming the RAPTC. *London Gazette*: Colonel (acting Brigadier) T. H. Wand-Tetley retires on retired pay on 17 January 1945 and is granted the Honorary rank of Brigadier. He remained on the Regular Army Reserve of Officers until his 58th birthday in September 1948. His OBE was advanced to CBE at the time of his retirement.

16. Marlborough College website: A Brief History of the College and its Site.

17. Marlborough College archive notes, collated by Dr Terry Rogers, College Archivist.

18. Harling, *Marlborough College: The Corps 1860–1960*.

19. The *Marlburian*, August 1935.

20. P. M. Wand-Tetley, letter dated 7 June 2000, to his great-niece, Hannah Sheard, the elder of two daughters to Sally-Anne (née Scott), Emily being the younger.

21. Downing College, Cambridge, P. M. Wand-Tetley Tutorial File: Ref. No. DCAT/1/2/2060. Letter by R. A. U. Jennings, MA Oxon, dated 25 Sep 1937.

22. Notes and Interview, Angela Carter (née Tatham), niece of Cécile Wand-Tetley, with Author.

23. Downing College, Cambridge, P. M. Wand-Tetley Tutorial File: Ref. No. DCAT/1/2/2060. Letter by T. H. Thompson, BA Cantab, dated 7 June 1938.

24. Downing College, Cambridge, P. M. Wand-Tetley Tutorial File: Ref. No. DCAT/1/2/2060.

25. Downing College student magazine, *The Griffin*, Michaelmas Term 1938 and Lent Term 1939.

26. Downing College, Cambridge, P. M. Wand-Tetley Tutorial File: Ref. No. DCAT/1/2/2060. Letter, T. H. Wand-Tetley dated 13 April 1939.

27. Johnson, *Regimental Fire! The Honourable Artillery Company in World War II, 1939–1945*. Ch. 2.

28. NA Kew, WO 166/1462; WO 166/6964; WO 175/307; WO 169/9462; WO 170/918; WO 170/4832: War Diary of 12 (HAC) RHA.

29. Kenrick, op cit, Ch. 18.

30. Ibid.

31. Gibson, Tom. *Famous Regiments: The Wiltshire Regiment*.

32. Discussion, Peter Wand-Tetley with author.

33. Ibid.

Chapter 2

Army Commando

Special Service Volunteer

6 December 1940. After just four months' commissioned service with 2nd Wiltshires, Wand-Tetley reported for duty with No. 3 Special Service Battalion which had been formed the previous month from No. 4 and No. 7 Commandos. The CO was Lieutenant Colonel Dudley Lister MC, of the Buffs. It was the policy at this stage that individual COs selected their own officers, so this was not the first time that Lister had met Wand-Tetley, having previously interviewed him to assess his suitability. At this stage the Battalion Headquarters and half the unit (No. 2 Company) was at Girvan on the west coast of Scotland, with the other half of the unit (No. 1 Company) about twenty miles farther north at Troon. However, on the very day of Wand-Tetley's arrival a movement order was received by Lister and the entire battalion moved north to Gourock, just west of Glasgow, and, on the 9th, embarked in HMS *Glengyle* for the Isle of Arran. Wand-Tetley was assigned to No. 1 Company under the command of Major M. G. Kerr. As a young subaltern he was appointed as a Section Leader within a Fighting Troop. Commanded by a captain, each Troop had fifty commandos and was divided into two Sections, each led by a subaltern. Having left Gourock, No. 3 SS Battalion made the short trip through the Firth of Clyde and anchored in Lamlash Bay on the east coast of Arran.[1]

British Army Commandos had been raised in June that year, shortly after the evacuation of Dunkirk, at the behest of Prime Minister Churchill, to strike back hard at enemy-held Europe. Comprised of hand-picked volunteers from the regular British Army, Commando units were raised to conduct sea-borne 'butcher and bolt' raids against the *Heer*. Commando units were expected to train for specific operations, forming sub-units of the size and shape required depending upon the specific enemy target. The raiding unit so formed would be expected to operate independently for up to twenty-four hours, be capable of very wide

22

dispersion and individual activity, and specialize in 'hit and run' tactics that depended upon surprise, speed and ingenuity for success.[2]

Upon joining his unit Wand-Tetley immediately found himself engaged in a maelstrom of intensive Commando training. Raiding operations called for irregular fighting methods as opposed to conventional tactics, so there was little focus on defensive tactics in the early years. The requirement was to strike quickly and withdraw while the enemy was still recovering from the shock of the attack. Pitched battle with conventional enemy troops in well defended positions, greater in number and better armed than the Commando raiding parties, was to be avoided. Highly aggressive light-role infantry tactics were therefore called for: shock effect, deception and mobility to gain the upper hand and achieve decisive effect, followed by a quick withdrawal before the enemy could bring their heavier numbers and weapons to bear, was the order of the day. The indirect approach, using the sea and landing at the bottom of cliffs, rocky shorelines and other unlikely routes, were key. Operations at night, under cover of darkness, and relying on surprise, speed and stealth, followed by a violent attack upon the enemy and a quick withdrawal back to base were to be the norm.

In line with the concept of developing self-reliance, Commandos did not receive Government quarters or rations, but were provided with a ration card and daily subsistence allowance to find their own accommodation and cover the cost of their food. This was quite generous in wartime Britain – 13 shillings and 4 pence for officers and 6 shillings and 8 pence for other ranks. There was some generally left over towards the cost of beer and cigarettes when off duty. There were other advantages to living in 'Civvy Billets', for there were no barrack guards, or cook-house fatigues – the general lot of those living in barracks.

On formation in 1940 commandos wore standard British Army battle-dress uniform and 37-pattern webbing and equipment. All volunteers were technically seconded to the Commandos and head-dress and insignia of parent regiments was initially worn, so Wand-Tetley remained on the books of 2nd Wiltshires for pay and continued to wear the beret and cap-badge of the Wiltshire Regiment. The introduction of the Commando green beret in 1942, along with common unit insignia, eventually introduced uniformity. However, such was the Commando *esprit de corps* that although he continued to harbour feelings of pride and loyalty towards his parent regiment, allegiance was quickly developed and focused towards his new unit and his fellow commandos.

In the UK at this time COs of Commando units were responsible for training their own men, for the Commando Basic Training Centre (CBTC) had not yet been set up. This was established in February 1942 under the command of Major Charles Vaughan of the Buffs, at Achnacarry, near Spean Bridge, Invernessshire, at the family seat of

Cameron of Lochiel. In December of that year the Commando Mountain Warfare Training Camp (CMWTC) was also set up at Braemar, Aberdeenshire, to cater for training towards operations in Norway. In the interim Commandos made use of the Combined Training Centre (CTC) at Inveraray. Located at the family seat of the Duke of Argyll on the banks of Loch Fyne and run by Vice Admiral Hughes-Hallett, the CTC offered excellent training facilities. Until Achnacarry was set up Commandos also used the SOE Irregular Warfare School (later the Special Training Centre), established in 1940 and based at Arisaig House on the shores of Loch Ailort on Lord Lovat's Inverailort estate.

The Commando training regime was acknowledged as the toughest in the UK and was designed to produce a highly motivated, self-reliant, first class light-role infantry soldier. Irregular warfare meant that commando officers and men were expected to be physically fitter and more capable than their counterparts in other units, better able to operate independently as well as in groups, and to be more versatile and flexible of mind. Independence of thought and action, along with self-reliance and self-discipline were encouraged. Military training exercises were designed to test a man's endurance to the very limit. Unsuitable volunteers were quickly weeded out. Many, both officers and other ranks, were returned to unit (RTU'd) and this unhappy prospect hung over many a head during training, acting as a spur to the men to push themselves to their limits. Wand-Tetley was not immune from such considerations, but he had every intention of staying.

As befitting their role as light-role infantry, Commandos, for the most part, utilized conventional infantry equipment but at light scales. For raiding they dispensed with all heavy equipment, including anti-gas protective equipment. Heavy ammunition boots were replaced with silent rubber-soled boots or shoes. Lifebelts were worn and toggle-ropes, which could be joined together into lengths of rope for cliff-scaling or obstacle crossing, were individually carried. Bergen rucksacks and, in 1942, assault jerkins, were adopted.

Much of the basic training called for the same skills as those developed by standard infantry regiments: physical training, gym work and boxing, weapon-training, bayonet drill, speed and endurance marching, cross-country runs, and navigation with map and compass. However, the Commandos were expected to achieve higher standards across the board, as well as mastering a number of new skills.

The Commandos called upon subject experts and special training facilities to fit them for their new role. The indirect approach called for cliff-climbing skills, mountaineering, and boat-work, all of which were practised by night as well as by day. Watermanship skills were key, both to amphibious operations and raids, as well as the crossing of water-obstacles. Demolition and sabotage, the preparation of explosive charges using blocks of gun-cotton and safety fuses, both in the dark and under water, was also taught. Clandestine operations by night, stealth, and the ability to stalk quietly over rough terrain, were all practised. The aim was to produce a fighter who had something of the night about him, able to strike swiftly and silently at the enemy before withdrawing back into the mist and fog from which he had come.

As a Section Leader Wand-Tetley's men looked to him to set the example and lead them from the front. And so, against the rugged backdrop of Scotland's wintry mountains, glens and lochs, they trained hard together, all the time perfecting their operational skills. Together they struck out across moor on endurance marches, and practised cliff climbing. Seamanship and boat-work featured frequently, and the men swam with full kit in the icy lochs. Fieldcraft, map-reading, and stalking at night became second nature. They became expert in close-quarter and unarmed combat, and constant exposure to Scotland's winter elements made them tough and inured to hardship.

Nor did Wand-Tetley and his Section ignore the essential tools of their trade, and advanced weapon-training, including enemy weapons, featured prominently in all they did. Commandos were issued with the same weapons as other infantry units, but to different scales, including .303 Lee-Enfield rifles, .45 Thompson sub-machine guns, .303 Bren light machine guns, and .38 revolvers. However, apart from the Boyes .55 anti-tank rifle (replaced by the Projector Infantry Anti-Tank (PIAT) in 1943) they were generally not issued with heavy weapons, such as 3-inch mortars, or medium (.303 Vickers) or heavy machine guns, for it was not intended that they would be expected to overcome well-established enemy defences or themselves take part in a defensive operation.

The bolt-action .303 Short Magazine Lee-Enfield (SMLE) rifle Mk 3, with long sword bayonet, later replaced by the Mk 4 version (with unpopular spike bayonet) and a ten-round magazine, first introduced into British service in 1907, was a superb and beautifully crafted weapon. In skilled hands it could achieve fifteen rounds per minute, and was not prone to stoppages. The commandos practised rapid fire and snap shooting at pop-up targets, usually at ranges up to 300 yards, by both day and night. However, it was very accurate over much longer distances and snipers would carry a standard rifle with a 3× magnification telescopic sight.

The .45-inch calibre Thompson sub-machine gun, or Tommy-Gun, became the iconic Commando weapon. It had become infamous in America in the 1920s and 30s as the favoured weapon of organized crime syndicates in gang warfare, although it had earlier been used by Irish republican guerrillas in the so-called Anglo–Irish War of 1919–21. Large numbers were imported from the United States in the early war years, and far higher proportions were carried by Commandos than by conventional units. The 20-round box magazine was favoured over the 50-round drum magazine, owing to greater reliability and the relative ease with which it could be carried in web equipment and jackets. Ideal for short-range fire and close-quarter work, it was devastating in short automatic bursts.

The reliable .303 Bren light machine gun was carried in higher numbers than was the case with conventional units, for it was portable and practical whereas the Vickers medium machine gun could not be carried for raiding. Based on a Czech design, this bipod-mounted, gas-operated weapon was one of the best machine guns in the world, capable of providing highly accurate firepower to 800 yards, in single shots or automatic bursts of up to 500 rounds per minute.

For personal protection the .38-inch revolver, replaced later by the US Colt .45-inch automatic pistol with seven-round magazine, was standard issue. For close work the Fairbairn-Sykes Commando fighting knife, designed by Major Bill Fairbairn and Captain Eric (Bill) Sykes, would, in time, become standard issue. Fairbairn, a colonial policeman known as the 'Shanghai Buster', had met Sykes, an employee of the Remington rifle company, while in China. Putting to good use experience gleaned from close-quarter fighting, they developed the double-edged, eight-inch bladed knife. It was primarily a thrusting weapon but, being well-balanced, it could also be thrown. Initially manufactured by Wilkinson Sword, various models were produced over the war years, the Mk 3 becoming the mass-produced version. They also taught unarmed combat (i.e. no firearms, but including knives) and Fairbairn, a ju-jitsu expert who had produced self-defence manuals for British imperial police forces across Asia, specialized in silent killing techniques with coshes, bows, sticks, garrotting and neck-breaking, disabling techniques such as eye-gouging, mouth-slitting, shoulder and jaw dislocation, nose-chopping, shin-scraping, ear-tearing and eardrum-breaking, and releases to escape from any hold. Every demonstration of a technique ended with the advice, 'and then kick him in the testicles'.

Close-quarter indirect fire-support was provided by the lightweight 2-inch mortar, firing high explosive, smoke, or illumination rounds. A maximum range of 500 yards, but effective range of 300 yards, could be achieved. For close-quarter work grenades were used, including the No. 36 Mills bomb (or 'pineapple' grenade), No. 69 concussion grenade, and the No. 77 phosphorous grenade for producing smoke screens, or for trench clearing. The No. 36 Mills bomb could also be fired out to 200 yards using specially adapted SMLEs.

The .303 Vickers machine gun was only introduced to the arsenal with the advent of Commando support troops in August 1943. This effective and reliable, water-cooled, tripod-mounted, medium machine gun had a greater rate of sustained fire than any other infantry weapon. Its slow rate of fire was sixty rounds per minute, standard rapid fire was 250 per minute (and, in extremis, up to 500 per minute).

The British commando concept had been the brainchild of Lieutenant Colonel Dudley Clarke, Royal Artillery, at the time General Staff Officer Grade 1 (GSO1) to General Sir John Dill, Chief of the Imperial General Staff (CIGS). His inspiration had been the Boer commandos of the South African War of 1899–1902 and their extremely successful guerrilla tactics and lightning strikes against vastly superior British forces. Churchill approved of the title, remembering no doubt his own exciting encounters with Boer commandos when in South Africa as a war correspondent.

However, the British commando genesis had been in the earlier 'Independent Companies'. These had initially been proposed by the Military Intelligence (Research) Branch of the War Office. MI(R), prior to its reorganization in the spring of 1939 had, in its earlier guise as the General Staff (Research) Branch (GS(R)), been established in the mid-thirties to study the art of irregular warfare. By 1939 Lieutenant Colonel Colin Gubbins MC, Royal Artillery, and Major Joe Holland DFC, Royal Engineers, heading the MI(R) branch, were busy producing pamphlets on guerrilla warfare based on studies of Boer tactics, various contemporary civil wars, and the tactics of T. E. Lawrence (of Arabia) in the First World War Arab Revolt. Holland had flown in support of Lawrence and his Arabs; Lawrence's raids were essentially the prototype in that war to the 'special forces' operations that were developed from the Second World War onwards.[3]

The nascent Commando force had, since formation, undergone, and would continue to undergo, a number of reorganizations and changes in title. However, none of this unduly worried Wand-Tetley who, in early December 1940, was delighted to have been posted to a Commando unit and would barely have time to find his feet and train himself and his men for their role before they found themselves bound for the Middle East in the New Year.

Layforce

When No. 3 SS Battalion had sailed from Gourock to the Isle of Arran in HMS *Glengyle* it had been accompanied by No. 4 SS Battalion in HMS *Glenroy* and No. 2 SS Battalion in HMS *Royal Scotsman*. All three units were placed on an operational footing on 13 December, but a gale blew up for the next few days which seriously hampered their Assault Landing Craft training. Accordingly, all three ships steamed a few miles farther north to Brodick Bay which provided better shelter and allowed them to get on with the business of practising their boat-work and landings. In view of the operation for which they had been warned, all three ships returned to Gourock on 17 December to take on water, oil and victuals. However, their scheduled return for the next day was postponed because the victualling ship sank in the harbour with all its stores on board. Nonetheless by the 19th all the ships were back at Arran. The following day Wand-Tetley and his fellow subalterns were directed to muster their Sections on the deck of HMS *Glengyle* to hear Admiral of the Fleet Sir Roger Keyes address the battalion. Having been piped aboard, Keyes informed the men that the operation had been indefinitely postponed, but to mitigate their disappointment told them that he believed it would not be too long before a date was fixed and that a similar delay had occurred prior to the famous raid on Zeebrugge in the previous war. The following day Dudley Lister therefore took his unit over to the west of Arran to continue his battalion's programme of intense training. He established Battalion Headquarters at Blackwaterfoot, with No. 1 Company nearby at Shiskine, and No. 2 Company at Lochranza in the north of Arran, and for the next three weeks Wand-Tetley and his fellow subalterns focused on honing the battle skills of their respective Sections.[4]

On 14 January 1941, having been informed that the operation was back on the cards again, Lister was able to grant his battalion two weeks' embarkation leave. The commandos returned to Gourock on 28 January, where HMS *Glengyle* was moored, and the following morning the ship steamed back to Arran. Having dropped anchor at Lamlash Bay, Lister disembarked with his Battalion Headquarters and No. 1 Company and from this basis would, by the end of the following month, re-establish No. 4 Commando. However, Wand-Tetley was one of four officers and ninety-one other ranks from No. 1 Company who contrived to remain on board *Glengyle* to make No. 2 Company fully up to strength. On 30 January No. 2 Company, now under the independent command of Major Felix Colvin of the Dorsets, reverted to its former title of No. 7 Commando. Admiral Sir Roger Keyes was piped aboard that same day and this time he was able to confirm that the operation was definitely on. He spoke in stirring terms to the men of the Commando, but he was careful to give nothing away that might indicate their destination. The following day their Brigade Commander, Haydon, also came aboard to bid them farewell, reminding them that they 'carried with them the good name of all'. By this stage the new contingent had been allocated their appointments, Wand-Tetley having been selected as CO's liaison officer. As such, besides providing direct support to Colvin, he would work closely with the Adjutant, Captain J. M. Flood, thus gaining a rare insight into the working of the entire Commando.[5]

Conspicuous by their absence were Captain 'Gus' March-Phillips and Lieutenant Geoffrey Appleyard, neither of whom had returned to No. 7 Commando following leave. In part this was behind the reason for the required uplift in new officers. Although their fellow subalterns did not know it at the time, they had in fact both been purloined by SOE as instructors, and the following year would lead the highly successful, buccaneering raid in the converted trawler, *Maid Honor*, against Axis shipping at Fernando Po, West Africa.

Thus it was that some two months after having arrived in Scotland Wand-Tetley found himself as part of the 1,500-strong 'Z Force', bound for the Middle East. Under command of Lieutenant Colonel Bob Laycock, Royal Horse Guards, Z Force consisted of the newly reconstituted Nos 7, 8 and 11 Commandos, A Troop of No. 3 Commando, and the Folbot Section (from No. 8 Commando) under command of Captain Roger 'Jumbo' Courtney, King's Royal Rifle Corps. Z Force, therefore, led the way in reverting to the revised Commando structures. 'Lucky' Laycock, its commander, was a natural leader and a well-heeled socialite about town. As the former CO of No. 8 Commando there was more than a little truth to the rumour that he had selected his subalterns on the basis of a gin-and-tonic interview at the bar of White's Club. The officers' mess of No. 8 Commando, in particular, having recruited from the Household Division, included a number of officers of noble lineage. This 'smart set' would become known for the high stakes card-games played on the passage to the Middle East. Amongst those at the card tables was Second Lieutenant George, The Lord Jellicoe, son of the First World War hero Admiral John Rushworth Jellicoe, who lost three years' salary but managed to win it back again before reaching Suez. He and Lieutenant David Stirling, son of retired General Archibald Stirling of Kier, Member of Parliament and Deputy Lieutenant of Perthshire, and of The Honourable Margaret Fraser, daughter of Lord Lovat, were both destined to distinguish themselves later in the war.

Admiral Sir Roger Keyes had been keen to put into practice the larger raids involving 5,000 to 10,000 commandos that Churchill envisaged. Conscious that such operations would not yet be feasible against the German-held coastline of France he had considered the possibilities of the Mediterranean. There it would be possible for such a raiding force to operate in conjunction with a large-scale offensive in the Middle East, something not possible at that time in Europe. In the Middle East objectives for such a force, along the North African coastline, would be more accessible than those on the Western European coastline, and would amount to 'flank', rather than 'frontal' attacks, which would be better suited to the Commando style of operations.

Italy's entry into the war in June 1940 had opened the theatres of North Africa, the Mediterranean, and East Africa. Benito Mussolini aimed to challenge Britain for control of the Mediterranean, secure Egypt and the Suez Canal – vital to Britain's lines of communication – and expand his African empire at the expense of the British East

African colonies. He made his first move in July 1940, capturing British border posts in Sudan, and his second in August with an invasion of British Somaliland launched from Abyssinia. General Sir Archibald Wavell, Commander-in-Chief Middle East since August 1939, launched a counter-offensive to capture Italian East Africa in early 1941, and both Eritrea and Abyssinia were captured by November the same year, restoring Emperor Haile Selassie, Lion of Judah and King of Kings, to his throne in Addis Ababa in the process.

Meanwhile, Wavell's attack on Italian forces in Egypt commenced on 9 December 1940 with Operation COMPASS. Taken by surprise, the Italian positions were quickly overrun by Lieutenant General Richard O'Connor's Western Desert Force, and the Allies moved rapidly west, capturing the port of Bardia on 5 January 1941, and Tobruk on 22 January, before driving the Italians before them to the port of Benghazi. By early February the Allies had captured some 120,000 Italian prisoners of war, and the battle of Beda Fomm, south of Benghazi, was the culmination in the capture of the entire eastern Libyan province of Cyrenaica.

This proved to be the British Army's first major victory of the war but, in the event, the triumph would be relatively short-lived, for General Erwin Rommel was waiting in the wings. Thus commenced a campaign that would see the Germans, and then the British, chase one another back and forth across the Libyan desert in what became known as the 'Benghazi stakes'. The objective was always to outpace the enemy, whether withdrawing in the face of him, or advancing and attempting to break through and cause havoc in his rear echelons. The ebb and flow, and success or otherwise, of operations would often be dictated by logistic and supply considerations, for the farther a force advanced the weaker it became and the more vulnerable did its lines of communication become. From Tripoli, in the west, which Rommel held as his main supply harbour, to British-held Alexandria, in the east, was 1,400 miles: the oft-quoted 'tactician's paradise, but quartermaster's hell'.

Against this backdrop Keyes had proposed to the Chiefs of Staff on 30 October 1940 that Pantellaria, a small island between the North African coast and Sicily, should be captured. The intention was that it could then be used as an alternative naval base to Malta, as well as providing an airbase from which to attack Italian lines of communication in the Mediterranean. Operation WORKSHOP, as it was code-named, was given the go-ahead, provided that it did not interfere with Operation BRISK, the intended capture of the Azores should Spain enter the war in support of the Axis powers. Keyes immediately set about planning how the SS Brigade would approach the task.

Although WORKSHOP had Churchill's support, Admiral Sir Andrew Browne Cunningham, ('ABC'), Commander-in-Chief Mediterranean Fleet, was opposed to it because he did not believe his overstretched resources would be capable of holding on to Pantellaria once it was captured. He also initially voiced his concern over Keyes's other scheme, codenamed MANDIBLES, which was to capture islands in the Dodecanese. Throughout December the debate swung to and fro. In mid-December Wavell's success in the Western Desert gave prominence to WORKSHOP, and accordingly Z Force was stood by to sail on 14 December. It seemed to some planners that an assault on Italy or at least Sicily might not be far off, and the capture of Pantellaria would be an advantage in terms of a stepping stone between North Africa and Sicily. However, the sailing of Z Force was then postponed because of fears over a possible invasion of Spain by Germany. Cunningham believed greater mileage could be achieved from MANDIBLES, particularly after the *Luftwaffe* had been deployed to Sicily in early January 1941, as the Dodecanese would facilitate an Allied hold on the Eastern Mediterranean. The final objective in MANDIBLES was to seize the island of Rhodes. Finally it was agreed that MANDIBLES would go ahead.

From the time of Wand-Tetley's arrival at the beginning of December 1940 until the departure of Z Force at the end of January 1941, he had trained hard in Scotland with his Commando unit, but for which particular operation, WORKSHOP or MANDIBLES, had been uncertain. Only a select few knew their destination and the likely target, for they were under sealed orders. This was to limit the intelligence the enemy might gain if survivors were plucked from the sea following a naval action, for enemy submarines were on the prowl in the Atlantic. Nonetheless, given the nature of their training on Arran, many of the commandos had concluded that the capture of an island might be involved. Indeed, such was security and the extent of last minute deliberations that Laycock was only formally appointed to command Z Force on the day it sailed, and the remark of Haydon's Brigade Major to him just prior to departure is particularly telling: 'You appear to be going to command a force of over 100 officers and 1,500 ORs with one staff officer, a note book and three wireless sets which nobody can work.'[6]

Finally leaving Arran on 31 January with No. 7 Commando in HMS *Glengyle*, No. 8 Commando in *Glenroy* and the men of No. 11 Commando split between these two ships, Z Force set sail for Egypt via the Cape of Good Hope. *Glenearn*, the third of the 'Glens', with Mobile Naval Base Defence Organisation (MNBDO) 1 – a Royal Marines unit whose role it was to capture or protect naval bases – set sail a few days later. Wand-Tetley was satisfied to be heading to what at the time was, as he and many of his fellow officers had correctly surmised, the only active theatre of operations, the Middle East. For the first part of the journey the Glen ships and the cruiser HMS *Kenya* joined several destroyers providing escort to a large convoy destined for America. They headed out into the Atlantic, passing between the Mull of Kintyre and Ireland and into the teeth of a violent storm that did not let up for three days. Very few were unaffected by seasickness and the first part of the voyage was generally miserable for all concerned. However, as the ships headed farther into the Atlantic the weather improved and with it so did morale.

Upon reaching American territorial waters the Glen ships left the convoy and headed back across the Atlantic, their destination Freetown in Sierra Leone. Moving into tropic waters, flying fish skittered across the bows, tropical kit was issued to the men, and then land was sighted – palm trees along a white beach. Having anchored on the 10th the ships took on board fuel and water for the voyage ahead. Liberty was not granted and only a few officers on official business went ashore, happy to have firm ground beneath their feet once again. As the ships lay in harbour the locals in their small boats plied their trade, selling carvings and fruit to the troops and Wand-Tetley and others amused themselves by throwing coins into the water for small boys to dive and collect. The following day the three Glens weighed anchor and, escorted by HMS *Dorsetshire* and three destroyers, steamed on towards South Africa.[7]

The day after departing Sierra Leone *Glengyle* reached the equator and Neptune was invited by signal to come aboard to oversee the Crossing the Line Ceremony which was conducted with 'skill, vigour and aplomb' for those to be initiated. Now that it was warm many of the subalterns took to sleeping on deck under the stars to escape the stifling and cramped conditions inside. Reaching Cape Town early on the morning of the 19th Captain Petrie RN berthed the *Glengyle* alongside the quay and the men heard to their satisfaction that they would be here for the next two days and that, following a route march to be conducted each morning, shore leave would be granted from noon until midnight. There was a very warm welcome awaiting the commandos as they disembarked on to the quayside, with a throng of well-wishers and families waiting there, all keen to show the soldiers the local sights and invite them home. South Africa was a country with which Wand-Tetley was of course familiar, given his family connections and his time spent there in Natal prior to university. The warm sunshine and familiar sights and smells evoked happy memories. There was time enough to visit Table Mountain, and relax on the beaches and swim. The Force set sail early on the 21st, and apart from a number of cases of soldiers arriving back late from liberty there were few disciplinary problems. The Capetowners were reported to have said that the commandos had behaved very well, to which the wry

32

observation was recorded by Flood in the No. 7 Commando War Diary, 'not surprising since the convoy before ours was Australian'.[8]

It had been intended to stop next at Durban but, pressed for time, the convoy steamed past, and the officers busied themselves in conducting military appreciations on how to invade and seize Rhodes. At this stage HMS *Dorsetshire* left the convoy to hunt for a German raider that had been reported off the coast of Madagascar, and the Glen ships headed north as planned, passing Dar-es-Salaam, Tanga and Mombasa. Little did Wand-Tetley realize at the time, but he would spend time working in Kenya and Tanzania after the war. Others in Z Force were also familiar with East Africa, not least 'Jumbo' Courtney, who before the war had engaged in gold-prospecting and big game-hunting there. He had also undertaken long-distance expeditions by canoe, including one down the White Nile, in between his hunting safaris. Indeed it was his interest in canoes that had prompted him to persuade Laycock (at that time CO of No. 8 Commando) to allow him to experiment militarily with canoes, with the aim of sabotaging enemy ships with limpet mines. His small unit, equipped with canvas-covered Folbot (or Foldboat) canoes that were collapsible and could be man-packed or stored in a relatively small space, became No. 1 Special Boat Section (SBS). Initially it had been the intention to form such a section within each of the Commandos, but except for one within No. 6 Commando, which was called 101 Troop, no others were established.[9]

Entering the Gulf of Aden, the *Glengyle* and the remainder of Layforce cruised north up the Red Sea and dropped anchor in Suez on 7 March 1941. Here Laycock heard from GHQ Middle East, based in Cairo, that two weeks earlier the War Office had renamed Z Force as 'Layforce' (after its commander) and that for security reasons no reference was to be made to the Commando title or for that matter to the Royal Navy. The reason behind this increased security was Operation CORDITE, the imperative within the MANDIBLES plan quickly to capture the island of Rhodes.

Having disembarked on the 11th No. 7 Commando marched to a tented camp at Geneifa, site of the Middle East Commando Depot, on the canal east of Kabrit. Two days later, having settled in, they were visited at Camp 50 by Sir Archibald Wavell and Sir John Dill, both of whom welcomed the assembled commandos to Egypt. The soldiers were engaged in shooting and bayonet practice, and Wavell evidently enjoyed the opportunity that was offered him to fire the Tommy Gun. Layforce was placed under Major General John Evetts, commanding 6th Division, who until recently had been on the North West Frontier of India. Also in 6th Division, which had been informed they were to seize Rhodes, were 22 Guards Brigade and 16 Infantry Brigade. Here

Layforce was reinforced by two Middle East Commandos, Nos. 50 and 52 which, being understrength, were amalgamated at the end of March.

In April Laycock would be promoted to colonel and be given a Brigade Major, Freddie Graham, and a headquarters from which to run his now expanded brigade-sized force. By this stage the novelist, Lieutenant Evelyn Waugh, Royal Marines and subsequently Royal Horse Guards, had already handed over the responsibility for writing No. 8 Commando's War Diary to Lieutenant Randolph Churchill of the 4th Hussars and had been appointed to Laycock's staff as his Intelligence Officer. For his part, Wand-Tetley assumed the responsibility for writing No. 7 Commando's War Diary at the beginning of April, his first entry at Geneifa being, 'Lt Col Laycock, Major Graham, Lt Comdr Parkinson RN, Lt Comdr Oarmauney RN and Lt Collar RN dine as guests of the Officers' Mess'.[10]

The Commandos were redesignated as 'battalions' in line with the security decree. A Battalion (No. 7 Commando) was commanded by Felix Colvin, now promoted to lieutenant colonel; B Battalion (No. 8 Commando) by Dermot Daly, Scots Guards; C Battalion (No. 11 Commando) by Dick Pedder, Highland Light Infantry; and D Battalion (No. 50/52 ME Commando) by George Young, Royal Engineers. The organization of this amalgamated ME Commando was slightly different, for it had five companies, each having two 50-man Fighting Troops, and each Troop having two Sections.[11]

The ME Commandos had been raised in 1940 by order of the War Office. GHQ Middle East had accordingly followed the lead of developments in the UK. Specifically, it was the MI(R) Branch, responsible for irregular forces under Colonel Adrian Simpson, that was set the task of raising the force. Three units were set up, the first of which, No. 50 ME Commando, with some seventy Spaniards in its ranks, under George Young, was raised in August 1940. This was followed in October by No. 51 ME Commando, comprised of Palestinians, both Jews and Arabs, under Henry 'Kid' Cator MC, Royal Scots Greys, and in November by No. 52 ME Commando, under Harry Fox-Davies, Durham Light Infantry. The ME Commando Depot, for training and reinforcement of the three units, was set up at the end of the year under Major D. W. Melville MC. They adopted, as their fighting knife, the 'Fanny', a knife with knuckleduster handle, which also featured as their cap-badge, wore the Australian slouch hat, and private soldiers were given the title of Raider.

Operation CORDITE

Training for the capture of Rhodes swung into action immediately after arrival, and for the first month Wand-Tetley found himself with A Battalion (No. 7 Commando) at the newly-opened Combined Training

Centre (CTC) at Kabrit on the Bitter Lakes, where all amphibious training was now taking place. The Layforce part of the plan was that, having conducted an assault landing on Rhodes, it would capture the airfield. Geneifa and Kabrit were well sited for training, with the Bitter Lakes available for boat practice and the Sweet Water Canal close by for raft work. Inland there were miles of barren desert, scrub and rocky plains available for endurance marching and tactical training. By the time Layforce arrived, No. 51 ME Commando had already set the bar particularly high by recording an Army marching record of fifty miles over hilly and rough jebel country while carrying full kit, in fifteen hours and forty-five minutes.[12]

As a preliminary to CORDITE, Courtney's Folbot Section, assisted by Lieutenant Commander Nigel Clogstoun-Willmott RN, conducted a daring and detailed three-day reconnaissance of the Rhodes beaches, launching from the submarine HMS *Triumph*, for which the two men were to receive the MC and DSO respectively. The reconnaissance included the hotel beach at the north of the island just outside the main gates of the city of Rhodes. The men managed to evade notice, test wire defences, and make sketches. Successfully avoiding the enemy, the moment of most unpredictable tension was on account of a dog, which kept pace with Courtney on the other side of the wire on the beach in front of the hotel, but since it confined itself to growling rather than barking, the game was not given away. Throughout 1941 Courtney would operate with the Commandos, but was attached to the 1st Submarine Flotilla in HMS *Medway* in Alexandria harbour, for it was from submarines that the Section launched their Folbot canoes.

At the end of 1941 Courtney returned to England to raise No. 2 SBS which, formed primarily on the basis of Captain G. C. S. Montanaro's canoeists of 101 Troop of No. 6 Commando, would operate until the end of the war, in one guise or another, in Europe, North Africa, the Mediterranean, the Far East, and Australia. Late in 1943 Courtney's original No. 1 Special Boat Section would provide the basis for the formation of Captain The Lord Jellicoe's Special Boat Squadron.

However, the situation in the Mediterranean then changed rapidly. On 6 April 1941 the Germans invaded Yugoslavia and Greece and, with all available Allied air and naval assets now required to support Greece, CORDITE was called off. The German Blitzkrieg tactics were supremely successful, and by the end of the month the Allied evacuation of Greece had commenced. By this stage the Allies were also experiencing worsening fortunes in Libya. In January 1941, with Italian forces defeated and in disarray, Hitler had deployed *Luftwaffe* forces to Sicily to aid the Italians in the air assault on Malta, Britain's strategic base. He had also despatched two divisions and additional aircraft to Libya. The commander of this *Deutsches Afrika Korps* (DAK), which arrived in Tripoli in

February 1941, was General Erwin Rommel, who wasted no time in reversing earlier British successes in Libya.

Having arrived in North Africa, Rommel launched an offensive at the end of March that captured Bardia and Sollum, in Cyrenaica, and successfully pushed XIII Corps (previously the Western Desert Force, and later to become part of Eighth Army) back towards the Egyptian border. The Allies, surprised by the speed of Rommel's advance, lost both Lieutenant General Philip Neame VC, the new commander of Cyrenaica, and Lieutenant General Sir Richard O'Connor, as prisoners during the confused withdrawal. The Allies nonetheless retained Tobruk, which lay astride Rommel's main lines of communication between his front and his supply bases to his rear. The Australian and British troops there would remain under siege for eight months until 7 December. With many Allied troops diverted to Greece, reinforcements were now needed desperately and Layforce was briefly placed in GHQ's Reserve, but not for long.

Raid on Bardia

On 11 April 1941 Laycock received orders to carry out a reconnaissance of the Libyan coast and to be prepared to conduct raids, 200-men strong, behind enemy lines. Wand-Tetley learnt of this on 13 April when, in anticipation of these raids his CO, Colvin, was ordered to move A Battalion from Kabrit to Alexandria to be close to the Mediterranean Fleet. At this stage Layforce in its entirety left 6th Division and came under command of XIII Corps (although the Western Desert Force title was still in use). Laycock attended a planning conference on board HMS *Warspite* over 14/15 April. The plan that was developed called for A and C Battalions to raid the enemy-held port of Bardia on the Libyan coast, while B Battalion raided the coast road, the *Via Balbia*, at Bomba.[13]

Bardia, thought to be an important enemy headquarters, was the first Libyan town, some twenty miles west of Sollum on the Egyptian border. Its picturesque white-walled houses sat upon tall cliffs overlooking the sea, and on the landward side a strong defensive double perimeter had been built by the enemy. The arrival of Laycock's Intelligence Officer, Evelyn Waugh, now a captain, wearing a solar topee, shorts and a beard, served to lighten the mood somewhat during the serious business of planning. Laycock, feeling rather harassed and under pressure, brusquely queried him saying 'What brings you here?' Back came Waugh's somewhat flippant response, 'Merely loyalty, sir.'[14]

Speed of operation was deemed paramount and by the evening of 15 April Brigade HQ, with A and C Battalions, had embarked safely in HM Ships *Glengyle* and *Glenearn*. B Battalion in HMS *Decoy* sailed at 2200 hours that same evening, and the *Glengyle* and *Glenearn* sailed at 0400 hours the following morning. By early evening an easterly wind was blowing at Force 5 and there was very heavy surf on the beaches. The submarine HMS *Triumph* also reported that it would not be able to launch its Folbots owing to the worsening weather. The concern was as much over re-embarkation as it was on the landing itself. The raid on Bardia was therefore postponed, and that planned on Bomba was in the event cancelled.

On 18 April, with a break in the weather, the plan was put in motion again, but this time with just Layforce Brigade HQ and A Battalion operating from HMS *Glengyle*. B Battalion were, needless to say, disappointed to have been stood down, but Wand-Tetley and the rest of A Battalion received with relief the news that they were still involved. Attached for the mission was a small contingent from the Royal Tank Regiment, comprising an officer and nineteen other ranks, who would assist in the event of the capture of any enemy armoured vehicles. The *Glengyle* sailed from Alexandria at 0230 hours on 19 April, the mission being to harass the enemy's lines of communication and to inflict damage on his supplies. She was escorted by the anti-aircraft cruiser, HMS *Coventry* and three Australian destroyers, HMA Ships *Stuart*, *Voyager* and *Waterhen*. HMS *Triumph*, with Courtney's Folbot Troop aboard, was also there. However, *Triumph*, which was to have shown a white navigational light two and a half miles off the coast of Bardia, was mistakenly attacked by Allied aircraft on her way and so arrived late. Courtney had thus also been a little late in reaching an islet from where it was planned he would show a green navigational light, and one of the Folbots had been wrecked while trying to launch it from the submarine conning-tower in a heavy swell.[15]

The plan called for A Battalion, divided into seven detachments based on its 50-man Troops, to land by Assault Landing Craft (ALC) on one of four beaches, depending upon the specific tasks allocated. The first four detachments were to land on A Beach, the fifth on B Beach, the sixth on C Beach, and the seventh on D Beach. *Glengyle* was due to arrive at her rendezvous at 2205 hours on 19 April, and the ALCs to depart from her between 2215 and 2220 hours. The ALCs were then due to leave the beaches on the homeward trip at 0230 hours on 20 April, allowing *Glengyle* to depart by 0400 hours. Thus timings were extremely tight, with only some three hours ashore for the commandos to accomplish their mission, but this was necessary to ensure that the ships would not be exposed to enemy air attack during daylight hours while they were beyond the reach of friendly fighter cover.[16]

At none of the beaches was enemy opposition encountered. Indeed, throughout the entire operation the enemy was particularly scarce. No. 1 Detachment (i.e. B Troop) successfully secured and held A Beach for the arrival and subsequent withdrawal of Nos 2, 3 and 4 Detachments. All went well in this respect except that one officer, Lieutenant

D. F. Passmore, who failed to answer correctly a sentry's challenge was tragically shot and died the following morning of his wounds. It was believed that he thought the sentry was challenging an unknown person in the opposite direction. No. 2 Detachment (i.e. F and H Troops) established a roadblock at the designated place with the aim of intercepting enemy vehicles, but in the event none were encountered.

No. 3 Detachment (i.e. D and J Troops) was to attack the 'square camp' and destroy any enemy stores found. No enemy was encountered, but a store of vehicle tyres found there was set on fire with incendiary bombs, and burnt furiously for the next two hours. On the way back to A Beach half of this party lost its way and so then headed for B Beach but, unknown to them, no ALC had landed there as initially planned. Twenty of these men were eventually picked up from C Beach, but the remainder, including five officers and sixty-five ORs, had to be left behind and were subsequently made prisoner by the Italians. These included Captain G. E. Ruggles-Brise of D Troop, Captain J. Colbeck and Lieutenant W. M. Royds of J Troop, as well as Captain B. Richards, recently appointed as Adjutant, and Major B. H. Ashford-Russell, the Administrative Officer.

No. 4 Detachment (i.e. E Troop) had been ordered to raid Bardia town. Approaching from the south the Detachment reached the edge of the town which it found deserted but, running out of time, it returned to A Beach without incident. No. 5 Detachment (i.e. I Troop and half of C Troop) which had mistakenly been landed at A Beach, rather than B Beach, and whose task was to attack Bardia town from the north was unable to conduct its task, there being not enough time to get to B Beach.

No. 6 Detachment (i.e. A Troop and the other half of C Troop) landed on C Beach. Its tasks included destroying a road bridge, a pumping station and reservoir, and the cratering of roads. Upon landing the detachment split into two parties to accomplish these tasks. The pumping station party encountered difficulties following the directions provided by the Intelligence Branch. By the time it arrived at the target available time was running out rapidly and so it was only able to impose limited damage. The other party set out to crater the road on the escarpment which it duly did, but due to the bedrock underlying the road only limited damage could be achieved. It met with greater success in tackling the bridge, which consisted of a 3-inch thick tarmac road running over 12-inch-by-12-inch timber baulks, supported by wooden trestle supports. The seventy-two pound explosive charge blew away a large part of the road and rendered it impassable to vehicle traffic but not to infantry, so once the dust had settled the party returned to the bridge, doused the wooden trestles in petrol, and set fire to it. This, like the tyre dump, was still burning when the commandos departed the beaches.

No. 7 Detachment (i.e. G Troop) landed on D Beach with the task of destroying coast defence or anti-aircraft guns on the peninsula which had been reported as being in action several days earlier. No trace could be found of such a gun, but the Detachment did find four 5.9-inch naval guns, and their breeches were duly blown up with gelignite charges.

Colvin's Battalion Headquarters party including Wand-Tetley went ashore with No. 3 Detachment, although the Second-in-Command, Major Ken Wylie of the Royal Engineers, attached himself to the demolition party of No. 6 Detachment. Laycock and his Brigade staff followed Colvin's party in to A Beach with No. 4 Detachment. An extraordinary episode in the Bardia raid to Wand-Tetley's mind concerned the participation by Admiral Sir Walter Cowan Bt KCB DSO MVO, an old shipmate of Sir Roger Keyes. Despite being seventy-one years of age he obviously felt that his active service days were far from over, and managed to persuade the powers-that-be to allow him on the raid. This was to be his first commando raid and he next attached himself to, and fought with, an Indian cavalry regiment until he was captured by the Italians in 1942 at Bir Hacheim while attacking an enemy Panzer single-handed with his revolver. Repatriated by the Italians, he was soon back in action in Italy first with one commando unit and then with another in January 1944. A fearless officer and exemplary leader, Cowan was to win a bar to his DSO, the first of which he had won some forty-six years earlier in 1898 while commanding a gunboat on the Nile during the Omdurman campaign.[17]

Apart from that element of No. 3 Detachment which had ended up on B Beach without an ALC to carry them back to the ship, the remainder of A Battalion managed, despite difficulties, to make it back. Nonetheless, the loss of five officers and some sixty ORs as prisoners of war was no small matter. Faulty compass equipment in the ALCs made it difficult to locate *Glengyle* lying four miles offshore in the dark, and one ALC which became stranded on the beach owing to the strong surf had to be destroyed *in situ* to stop it falling into the hands of the enemy. Another ALC with a defective compass never did locate *Glengyle*, but successfully made it back along the coastline to Tobruk, still at that stage in Allied hands, under her own steam. From here the coxswain, Sub Lieutenant England RN, the two commando officers, Lieutenants G. M. Milton and J. M. Kinross, and thirty-nine ORs made it back to Alexandria in HMS *Greyhound*. The *Glengyle* was, nonetheless, able to depart by 0500 hours and made it back by 2300 hours on 20 April.[18]

No liberty was granted on 21 April and the men of A Battalion remained aboard the *Glengyle* in harbour. The exception was the small funeral party which included the Padre, Captain R. G. Lunt, and Wand-Tetley, both of whom went ashore that afternoon to bury Lieutenant D. F. Passmore at the British Cemetery behind the 8th General Hospital. Layforce Brigade HQ and A Battalion disembarked from the *Glengyle* the following day and proceeded to their camp at Sidi Bishr. With the best part of D and J Troops lost during the Bardia raid, a degree of reorganization was needed, focused upon the Battalion's remaining eight Troops. Wand-Tetley was posted to B Troop, under Lieutenant D. J. P. Thirkell-White of the Suffolks, to take over Passmore's Section and at the end of April he also relinquished responsibility for writing the Battalion's War Diary.[19]

The raid on Bardia achieved mixed results, the destruction of the bridge undoubtedly causing the enemy temporary difficulty. More importantly, from a strategic perspective, the Germans were forced to divert the best part of a brigade from Sollum to Bardia, and to build boom defences in Bardia harbour in case of a repeat raid, thus relieving pressure against the Allies at Sollum. Nonetheless, it was evident to the military hierarchy that poor intelligence from GHQ Middle East had committed and risked substantial forces – a Glen ship, a cruiser, three destroyers, a submarine and a Commando – on a raid against a town that was largely deserted. However, to the commandos of A Battalion it was nonetheless 'one in the bank', and it was satisfying to have finally completed a raid after all their hard training.

There followed a period of extreme frustration for the Layforce commandos, with planning and orders given for raids which would then be cancelled at the last minute. It would not be long before Wand-Tetley and the rest of A Battalion would find itself engaged in fierce fighting on Crete. However, the general sense of exasperation felt by A Battalion, which remained afloat on HMS *Glengyle* until May, can be gleaned from an irreverent comment on Churchill's Battle of Britain speech, left as an inscription on a partition in one of the mess decks, 'Never in the whole history of human endeavour have so few been buggered about by so many'.[20]

Crete

On 20 May 1941 the Germans launched an airborne invasion of Crete, codenamed Operation MERCURY. During fierce hand-to-hand fighting the Allies were forced to retreat across the island in the face of the enemy. A and D Battalions of Layforce were despatched to assist in the evacuation of the island. Arriving on Crete a week after the invasion, the two Layforce battalions fought a gallant rearguard action among the rocks, vines and olives to cover the evacuation, a role for which they were neither organized nor equipped. Designed for close-quarter fighting, the Commandos had no transport and no long-range weapons such as mortars or heavy machine guns capable of halting the enemy at the required range. Nonetheless, the Commando rearguard action successfully enabled the evacuation to take place, but the cost was extremely high, and of the 800 commandos sent to Crete some 600 were lost, killed or captured.[21]

The Cretan garrison – Creforce, as it was called – under command of Major General Sir Bernard Freyberg, had been anticipating and preparing for a German seaborne invasion. It was entirely caught out by the nature of the lightning airborne assault, this being the first strategic use of airborne forces in history. Crete's principal importance to the British lay in its naval base at Suda, which provided refuelling facilities for ships being used in the protection of Malta. The defence of the island until March had been in the hands of Major General E. C. Weston, Royal Marines, who had at his disposal the MNBDO along with 14 Infantry Brigade. However, following the evacuation of Greece, Crete had been reinforced with the 2nd Australian Division and the 2nd New Zealand Division. Overall command for Creforce was at this time handed by Churchill to Freyberg, commander of the New Zealand Division, a charismatic leader who had won a VC as a young man in 1916 at the battle of the Somme.

Germany's bold airborne invasion planned to deliver 10,000 troops by parachute, 5,000 by transport aircraft, as well as a number by glider. This required some 500 transport aircraft, a number of gliders, along with 600 combat aircraft to protect the transport fleet. Quick seizure of airfields was key to the German plan and those at Maleme and Canea were earmarked as initial targets, with those at Rethymno and Heraklion marked for subsequent attention. The surprise and nature of the German operation meant that the enemy was quickly able to secure the airfield at Maleme on the north-west coast of the island, and then to build up its force rapidly from 3,000 to 22,000 within the first two days of operations.

GHQ Middle East believed that if Maleme could be recaptured it might be possible to stem the invasion. Laycock was informed in the early hours of 23 May that his Commandos were likely to be required for service on Crete, and they were duly placed on four hours' notice to move. Wand-Tetley had been training at Aboukir with B Troop and the remainder of No. 2 Company when they were recalled at 0330 hours to their camp at Sidi Bishr. The plan envisaged Layforce landing on the south of the island at Castel Selino and then marching north to attack the Germans at Maleme, in their flank and rear. This would involve a cross-country march of some forty miles with its inherent supply problems. An alternative plan, involving a shorter march of thirty miles, to land the Commandos at Kastelli on the west coast, was quickly dismissed because of the increased risk to their shipping.[22]

For the operation, Layforce was to comprise Brigade HQ, A Battalion under Colvin, and D Battalion under Young. B Battalion was to remain behind at Mersa Matruh and C Battalion had by this stage been deployed to Cyprus to reinforce the garrison, now under threat from the Axis powers based in Greece. After the frustration of experiencing a number of planned, but then cancelled, operations, Wand-Tetley felt a sense of elation that A Battalion had been selected for the operation. However, neither he nor the men in his Section would have felt quite the same way if they had had any perception of what would transpire in the coming week.

On the afternoon of 23 May Colvin, his Battalion Headquarters, and the 200 men of No. 1 Company (A, F, H and I Troops) embarked at Alexandria on the fast mine-laying cruiser HMS *Abdiel* and landed the following morning at Suda Bay in the north of the island just east of Canea, to act as the Commando Advance Party. A Battalion's No. 2 Company (B, C, E and G Troops), and the reminder of Layforce was placed on twelve hours' notice to move.[23]

Early the following morning Laycock was asked whether he could get the balance of his force to Alexandria docks within the next two hours. Regardless of their notice to move status, Laycock responded that his men would be ready so long as the necessary motor transport could be provided for them. Having lost their Glen-type ships to the campaign in Greece, it was planned that the commandos would embark in the four destroyers, HM Ships *Isis*, *Decoy*, *Hero* and *Nizam*. It soon became clear to the men of No. 2 Company that not enough transport had been provided to get them all down to the docks in time. As a result E and G Troops and one of the Sections from C Troop left Sidi Bishr in the first wave and managed to embark upon HMS *Isis* just before she sailed for Crete. This left B Troop and Wand-Tetley, along with the remaining Section from C Troop, stranded and wondering quite how they were going to join their battalion on Crete. However, in the early hours of 25 May, in poor visibility and a gale which precluded the lowering of the boats that would have taken the Commandos ashore, and with dawn rapidly approaching, the landing at Castel Selino was aborted. The destroyers returned to Alexandria for, following significant naval losses on 22 May, the Admiralty would only allow ships to make the dangerous trip through the Mediterranean to Cretan waters in the hours of darkness.[24]

Arriving back in Alexandria that evening, Laycock was given fresh orders. The Commandos would now land at Suda Bay. Those embarked in HM Ships *Isis* and *Decoy* first transferred to HMS *Abdiel*, which had by now returned from her original task of dropping Colvin with the Commando Advance Party at Suda. Wand-Tetley and the others who had been left behind on the first sailing now managed to embark upon

Abdiel and join the rest of No. 2 Company aboard. The convoy of *Hero*, *Nizam* and *Abdiel* then put to sea again at dawn on 26 May bound for Crete, which it reached just before midnight.[25]

The situation on Crete had deteriorated over the last couple of days. Although the Germans had been repulsed by the New Zealanders at Galatas, they had managed to make inroads into the Greek positions on the flank of the Australians and New Zealanders. Freyberg subsequently made a recommendation to Wavell for evacuation, which was to receive his endorsement on the 27th. It was planned that Creforce would withdraw over the White Mountains to Sphakia, a small fishing village on the south coast, with a rearguard covering the retreat from Suda. At this stage the Allies were holding a north-to-south line of some twenty-five miles, from just west of Canea, to the vicinity of Perivolia.

Having only just arrived at Suda, Laycock learnt for the first time that Crete was to be evacuated. Until this stage the Commandos had believed they would be used to raid enemy-held airports and seaports. Indeed, back in Alexandria they had been led to believe that, with the exception of Maleme airfield, the situation in Crete was well in hand. This news was reinforced by the arrival of a liaison officer from the Commando Advance Party, who also stressed that there was no transport, little chance of food or ammunition other than that which the men already held, and that the Commando Advance Party, under Colvin, was holding a position to the south-east of Suda.

Laycock disembarked immediately and with the aim of confirming the situation with Freyberg, departed with Graham and Waugh and encountered Weston, now in charge of the forward area. He was instructed to form a rearguard to protect the main body of Creforce as it withdrew the some twenty miles over the mountains to Sphakia. This was subsequently confirmed by Freyberg. Neither of the Allied generals managed to make a particularly favourable impression on Waugh though, or escape his scathing wit, but he did not confine his flippancy to generals, for even a heavy German air attack against their position was condemned as being 'like everything German – overdone'.[26]

The newly arrived commandos quickly completed the business of disembarkation. Orders were to leave all heavy equipment on board since there was no transport available to carry it. The commandos had, in any event, been instructed to leave their kitbags and blankets behind in Alexandria. Everything would need to be carried on foot, with ammunition and food being the priority. Wand-Tetley and his Section stuffed their battledress pockets with loose clips of ammunition, tins of bully beef and M&V (meat and vegetables) and hard-tack biscuits. Most heavy equipment, including wirelesses, cook-set equipment and broken-open Bren gun magazine boxes, were left on board or dumped in the harbour. All was conducted with the utmost speed, because the ships needed to be under steam and away from the harbour before dawn because of the German air threat.

The plan was that A and D Battalions of Layforce were to leapfrog southwards, moving alternately through each other's positions from one rearguard position to another, covering the withdrawal of Creforce along the line of the mountain road to Sphakia on the south coast. This was to prove to be a gruelling marathon of endurance, for they would be forced to move on foot at night under cover of darkness and then fight during the day. The enemy, on the other hand, would rest at night and then, with the advantage of air superiority and motor transport, rapidly bring the fight to the commandos during daylight hours, offering them no respite.

Wand-Tetley and the newly arrived members of No. 2 Company marched off under Wylie to join Colvin and the rest of A Battalion at No. 1 Company's position south-east of Suda. D Battalion followed and took up a position some six miles east of Suda Bay on a ridge. As the commandos marched to their locations it was evident that the withdrawal was already in full flood, with Creforce soldiers streaming down the road east from Suda. Layforce was in its respective battalion positions by dawn on the 27th, which was just as well because through-out that day both battalions were subjected to Stuka dive-bomb and machine-gun attack; however, having found good cover there were fortunately few commando casualties.[27]

In the afternoon of the 27th, Young, CO of D Battalion, went to reconnoitre new defensive positions some twelve miles south of Suda Bay on the Sphakia road at Babali Hani, to which the battalion would move that night, less a company which was left to cover the forward road junction where the main road running south forks off the coast road. Moving under cover of darkness, the battalion would be in its new positions by dawn on the 28th.

A Battalion had meanwhile remained in its original position forward of D Battalion throughout the 27th, watching over Creforce as it with-drew and headed south. Wand-Tetley and the men of B Troop, along with G Troop, were initially positioned a mile or so to the rear of A Battalion's main position to cover the withdrawal of their battalion as it fell back towards D Battalion's positions. By 2100 hours, the Creforce stragglers and the bulk of their own battalion having passed through their lines, B and G Troops bore the brunt of the probing German patrols until the early hours of the 28th. It was then their turn to fall back, with G Troop moving first. In the early stages of this move G Troop along with A and C Troops was attacked in the flank by the Germans; although the enemy were beaten back, a number of men fell into their hands. Wand-Tetley and B Troop were meanwhile able to break contact with the enemy to their front and make their way back through their own lines.[28]

By dawn on the 28th the main body of A Battalion had managed to pass through D Battalion's forward company at the road junction, and take up an intermediate position in the vicinity of Stylos. By this stage D Battalion's forward company had been reinforced by two Maori Companies which, wishing for a chance to fight the Germans, had asked if they could remain behind with the commandos rather than withdraw with the remainder of Creforce. They had their desire, for within three hours they were heavily engaged by German airborne troops. The fighting was at close quarters and this company, along with the Maoris, was gradually forced back south through the olive groves and A Battalion's position at Stylos, to join the remainder of D Battalion at Babali Hani.

A Battalion now took up the gauntlet and bore the brunt of the German attack. By this stage battalion command had fallen to Wylie, soon to win the DSO, Colvin having been taken ill. As usual the commandos were first engaged by German mortar fire, to which they could not respond since they had no heavy weapons of their own. However, they were assisted by two Matilda tanks of 7th Royal Tank Regiment. The Germans were initially driven off in a spirited counterattack led by Wylie. Captain Jocelyn Nicholls, a Gunner, led a similarly successful counterattack with the bayonet, driving the Germans from a hill from which they were enfilading A Battalion's position. Nonetheless, forward on a limb and fighting at close quarters, the battalion was in serious danger of being cut off, and had trouble disengaging with the enemy to fall back to Babali Hani. However, they eventually accomplished this, but in the process a significant number were killed or captured by the German mountain troops.

Throughout A Battalion's engagement Laycock and his Brigade Major, Graham, had been positioned close to the battle to witness and control the action, but they had then made their way south to Babali Hani on one of the Matilda tanks. In fact they had been so far forward that they had very nearly been captured by the Germans. Wand-Tetley and the remnants of A Battalion, which had by now received a significant mauling by the enemy, also made their way back through D Battalion's lines. At this stage, with significant casualties taken, Laycock decided it was best to merge his force into a single unit. He based this on D Battalion, which still had at its helm its CO, Young.

Laycock now prepared his force to slow the enemy's progress at Babali Hani. At this stage Weston reinforced Layforce with an Australian infantry battalion to provide depth to the Commando position and six Matilda tanks. Laycock positioned his Brigade HQ in a house on the edge of the village so as to maintain close command of the action to come. By midday on the 28th the enemy was on the outskirts of Laycock's defensive position and proceeded to rain down mortar fire upon the commandos, to which, again, they had no effective response. The initial attack came from two battalions of the German 5th Mountain Division advancing south down the road, which was eventually repulsed after an hour. The enemy next attacked the left flank, which was where a composite company of the original A Battalion including B Troop had taken up its position. This too was beaten off after fierce fighting, and by the evening of the 28th it was clear that the Germans had been successfully held back for that day, at least. The enemy had been dealt a bloody nose, for after the event it became clear from those burying the dead that between eighty and 200 Germans had been killed, with many more wounded, at a cost of just three commandos killed and fifteen wounded.

Although Laycock had initially intended to hold the position at Babali Hani until midday on the 29th, now that the main body of Creforce was on the south coast the decision was taken to withdraw south towards the Askifou plain that very night. The commandos did this, leapfrogging back, company by company, through the olive groves and fields, with the remnants of the A Battalion troops being the first to move. Under cover of darkness the commandos were able to extricate themselves from Babali Hani without undue hindrance from the enemy, and Layforce headed south down the mountain road past Vryses towards its assembly area, some three miles east of the Sphakia beaches. A New Zealand brigade had by now been ordered to relieve Layforce of its rearguard duty, and the commandos marched through the night and by dawn of the 29th had reached Imvros, the site of Weston's headquarters, where they remained a while. Battle-weary, thirsty, and hungry, the exhausted men made their way on through the mountain-passes and hairpin bends, all the time subject to enemy fire from both snipers and Stukas until by the evening of the 29th they had reached their assembly area at Komithades. Here they reconnoitred their positions to the east of the village for their next task as the right flank perimeter guard for the Sphakia beach evacuation.[29]

On the 30th A Battalion's composite company remained in their defensive positions, as did those from D Battalion. By this stage the Commandos were at half-strength. Laycock and Waugh had set off early to find Freyberg, but returned unsuccessful after many hours. The Brigade Major, Graham, then set off to try his luck, and eventually managed to find HQ Creforce in a cave at the base of the Sphakia Ravine. At this stage Freyberg made clear that Layforce were to be the last of the regular troops to leave the island, following the Creforce fighting troops. Freyberg, with many of his staff, was to leave the island later that evening in two Sunderland flying-boats despatched for the task by GHQ Middle East.

The following day Laycock received a refined set of orders from Weston that Layforce was to depart Crete only on the orders of HQ Creforce, after the Creforce fighting troops but before the stragglers. Late that afternoon of the 31st Weston dictated to Graham, in the presence of Colvin, the orders for surrender of the island. The written order was addressed to Colvin and instructed him to capitulate to the enemy the following morning. Weston left the island later that evening by flying-boat. Graham met Laycock, who informed him that he also had received orders to leave the island that same evening with his Brigade HQ and as many of his commandos as he could take with him on the grounds that, irrespective of any commandos that they might be forced to leave behind, Layforce still had B and C Battalions to command (in Cyprus and Egypt respectively). By now it was becoming very clear that the last ship would depart Sphakia that very night of 31 May/1 June.

HQ Creforce had initially intended that, as far as the evacuation from Sphakia was concerned, 1,000 men would be evacuated on the first night of the 28th/29th, followed by 6,000 men on the 29th/30th, 3,000 on the 30th/31st and 3,000 on 31 May/1 June, but in the event the overall target could not be reached. The Royal Navy was forced to embark men only between 2359 and 0300 hours, having already lost ships to hostile air attack when evacuating the garrison at Heraklion on the north of the island. Therefore, only 700 men were taken off the first night, and, although the target of 6,000 was met on the second night, only 1,500 were evacuated on the third night, and 4,000 on the last night. Despite being unable to evacuate all the men, the Royal Navy accomplished all that really could have been expected under the circumstances and, justly proud of its work, the toast in many a Mediterranean Fleet wardroom after the event was 'To the three Services, the Royal Navy, the Royal Advertising Federation, and the Evacuees'.[30]

Once the remnants of HQ Creforce had embarked upon board ship for departure on the last evening, Laycock took it upon himself to strike out Colvin's name on the surrender order, and insert 'senior officer left on the island'. He did so because Colvin, still ill, was clearly not up to such a task. Laycock then ensured that the message was delivered by runner to Young, who was farther up the Sphakia ravine with the bulk of the commandos. Despite this turn of events, Young accepted his future fate as a prisoner of war; it was some consolation that he was later awarded the DSO for his inspired leadership throughout the entire evacuation.

A Battalion had taken up perimeter positions covering the Sphakia beach late on the afternoon of the 31st, with the remnant of A, B, E and

G Troops on the left and those from F, H, C and I on the right. Close on midnight the sorely depleted battalion was given the order to embark, and the commandos made their way down the 500-foot cliff on a goat-track to the beach. Those from the Troops that had been positioned on the left were ferried out to HMS *Abdiel* lying offshore, but those on the right were unable to force their way through the seething throng of refugees in time; Wand-Tetley and other B Troop survivors were among the fortunate few to embark. Barely any commandos from D Battalion, situated in the most northerly positions around the Sphakia ravine, made it down to the beach in time. Laycock, having managed to embark on the destroyer, HMS *Kimberley* with Graham and Waugh, did his best to delay the departure but, at 0245 hours on 1 June, Rear Admiral King, the Senior Naval Officer present, made the difficult decision to depart for fear of exposing his ships to unacceptable danger from dive-bombers during daylight hours. Laycock's Brigade HQ and only twenty-three officers and 186 ORs of Layforce managed to get back to Egypt.[31]

Those commandos still on the island now faced the unhappy prospect of being prisoners of war for the next four years. The following morning Young departed alone, having refused his Adjutant's offer to accompany him, to search for a suitably senior German officer to accept the surrender. However, he first encountered an Australian officer, Colonel Theo Walker to whom he passed on the surrender order in line with its recent amendment to the 'Senior officer left on the island'. Walker shortly afterwards offered the Allied surrender to an officer of the 100th Mountain Regiment in the nearby village of Komithades. All Allied troops left on the island were ordered to surrender at 0900 hours on 1 June.

Before capture, the commandos of D Battalion were instructed by their officers to dispose of their 'Fanny' fighting knives. These knives might well have singled them out for special treatment by the Germans, given their penchant for executing special forces – a trait that would be formalized in Hitler's infamous *Kommandobefehl* of 1942 ordering the immediate execution of all captured commandos. Most of these knuckleduster knives therefore very quickly ended up at the bottom of a village well. For similar reasons the Spanish Republicans in the ranks of D Battalion were instructed to assume the identity of Gibraltarians if interrogated, lest they were sent back to Franco's Spain, where a particularly grim fate would undoubtedly have met them.[32]

The majority of the commandos left behind on the island inevitably became prisoners. Young would eventually end up at Colditz Castle where, as head of the Escape Committee, he would be intimately involved in the planning of many of the dramatic escapes. However, some managed successfully to evade capture and make their way back to Egypt using Motor Landing Craft (MLC) left behind by the *Glengyle*.

One of these, *MLC 69*, brought back fifteen members of A Battalion and seven of D Battalion. Escaping on the evening of 1 June under heavy enemy machine-gun fire directed from the shore, the commandos eventually made it back to friendly territory in Sidi Barrani over a week later. This impressive escape provided the basis for an episode in Waugh's fiction trilogy, *Sword of Honour*.[33]

A few others made for the heights of Crete's mountains. From here, having made contact with SOE agents operating alongside Cretan resistance fighters, they were later evacuated from the island by submarine. Some, like Wylie who as second-in-command of A battalion had taken over from Colvin when he became ill, made a bid for freedom but were unlucky. Having escaped with a group of commandos over the hills to the west of Sphakia, and identified some fishing boats at Port Lutro with which to make good their escape, their hopes were cruelly dashed when these were bombed by the Luftwaffe; they were then subsequently rounded up.

The battle for Crete had proved a costly victory for the Germans, for the high killed-to-wounded ratio tells of the ferocity of the battle. Of Germany's 22,000 assault troops, some 6,500 were casualties, of whom 3,350 were killed or missing in action, and a third of the transport aircraft were lost. The British and Commonwealth forces suffered 3,500 casualties, of whom 1,700 were killed in action, and almost 12,000 were taken prisoner. The Greeks lost 10,000 men taken prisoner, but the number of their troops and of Cretan volunteers killed is unknown. The Royal Navy lost 2,000 sailors, with three cruisers and six destroyers sunk and a further two battleships, seven destroyers, six cruisers and an aircraft carrier badly damaged. As a result of the high German losses and the almost pyrrhic nature of this airborne victory, Hitler forbade any future strategic venture of this kind. Indeed, although Crete was arguably for the German airborne forces their finest hour it was also effectively their undoing, and was dubbed the 'Graveyard of the *Fallschirmjäger*'. Apart from a few small-scale airborne operations, the German paratroopers were utilized as elite infantry for the remainder of the war.

For those like Wand-Tetley who had managed to get away from Crete there was an understandable sense of relief, but with it came the inevitable soul-searching with regard to those comrades they had been forced to leave behind. This was particularly hard-felt in Layforce, with its strongly developed *esprit de corps* and Evelyn Waugh, for his part, expressed much of his personal sense of loss and disillusionment in his novel *Officers and Gentlemen*, published in 1955. Wand-Tetley would suffer from bad dreams about the death and bloodshed that he had experienced for many years.

Disbandment of Layforce

The fall of Crete was the low point for the Allies in the Middle East and afterwards there followed a particularly uncertain period for the Commandos, which would culminate in the disbandment of Layforce and the formation of a new, single 'Middle East Commando', one of a different nature to the three original ME Commando units.

On 2 June, the remnants of A and D Battalions, now numbering only a few officers and less than 100 other ranks each, were amalgamated at Sidi Bishr under the short-lived title 'Layforce Details'. Initially command went to Major Stephen Rose, Royal Fusiliers, previously the second-in-command of D Battalion, who had been unable to deploy to Crete with his unit owing to a training accident with explosives which had badly damaged his hand and perforated his eardrums. Within a couple of days he had to return to hospital, and Captain Jocelyn Nicholls, now the senior officer of A Battalion to have returned from Crete, assumed command briefly before this was in turn handed on to Major John Milman, second-in-command of D Battalion who, although shot in the leg during the fighting on Crete, had managed to be evacuated. From the end of June the men of 'Layforce Details' started their move to Geneifa, the location of the Middle East Commando Depot, and for the most part were transferred to the Depot's strength. Wand-Tetley reported there together with Nicholls and Captain J. R. H. Owen of the Manchesters, also of A Battalion, in mid-July.[34]

For the Allies in the Middle East this had been a frustrating and demanding period and one that was to directly affect the future of the Commandos. Wavell, distracted by the requirement to quell a revolt in Iraq in April, had also to contend with Greece and Crete being overrun and the requirement to invade Syria; he was thus under quite enough pressure without also having to contend with Rommel. On 15 May Wavell had launched Operation BREVITY in Libya which resulted in the capture of Capuzzo, Sollum and the Halfaya Pass, but, in a counter-attack the following day, Rommel had recaptured the first two locations and by the end of the month he had also reoccupied the Halfaya Pass.

On 8 June, following the evacuation of Crete, Churchill ordered Wavell to invade Vichy French-held Syria to prevent the French from allowing the Germans use of their airfields, in particular Aleppo. Although only token resistance was anticipated, this would prove a tough nut to crack, and it would be a full month before operations were concluded. Meanwhile, under further pressure from Churchill, Wavell also attempted to lift the siege of Tobruk, but Operation BATTLEAXE, launched on 15 June, failed in its objectives.

Disregarding Wavell's overstretched forces and his complex operational challenges, on 22 June Churchill replaced him as C-in-C with General Sir Claude Auchinleck. Given Wavell's reverses in the Western

Desert, Greece and Crete, this was perhaps inevitable. The timing of Churchill's change of generals coincided with the German invasion of Russia, which would influence the whole dynamic of the conflict; the Middle East would no longer be a relatively isolated theatre but would become part of a larger world strategy. It would also take time for many in the West to adjust to the idea of fighting alongside the Communists. Nonetheless, before the 'Auk' could turn his attention to Rommel he was forced in August to invade and occupy Iran, lest the Germans should launch an assault on the Middle East from the Caucasus.

Against this backdrop Laycock had been informed in mid-June of Wavell's decision to disband Layforce because the Brigade's strength had been so severely diminished by casualties to its two battalions on Crete and elsewhere. Furthermore, the Royal Navy was no longer in a position to provide ships for Commando amphibious operations due to high losses, particularly during the evacuation of Crete. Also, with the scarcity of manpower in the Middle East, it would not now be realistic to anticipate that the force could be replenished, for across the Middle East standard infantry units were thousands of men short. Furthermore, once in post Auchinleck reinforced this directive and made it clear that he concurred with his predecessor's judgement on the matter.

Disbandment of Layforce as a formation occurred formally at the end of July, but it was less than a straightforward matter, for a number of its elements continued in being. The ME Commando Depot at Geneifa remained, and continued to supply troops to No. 51 ME Commando in Abyssinia. B Battalion (No. 8 Commando), involved in operations in Tobruk, remained in being though in much reduced strength, and C Battalion (No. 11 Commando) continued in its garrison role in Cyprus. Courtney's SBS, now under command of Cunningham, C-in-C Mediterranean Fleet, also remained unaffected. It was therefore just 'Layforce Details', i.e. the remnants of A Battalion (No. 7 Commando) and D Battalion (No. 50/52 Commando), which had been depleted in the heavy fighting on Crete and were unsustainable as units that were primarily affected at this stage. The principal options offered to the commandos from these two units were to volunteer for guerrilla operations in a force, led by Jocelyn Nicholls, that was to become Mission 204 in the Far East, or return to their original regiments if these happened to be in the Middle East. A third option, one that Wand-Tetley elected to follow, was to remain on the strength of the Middle East Commando Depot and see what other opportunities for special forces might arise. One such opportunity arose in mid-June when a small force, codenamed Pencil Party, comprising two officers and ten ORs, formerly of No. 7 Commando, was deployed to Cyprus to operate in the vicinity of Nicosia airfield as a stay-behind sabotage team in the event of a German airborne invasion of the island.[35]

Meanwhile, Laycock had returned to England in June and had set about securing what support he could to ensure the future of Layforce. At this time Dudley Clarke, in writing to a colleague at the War Office, lent weight to the argument that the Commandos in the Middle East had frequently been inappropriately used and, moreover, had often suffered as a result of poor planning and intelligence from on high. Churchill was certainly grieved with how he perceived the Commandos had been handled by Wavell in the Middle East, and fired off a minute to General 'Pug' Ismay, Secretary to the Chiefs of Staff Committee, 'The Commandos have been frittered away, and now disbanded. The late regime in the Middle East showed no aptitude for Combined Operations.' This was quickly followed by a further minute, 'I wish the Commandos in the Middle East to be reconstituted as soon as possible. The Middle East Command have indeed maltreated and thrown away this valuable force.'[36]

Laycock discussed the matter with Churchill at Chequers over dinner on 19 July. Following this, Churchill spoke on the matter with Auchinleck, while the latter was paying a short visit to Britain. The result was that the Commandos in the Middle East would be reconstituted, but their future form at this stage was still far from clear. At the end of July Laycock returned to the Middle East as DCO, now back in his substantive rank of lieutenant colonel having lost his Acting Colonelcy, to reconstitute the Commandos on a smaller scale.

At the beginning of August C Battalion returned to Egypt from Cyprus, where it had been engaged in garrison duty. Two months earlier, in June, the Battalion had temporarily been deployed from Cyprus to take part in the invasion of Vichy French Syria, where it took part in an amphibious assault and the subsequent seizure of a vital bridge over the Litani river (in modern Lebanon). Here the battalion had suffered some twenty-five per cent casualties, including the death of its CO, Dick Pedder. The battalion, now under the second-in-command, Major Geoffrey Keyes, Royal Scots Greys (son of Admiral Sir Roger Keyes), who had distinguished himself at the Litani river action and won an MC and Free French *Croix de Guerre*, returned to Egypt conscious that they were to be formally disbanded on 1 September.

B Battalion, based at Mersa Matruh, had since April maintained a detachment, reinforced by sea as necessary, at Tobruk which had been under siege by Rommel. The initial detachment of some five officers and seventy-five men had been sent to take part in raids prior to, and in support of, Operation BATTLEAXE. Of these raids, that led by Captain Mike Kealy, with two other officers and forty other ranks, against the Italian strongpoint known as the 'twin pimples' on the night of 17/18 July was the most notable success. When Wavell's offensive to lift the siege of Tobruk failed, a detachment had stayed on in support of the Australian Commander, Major General Leslie Morshead, who had British infantry, tanks and artillery as well as 9th Australian Division with which to defend Tobruk's thirty-five mile perimeter. Dominating no man's land the commandos, amongst them George Jellicoe, became expert in raiding Axis lines and kidnapping soldiers from enemy trenches. However, by 20 August, with its detachments now back from Tobruk, it too faced formal disbandment at the beginning of September.

Although men from both battalions began to disperse back to their parent regiments, many of the commandos, like Wand-Tetley, who still saw their future with special forces, remained at the Middle East Commando Depot to see what Laycock might be able to resurrect.

On 11 October 1941 GHQ Middle East held a conference at which it was debated that the Special Service Troops should be formed into a single unit comprising six Troops. The suggestion was that No. 1 Troop would be Depot and Training; No. 2 Troop would be the recently formed L Detachment SAS; No. 3 Troop would be British (ex Layforce); Nos. 4 and 5 Troops would be Palestinian (ex No. 51 ME Commando); and No. 6 Troop would be SBS. The Depot and the LRDG were to remain separate from the plan. This suggestion never really got off the ground, and at a subsequent meeting on 25 October it became apparent that the G (Ops) and G (R) Branches at GHQ Middle East held opposite views on which organization the SBS should come under. As a result any decision was postponed. Although given overall command, Laycock certainly never supported the plan and made his feelings on the subject known to Auchinleck. In the event this plan was never carried through and resolution would wait until Operation CRUSADER, the imminent Allied offensive to drive Rommel out of Cyrenaica and relieve Tobruk, was over.[37]

Between July and November there was an apparent lull in the Middle East, with only the isolated garrison of Tobruk seeing any serious action. In fact Auchinleck was preparing his forces and at dawn on 18 November 1941 he launched CRUSADER, initially catching Rommel by surprise. The Eighth Army, under the command of Lieutenant General Sir Alan Cunningham, formed in September and comprising XIII Corps and XXX Corps, eventually forced *Panzergruppe Afrika* to withdraw from Cyrenaica to Agheila in Tripolitania. The port of Bardia, which had been bypassed by the Allies in their opening thrust, was captured in mid-December as the culmination to the operation. The situation in the Libyan desert was, as a consequence, reversed and almost mirrored that which had existed a year previously. However, quickly regaining the initiative, Rommel launched his second major offensive on 21 January 1942, managing to force the British eastwards before coming to a halt in February on the Gazala-Bir Hacheim line, just west of Tobruk.

As a preliminary to CRUSADER, two special forces operations were launched the evening before the main assault, but neither achieved the success hoped of them. It had been intended, in Operation SQUATTER, that L Detachment SAS would be dropped behind enemy lines in the Gazala-Tmimi region, with the task of raiding enemy airstrips and destroying aircraft parked on the ground. However, the aircraft transporting the SAS were delayed by anti-aircraft fire and blown off course by a fierce electric storm, in fact the worst rainstorm Cyreniaca had experienced in almost forty years. As a consequence the parachutists landed scattered far from their intended drop zones, and were forced to head directly to their pre-arranged rendezvous with the LRDG, whose task it was to transport them back through the desert to friendly lines.

Meanwhile in Operation FLIPPER elements of No. 3 Troop, based upon remnants of C Battalion, which insisted upon calling itself by its original title, No. 11 (Scottish) Commando, led by Geoffrey Keyes, now a lieutenant colonel, would land by submarine 250 miles behind enemy lines and set out to raid Rommel's HQ in the Jebel Akhdar. This dramatic operation, the aim of which was to capture or kill Rommel, was acknowledged to be a suicide mission from which, Laycock thought, it was highly unlikely that anyone would return, would result in a posthumous VC for Keyes.[38]

In November 1941, at the time that CRUSADER was launched, Wand-Tetley was one of five subalterns despatched by Major D. W. Melville, who had commanded the ME Commando Depot since its inception in January 1941, to the Suez docks to form a Commando Security Section. The other Section leaders sent with him were Second Lieutenants H. H. Gurmin of the Buffs, R. C. Robinson of the Essex, J. F. Nixon of the RNF, and S. Lepine of the South Staffords. Here they were briefed by Thirkell-White, Wand-Tetley's Troop Commander from Crete, that they would each head a ten-man Section and, working in concert, would be responsible for cracking down on the rampant crime and theft inherent within the docks, railways and the surrounding area from Suez Junction to a point north of Shallufa station by twenty odd miles. It was intended that they should test the security of the facilities and operate as ambush squads, rather than as guards.

After a couple of days and nights spent in observation it became apparent to Wand-Tetley and the rest of the Security Section that significant quantities of War Department (WD) stores were disappearing, either being stolen at the railway stations or being dropped off by local employees as the rolling stock moved past outlying villages. In testing the security of the docks, they found that these were easy to enter, especially from the seaward side by small boat. Once in the docks area it was also straightforward for pilferers to help themselves to anything, including arms and ammunition, and silently disappear with the loot by boat. Nor was it just the local Egyptian employees who were responsible for the pilfering, although they were indeed clearly the main culprits. Certain Allied naval elements were found to be offloading crates of beer and making off with far from insignificant quantities.

A number of raids were conducted, culminating in a large combined sweep at the end of November on the Ataka Quarry and labour camps, led by Wand-Tetley, Lepine and Gurmin with thirty ORs. Significant quantities of WD stores were found and the culprits detained and handed over to the Frontier Administration Police. During the course of the raid a number of warning shots were fired, all legitimate under the circumstances, in an attempt to keep the crowd from rushing individual commandos. Nonetheless, the strong-arm tactics, in which one culprit was killed and another wounded, allied to the success of the raid, caused a degree of professional jealousy within local police elements and minor political repercussions. In the event, the Commando Security Section was recalled to its Geneifa base at the end of the first week of January 1942, having concluded that the only real answer was to make the docks and railways stations a purely military area, not shared with the local Egyptian authorities, and to increase the guard on both the land and the seaward side of the docks.[39]

Middle East Commando

With CRUSADER over, Auchinleck returned to the matter of re-organizing the Special Service Troops. On 29 December 1941 he authorized a plan for the reconstitution of a new unit of Commandos which would be placed under command of G(R) Branch, itself controlled by the Ministry of Economic Warfare (MEW) Mission in Cairo, which was responsible for SOE operations in the Middle East and Mediterranean. The unit would comprise the old ME Commando Depot at Geneifa, the remains of Layforce and No. 51 Commando, and the SBS. It did not include L Detachment SAS, nor did it include the LRDG; both these units were now placed under direct command of Auchinleck.

By early January 1942 the new unit named the Middle East Commando was being formed at Geneifa. Under the command of Lieutenant Colonel J. M. Graham, Royal Scots Greys, the unit would have an overall strength of approximately 650 men, and its higher control was now very clearly in the hands of the SOE. There were three British squadrons, A, B and C. D Squadron was composed of Palestinians (of No. 51 Commando) and the surviving Spaniards. These squadrons (with an overall strength of eight officers and eighty-two other ranks), were established as an HQ, and three troops each of two officers and twenty-six men. E (Holding Depot) Squadron consisted of some one hundred all ranks, half of whom were officers. Additionally there was

No. 1 SBS, established for twelve officers and forty-four other ranks, whose force was by now split between Alexandria and Malta.[40]

The new Middle East Commando evolved rapidly. In mid-January, C Squadron moved to Kabrit to undertake parachute training, and thereafter groups of commandos, including Wand-Tetley, would regularly undertake parachute courses. After the war he would reminisce about some of the counter-productive training methods involved, including jumping off the back of a speeding truck to simulate a parachute landing. This inevitably resulted in a number of injuries, some of them quite serious, and Wand-Tetley counted himself lucky to have escaped with just a few cuts and bruises. Meanwhile, patrols in the Suez docks to tackle pilfering had commenced again. In February A Squadron was posted to Syria in case of a German invasion of Turkey, for if Syria was also overrun it would be the Squadron's task to organize local guerrilla resistance behind enemy lines. Also in February, in a relationship that would subsequently develop further, two officers and twelve other ranks from C Squadron were sent on attachment to the LRDG. This was not a new idea, for Laycock had suggested that commandos might provide such patrols at the time that Layforce was being disbanded following Crete. Then in March 1942 the Commando moved its camp from Geneifa, westwards down the coast to Burg el Arab.[41]

At this time D Squadron provided the basis for a new secret unit, under the cover-name of the Special Interrogation Group (SIG). Commanded by Captain Herbert Buck, a German linguist of the Punjab Regiment, the SIG consisted of German-speaking Jews whose role was to infiltrate Axis lines. Wearing German tropical uniform and equipped with captured German equipment, unpleasant torture and death almost certainly awaited those of the unit ever caught alive. Trained by two German NCOs, Heinrick Brockmann, a.k.a. Brueckner, and Walter Essner, a.k.a. Esser, both former members of the French Foreign Legion released from the prisoner pens, SIG's contact with British units was minimized for security reasons.

Also in March B Squadron was split, half being attached to Eighth Army and the rest joining C Squadron, which by now had moved from Kabrit to Jarabub. In April the unit moved camp again, farther down the coast to Mersa Matruh, and A Squadron returned from Syria, to be replaced by B Squadron, and later would reinforce the LRDG.[42]

On the wider Middle East stage, stalemate had existed in North Africa since February 1942 after Rommel had driven British forces back to the Gazala-Bir Hacheim line just west of Tobruk. On 26 May Rommel launched a further offensive, took Tobruk on 21 June, and pursued Eighth Army, at the time under command of Lieutenant General Neil Ritchie, eastward to El Alamein in Egypt, where early in July the British finally managed to bring him to a halt. However, in halting Rommel,

Auchinleck had felt compelled to remove the unfortunate Ritchie from command, take control of Eighth Army himself, stop plans for a defence of Mersa Matruh, and instead fortify El Alamein. The capture of Tobruk brought promotion to field marshal for Rommel – at fifty the youngest in the *Heer* – and an international reputation. With Tobruk captured, he now had his eyes firmly set on the Nile Delta, the Suez Canal and beyond the Sinai Desert and Palestine. Indeed, the key oilfields of Persia seemed within his grasp, and there Rommel might even meet victorious German armies rolling down through the Caucasus – Plan ORIENT.

Throughout June A Squadron and the SIG would be involved in operations while the remainder of the Commando, apart from B Squadron still in Syria, would be held in reserve to defend Cairo. Here they would busy themselves on a number of tasks, guarding key points, ever on the lookout for enemy parachutists or for frogmen in the Suez Canal, and also providing armed protection for VIPs. The SIG was involved in an SAS operation in mid-June to strike five enemy airfields concurrently on the North African coast as well as one on Crete. As the enemy had a heavy presence at Derna, the SIG was employed to infiltrate the Free French detachment of the SAS through the Italian lines in the Derna region to their target airfields. In the event the SIG and the Free French were betrayed by one of their German instructors, but the SAS were successful with their other targets, including Crete, where Commandant Georges Bergé, leader of the Free French SAS, and Jellicoe's party destroyed twenty-two aircraft and a bomb depot at Heraklion airfield. However, they were betrayed, and only Jellicoe and his Greek guide made good their escape.[43]

Long Range Desert Group

In May 1942, soon after arriving from Syria, A Squadron of the Middle East Commando deployed to Siwa Oasis and came under command of the LRDG. Wand-Tetley, promoted to lieutenant earlier in the year following eighteen months' war service, was now a Troop leader and had joined the Squadron, under command of Major W. A. Knowles, a Sapper. The squadron's task was to conduct raids on enemy lines of communication in Cyrenaica in the vicinity of the Barce-Slonta and Barce-Beda Littoria tracks, but with Rommel now very much on the offensive they were destined to suffer heavy vehicle losses to enemy air attack.

Before continuing with A Squadron's narrative it is perhaps worth focusing first upon the LRDG and the men who sported the distinctive 'desert scorpion' cap-badge, as it was arguably the most consistently successful of the special forces units, and saw the Desert War through from start to finish. Both the SAS and Popski's Private Army turned to the LRDG to learn the necessary survival skills of travel and navigation in the desert. In fact, the LRDG could trace its inception back to the First World War's 'Light Car Patrols', manned by the Yeomanry. Mounted in armoured Model T Fords with three-and-a-half-inch tyres, and armed with a Vickers machine gun they patrolled the interior while the horse cavalry patrolled the coastline. They had been responsible for developing the sun-compass for navigation and developing the condenser to stop radiators boiling over.[44]

During the late twenties and thirties, the flame of desert travel had been kept alive by one man in particular, Major Ralph Bagnold, Royal Signals. The desert, which is the largest on earth and about the size of the Indian subcontinent, stretches a thousand miles west from the Nile and the same distance south from the Mediterranean coastline. With encouragement from the Royal Geographical Society, Bagnold pioneered many routes across the desert from the Mediterranean to northern Sudan, and in 1935 was awarded the Society's Founder's Gold Medal for his achievements. Covering thousands of miles, he penetrated deep into the Egyptian and Libyan Desert, reaching the Gilf Kibir massif and Uweinat, 680 miles from Cairo and 300 miles from Kharga Oasis, on the border between Egypt, Sudan and Cyrenaica.

Vast sand formations exist over large portions of the desert, the largest being the Great Sand Sea, some 100 miles wide, which stretches from the rock cliffs of the Gilf Kebir at its southern end in Egypt, northwards by almost 500 miles to a line between the southern end of the Qattara Depression to the oases of Siwa and to Jarabub in Libya. Here at its neck it joins the Kalansho Sand Sea which lies to its west and which itself then stretches southwards to Zeighen and Kufra Oasis, thus forming a giant horseshoe. The huge dunes run on a north-south line, rising to 400 feet in height, with patches of gravel between them, particularly towards the southern end of the Great Sand Sea. At the Wadi Sura on the western side of the Gilf Kebir ancient rock etchings survive of animals and of human figures swimming, demonstrating that at one time a large inland lake existed here. This is also the presumed locality of the 'Lost Oasis of Zerzura' mentioned by Herodotus, the Father of History, and the basis of Michael Ondaatje's Booker Prize-winning novel *The English Patient*, subsequently made into an Oscar-winning film.

Bagnold developed a wealth of desert travel experience. He perfected the radiator condenser and designed a sun-compass that was superior to the Coles sun-compass on general issue in the Army. He developed steel sand-channels and canvas sand-mats to extricate vehicles from sand, the former for use under the rear tyres and the latter under the front tyres. He also developed balanced desert rations that would keep a traveller fit in the austere conditions. Besides being extremely practical, Bagnold's treatise, *The Physics of Blown Sand and Desert Dunes*, which was published in 1941, established him as a scientist of note in the somewhat esoteric academic field of sand formation.[45]

Much of the credit for the establishment of the LRDG must go to General Wavell, newly appointed as C-in-C Middle East, who was perceptive enough to realize the viability of Bagnold's proposal to form a desert reconnaissance force for gathering behind-the-lines intelligence on the enemy. Indeed, when Italy entered the war in June 1940, Wavell gave Bagnold just six weeks, and carte blanche, to raise, train and ready his force. Amongst Bagnold's fellow pre-war explorers whom he recruited to the LRDG were Guy Prendergast and Teddy Mitford, both of the Royal Tank Regiment. Bill Kennedy Shaw, tracked down by Bagnold in the Colonial Office in Palestine, was to become the LRDG's Intelligence Officer, and Pat Clayton, at the time in Tanganyika but with twenty years' experience in the Egyptian Survey Department, also readily accepted Bagnold's offer to join him. However, Rupert Harding-Newman, at the time in the Military Mission to the Egyptian Army, could not be released. This was a blow. Harding-Newman, educated at St Edward's School, Oxford, and of the Royal Tank Regiment, had been a veteran of many a pre-war desert expedition with Bagnold. Nonetheless, using his contacts in the Egyptian Army, Harding-Newman was able to look after Bagnold's interests by securing much-needed equipment from the Egyptians, including vehicles and sun-compasses that were more suited to the task than anything the British Army had to offer. After he had been posted to HQ Eighth Army, Harding-Newman continued to look after the interests of the unit. By the end of August the 'Long Range Patrols', as the force was known for the six months of its existence, was ready for operational service.[46]

Intelligence-gathering remained the LRDG's *raison d'être* throughout the war although, as a secondary role, it also proved itself extremely capable of harassing the enemy when it was called upon to do so. The LRDG 'Road Watch' on Axis lines of communication between Tripoli and Benghazi, mounted during critical periods of the Desert War, was assessed initially to have been one of the most useful sources of Allied intelligence. Recently the full extent of Ultra decrypts – the intelligence product derived from the German Enigma and *Geheimschreiber* code messages – has placed this in context, but nonetheless it was extremely significant.

Within its first year the LRDG underwent significant reorganization and expansion and became a lieutenant colonel's command. LRDG HQ, initially in Cairo, would by early 1941 be relocated to one or other of the larger desert oases, Kufra or Siwa. Upon promotion to colonel, Bagnold was relieved by Prendergast and he, in turn, by David Lloyd Owen of the Queen's Royal Regiment. Patrols were usually of five vehicles, each carrying three men, and were generally based on New Zealanders, the Guards, Southern Rhodesians, and British Yeomanry.

At the beginning of the war there was only one tarmac road in Libya – the coast road. Suitable four-wheel-drive vehicles were at first unavailable. Mounted initially in 30-cwt two-wheel-drive Chevrolet trucks, painted in their distinctive disruptive camouflage colours of rose pink and olive green, the LRDG nonetheless regularly ran their patrols some 1,200 miles from Egypt, through the southern desert, as far west as a line from Tripoli to Lake Chad. Suitable vehicles were not the only items of equipment difficult to come by. Initially there were only three theodolites – necessary for fixing position by the stars at night – to be found in the theatre. These were liberated from the Army's stores, the Egyptian Desert Survey Department, and from Nairobi, Kenya. For communications the LRDG relied upon sky wave, encoded morse, and routinely maintained communications over distances of up to 1,400 miles between LRDG HQ and its patrols. The Chevrolet trucks would be replaced in 1941 by Ford four-wheel-drive trucks, and these by 15-cwt and 30-cwt Chevrolets in early 1942 with an improved machine-gun armament consisting of a mix of .5-inch Vickers, .303-inch Vickers K, and 20mm Breda guns. Support was provided by 3-tonners which, with their greater range, created hidden forward dumps of petrol, ammunition, water and food, to increase the operating range of patrols and provide for emergencies.[47]

On the Axis side was the *Brandenburg* Special Service Regiment, not unlike the LRDG in concept although not as successful, under the command of the *Abwehr*, the German military intelligence and counter-intelligence service which was headed by Admiral Wilhelm Canaris. Specializing in Commando-style raiding operations behind enemy lines, the *Brandenburgers* ferried agents to Cairo and provided Hauptman Count Laszlo Almasy to lead the 4,000 mile expedition to drop enemy agents in Egypt – a compelling tale told by Saul Kelly in *The Hunt for Zerzura, the Lost Oasis and the Desert War*.

Wand-Tetley arrived with A Squadron, under Knowles, at the LRDG HQ at Siwa Oasis on 7 May, having driven from their initial deployment at Jarabub Oasis in Cyrenaica, south of Tobruk on the northern edge of the Great Sand Sea. Siwa, 350 miles west of Cairo, which is between the western edge of the Qattara Depression and the north-east edge of the Great Sand Sea, was a veritable 'Clapham Junction' for Allied special forces units as they crossed the desert back and forth behind enemy lines. The LRDG had established their headquarters and mess among the more modern Egyptian-built buildings. The Senussi Arabs were friendly and the ruins of their mud-built fortress town, which had taken a hammering from First World War shells, were clearly visible.

Earlier in its history, both Alexander the Great and Hannibal were reputed to have visited the ancient Greek Temple at Siwa to consult the Oracle of Jupiter Ammon. Herodotus tells the story of the Persian Great King Cambyses' army, a formidable 50,000 strong force, marching across the desert to attack 'the Ammonians' at the oasis in about 525 BC and being wiped out by a ferocious sandstorm, the dreaded *Khamseen*, whipped up by a south wind from the Sahara. Yet older ruins dated back to the time of the ancient Egyptians. In the war the oasis was particularly popular with the LRDG for the spring-fed 'Cleopatra's Pool', known in ancient times as the Fountain of the Sun, shaded by desert date-palms, which allowed the tired and dusty soldiers to take a swim, and for its other numerous springs of clear, sweet drinking water.

For the remainder of May the commandos of A Squadron concentrated on training, with practical lessons delivered by the LRDG. The CO, Prendergast, lectured the squadron and Major Jake Easonsmith, generally acknowledged as the best LRDG patrol leader, imparted desert skills and lore, while Captain Philip Arnold taught them the arcane art of desert navigation. There was no substitute for practical experience, and Wand-Tetley and the other Troop leaders would regularly disappear into the desert for training exercises of a few days in duration to practise and hone their skills. By the end of the month the squadron was ready to commence operations.[48]

Navigation by day was accomplished with sun-compass and speedometer readings, with care taken to account for wheel slippage, which could amount to ten per cent of speedometer readings. At night the position thus calculated by dead reckoning would be checked by astrofix with theodolite, and referenced to the Greenwich time signal received by civilian wireless. By day the theodolite would also occasionally be used to take bearings on the sun. When on the move by night the prismatic compass was used, but always taking care first to dismount and move at least thirty yards from the vehicle to avoid magnetic distortion. In many respects desert navigation was more akin to that conducted at sea by a sailor than on land, particularly given that maps of the desert were notoriously unreliable. Indeed, the Army trade of 'Land Navigator' was established and those qualified were paid an extra shilling a day.

It was an exacting and extremely disciplined lifestyle where the smallest mistake or lapse of concentration could spell disaster. In particular, the almost total lack of water, bar the few oases and birs (wells), meant that water conservation was of paramount importance. Patrols were always particularly vulnerable to enemy aircraft, against which there was little that one could do if caught out in the open. The contrast in temperatures, between the searing, desiccating heat of the day and the freezing cold at night took some getting used to, yet the desert life

61

did have its compensations. Not least was the sheer sense of space. Moments most savoured by Wand-Tetley were the early morning, when the air smelt clean and fresh before the sun had risen to exact its toll, and the early evening when it was cool, but not yet cold, and one could gaze at the thousands of stars against the huge expanse of sky and reflect upon the day's events. However, moments of pure relaxation were rare, for there were always radio reports to be made, vehicles to be repaired and camouflaged, weapons to be cleaned, meals to be cooked over a tin of sand with petrol poured in, courses to be plotted and plans to be drafted.

On 4 June Wand-Tetley set off with A Squadron from Siwa on a raid behind enemy lines, their destination Fort Marua on the Barce-Slonta track between Benghazi and Derna, in northern Cyrenaica. The squadron had eighteen trucks in total and was equipped similarly to the LRDG, but on lighter scales given the shorter range at which they would be operating. Squadron HQ, led by Knowles, was mounted in three 15-cwt Chevrolets, one of which carried the wireless. The HQ party included the second-in-command, Captain J. P. Power of the Hampshires, the Intelligence Officer, Captain D. O. Hamson and the unit medical officer, Captain Townsend RAMC. They also had attached to them Lance Corporal G. Arnold, an LRDG navigator, who would do sterling work in the days ahead. There were two Patrols, led by Wand-Tetley and Lieutenant J. S. W. Meikle of the RNF, each of which had five 15-cwt Chevrolets and in addition to their own personnel each carried a small sabotage party. Also present were Lieutenant Graham Taylor, another Wiltshires officer, and Second Lieutenants M. J. Duffy of the Hampshires and David Barnby, East Yorks. The heavy support section, led by Second Lieutenant R. C. Robinson of the Essex Regiment, had at its disposal five 3-tonners.[49]

The first day passed relatively uneventfully and the squadron reached Fort El Grein at dusk, where it rendezvoused with Robinson, who had come out with his section and the five 3-tonners from Jarabub to refuel the squadron. Here also was their CO, Graham, who had not been able to resist the opportunity of coming out into the desert to see the squadron on its way.

On the 5th the squadron headed off for Bir el Meddah, travelling in two parties with Squadron HQ and No. 1 Patrol in the lead, and No. 2 Patrol and the Heavy Section following on some thirty minutes afterwards. During the day they were all forced to halt and lie low, as an enemy reconnaissance plane flew overhead. This was a precursor of things to come, for enemy aircraft were to become increasingly and uncomfortably plentiful over the coming week. Early the next morning they set off once again, and after another uneventful day camped that night leaguered up in the open desert. On the morning of the 7th they established a forward base at a spot they had discovered that provided good cover, some ten miles north of their previous night's camp, and Robinson travelled back to Jarabub with three of his five 3-tonners to collect and bring back further supplies of water and fuel. The commandos were now some thirty miles from the Msus-Mechili track, which runs west to east in line with the two coastal towns of Beda Fomm and Tmimi, beyond the more southerly Trigh el Abd, an ancient caravan slavers' route now strewn with enemy 'thermos' bombs dropped by the Italian Air Force. They were now not far from their selected target. This was reinforced by the sound that night of a good number of enemy aircraft flying over the vicinity of their camp.

At dawn on the 8th the squadron set off north in the same two parties, but leaving behind the reserve sabotage party to protect their Forward Base and the remaining two trucks of the Heavy Section. By noon the two patrols had crossed the Msus-Mechili track and then called a halt at the Bir Commando for lunch but found the well to be dry. Knowles and Arnold, the LRDG navigator, then moved forward on a reconnaissance as far north as the El Abiar-Mechili track. Having returned and brought up the rest of the squadron, the commandos proceeded west down the track to Fort Tecasis, which was found to be devoid of the enemy, although they did encounter an encampment of Senussi in the nearby Wadi Sammalus. From here they drove north up the Abd el Krim track until last light and made camp in the cover of the Wadi el Ansal. That evening Hamson set off with two attached Senussi soldiers in an effort to make contact with local tribesmen to elicit any information on the enemy, but found none in the vicinity.

Early next morning Knowles, Hamson and Taylor set off in two vehicles to reconnoitre the squadron's next move and to see again if they could find any Senussi who might have information on enemy dispositions or movements. This time they were successful, and having returned to the main party the entire squadron headed north up the Wadi el Ansal until, at dusk, they came in sight of Maraua. That night the same three, along with Duffy, conducted a reconnaissance of the town and its fort, assessing that some 200 Italian soldiers were garrisoning Maraua. They also noted a motor transport park to the north of the fort and decided that the vehicles parked there presented a prime target for an attack.

However, on the morning of the 10th, while the commandos were planning their raid on the garrison, an enemy reconnaissance plane flew over their position. Feeling certain that their position had been compromised, they waited for it to fly out of sight and then moved out and headed back to their forward base. Having reached Bir Commando they stopped very briefly before heading off south again, with Squadron HQ and No. 1 Patrol in the lead. Late that afternoon the lead party had stopped briefly at a Senussi settlement when they noticed an enemy aircraft circling in the distance to the north, over the location which they estimated to be that of No. 2 Patrol. Shortly afterwards columns of thick black smoke were seen rising into the evening sky and they had to assume that No. 2 Patrol had been attacked by enemy aircraft. Their worst fears were confirmed shortly afterwards. Under cover of darkness No. 1 Patrol despatched a rescue party which found that four of the five Chevrolets had been attacked and set on fire. Miraculously there were no casualties for, as the enemy fighter had come in on its approach run, all the commandos had managed to jump out of their trucks and take cover in the desert scrub. With darkness approaching the pilot had seemed content with his 'bag' of trucks and had not returned to seek out the commandos hiding amongst the scrub.

Having ferried the survivors back to the Senussi settlement, the squadron set off in their overloaded trucks shortly after midnight in an attempt to put as much ground as they could between themselves and the enemy airfields along the coast. They were conscious that they were now passing close to the LRDG camp of Captain Alastair Timpson's G1 Patrol which had recently taken over surveillance of the inland tracks, particularly that of Msus-Mechili, from Lloyd Owen's Y1 Patrol. At dawn on the 11th the commandos camouflaged their vehicles as best they could and lay up for the day, watching several enemy aircraft quartering the desert to their north in the vicinity of the previous day's attack. Then at last light they set off under cover of darkness once more, reaching their forward base that same night.[50]

The following morning Robinson and his party arrived from Jarabub with three 3-ton lorries and much needed supplies of fuel and water. His party then drove on to Siwa that afternoon, taking with him those from No. 2 Patrol and the single truck that had survived the air attack. Meanwhile, Squadron HQ and No. 1 Patrol lay up for the remainder of that day and the next. On the evening of the 13th Knowles held an Orders Group in which he outlined his plan for going back to Marua Fort and mounting another attack on the enemy garrison and the nearby police post at Bu Gassal.

On the morning of the 14th the party set off again towards Marua, with Squadron HQ now in just one Chevrolet, and No. 1 Patrol with its original five trucks, carrying its sabotage section as well as Hamson and the two Senussi soldiers. The second-in-command, Power, remained behind to secure the Forward Base and had with him Squadron HQ's second truck, the wireless truck and the two remaining 3-tonners. That afternoon, while the raiding party was stationary and mending a puncture on one of the vehicles, an enemy reconnaissance aircraft flew in low from the east and spotted the patrol. Everyone jumped out of the trucks to hide in the scrub, although Knowles stayed in his and accelerated quickly forwards in an attempt to get it into the cover of a wadi a little way to his front. The plane fired a few bursts of machine-gun fire and then flew farther south in an attempt, it was presumed, to see if there were any further trucks following on. With the plane heading away from them the commandos grabbed their chance, leapt back into their vehicles and drove like the wind for the wadi to get into cover. However, only two vehicles had reached the wadi before two enemy fighters arrived on the scene and proceeded to attack with their machine guns, setting fire to four of the five trucks. Next a bomber arrived on the scene and, having circled the burning vehicles and taken in the scene, dropped anti-personnel bombs and fired bursts of machine-gun fire at Knowles's truck, which also burst into flame.[51]

Meanwhile the commandos were lying low, scattered up and down the wadi, hiding under what little cover they could find and keeping as still as possible. One of the fighters appeared on the scene again and proceeded to fly down the wadi at low level with machine guns blazing in an attempt to shoot the men hiding there. Fortunately, in the rapidly failing light and travelling at speed the pilot had difficulty in discerning his targets. When they felt certain the planes would not be back the men came out of hiding, dusted themselves down and assessed the situation. Again, almost miraculously, no casualties had been sustained, but they now had just one truck. They all clambered aboard and, with men hanging off the sides, the driver headed south into the darkness. All went well for the first five miles and then the truck hit an unseen boulder in a mud-pan which smashed the steering. The commandos jumped off the vehicle, ate a quick meal and set fire to the vehicle to deny it to the enemy before setting off on foot towards their forward base, guided by Arnold.

At dawn on the 15th the decision was taken in the interests of speed and security to leave the bulk of the party hidden in a wadi while Hamson and Meikle set off with Arnold to get help from their forward base. This small party had not gone far when a truck appeared from the south and circled them. It turned out to be from Captain Alastair Timpson's G1 Patrol, which had been despatched to investigate the cause of the smoke seen during the attack of the previous day. The LRDG truck was carrying Lance Bombardier Fassam, who had become separated from the main commando party on the previous day. He was now given a jerrycan of water and was instructed to make his way the short distance to the main party and wait there. The others climbed into the truck and headed back to the LRDG patrol camp. From here they marched to their forward base and that night, under cover of darkness, headed back north in a 3-tonner to collect their main party, which was still hidden in the wadi. However, locating them in the darkness proved difficult, so they fired off some Very flares and waited just off the Msus-Mechili track for an answer. Seeing a fire in the distance they set off in that direction.

By this stage dawn was approaching rapidly, and when they met the main party they found it to be in reasonable order but suffering from exposure and lack of water. They all jumped quickly into the 3-tonner and were back before noon on the 16th at their forward base. From here they continued on their journey, making camp for the next two evenings in the desert and arriving by mid-morning on the 18th at Siwa Oasis.

This entire episode was etched in Wand-Tetley's memory, and after the war he would reminisce about the disquiet of being the object of 'target practice for Messerschmitt fighters' and of the discomfort of having to survive thereafter with little or no water. He and the rest of A Squadron did not know the full facts at the time, but it was not only them that had received a bloody nose. The previous day the entire Eighth Army had started to pull back in the face of the *Panzerarmee Afrika*; Tobruk being left isolated, it was promptly captured by Rommel along with 25,000 Allied prisoners of war.

A Squadron remained at Siwa for the next few days sorting themselves out, before departing up the Garawla track on the 22nd for Mersa Matruh. Wand-Tetley's Troop remained behind at Siwa to act as rear party. That evening the main party camped at Bir Fuad and the following morning set off again in two parties with Knowles, Power, Duffy and Barnby leading, and the Heavy Section following at a suitable interval behind. As they approached Mersa Matruh they found Allied traffic on the coast to be extremely heavy, with a diversion in place which meant they were not able to join the main coast road until some miles farther east at Fuka. From here they were able to make better time, although the road was still extremely congested by Eighth Army traffic withdrawing eastwards with Rommel hot on their tail. The squadron reached Burg el Arab, just west of Alexandria, at midday on the 24th and Wand-Tetley and Taylor arrived two days later.[52]

They now came back under command of their Middle East Commando CO, Graham, and received orders to take up defensive positions at Dekheila. Two days later the LRDG was forced to withdraw from Siwa Oasis and would set up a new headquarters, away from the advancing *Panzerarmee*, at Fayoum Oasis, south of Cairo, by which stage the triumphant Rommel had reached El Alamein.

1st Special Service Regiment

Meanwhile the turf war for control of the Middle East Commando had not let up. With Eighth Army appearing to gain undue influence in Commando matters, Colonel Terence Airey of G(R) Branch had a couple of months earlier reminded all concerned that the Middle East Commando was under control of SOE Middle East and Balkans and not under GHQ Middle East. In particular, he had expressed concern that A Squadron's return from Syria and the move of the Commando base, at the end of April, from Burg el Arab to Mersa Matruh meant that Turkey, Syria and the Balkans would receive less attention than they warranted. He also stressed that the Middle East Commando had been raised to conduct fifth column work behind enemy lines, and that the Commando title had been retained as a suitable cover for such work and to satisfy Churchill's desire for Commandos to continue to exist in the Middle East.

As a result the Middle East Commando title was changed at the beginning of July 1942 to 1st Special Service Regiment (not to be confused with 1st Special Air Service Regiment). This renaming was to emphasize the nature of 1 SSR's special SOE work rather than the traditional raiding operations. At this time the SBS also moved to the command of C-in-C Mediterranean Fleet, while the LRDG remained under GHQ Middle East.

Having been forced back to El Alamein in July the C-in-C Middle East, Auchinleck, stood firm on this line, for beyond there was only Cairo and the Nile Delta from which to make a last-ditch defence. With Rommel on the El Alamein line, sixty miles from Alexandria and 150 from Cairo, British headquarters prepared for the worse and set about burning their classified documents. Known as 'The Flap' or 'Ash Wednesday', such was the volume of classified documents burnt that Cairo was coated with a fine layer of ash and charred paper. For the same reasons HQ Mediterranean Fleet moved from Alexandria to Beirut, as did 1st Submarine Flotilla. Fortuitously, the El Alamein line was tactically excellent for defence, being only forty miles long with its northern end based on salt lakes by the sea and its southern end upon the Qattara Depression and its quicksands. Every other line in the desert had been able to be turned by the enemy because the southern end lay in the open desert. Eighth Army counter-offensives in July were unsuccessful, and stalemate ensued.

Churchill, disappointed with the lack of success, flew to Cairo in early August. He decided changes were again in order and replaced Auchinleck with General Sir Harold Alexander. Lieutenant General William 'Strafer' Gott, who had commanded both 7th Armoured Division (The Desert Rats) and XIII Corps, was chosen to replace Ritchie, but his plane was shot down while en route to Cairo and he was killed. As a consequence Montgomery was selected as a replacement and flew out from England to take command of Eighth Army. He was fortunate to take over an experienced Army consisting of the British 1st, 7th, 8th and 10th Armoured Divisions, the 44th, 50th (and later the 51st) Infantry Divisions, and infantry divisions from South Africa, Australia, New Zealand and India. Alexander and Montgomery echoed Auchinleck's earlier resolve that British and Commonwealth forces would retreat no further.

In early July when Rommel reached El Alamein, GHQ Middle East had sought all available troops for the defence of Cairo and the Delta, and 1 SSR had been roped in to help in the defence of Alexandria. Wand-Tetley found himself digging in with A Squadron at a number of locations, first Dekheila, then Sidi Bishr and Hosh Isa, before finally ending up at Mustapha Barracks, where his father had served in more peaceful times back in 1930.

A GHQ signal on 11 August ordered A Squadron back to Syria. The Commandos had maintained a squadron-sized presence in Syria ever since February that year, when A Squadron had deployed there prior to its attachment to the LRDG. They had been replaced by B Squadron in April. It had initially been intended that D Squadron would relieve B Squadron at the beginning of June, but the defence of Alexandria had become the priority. Now it was decided that A Squadron would go instead, to complement B Squadron's presence in the Levant. Furthermore, C Squadron would provide half of its manpower to reinforce the somewhat depleted B Squadron. Departing by road in twelve 30-cwt trucks, on 15 August, the A Squadron party consisted of five officers and seventy-two ORs, and with them in the same convoy were one officer and thirty-nine ORs as reinforcements for B Squadron.[53]

The British had sustained a significant military presence in Syria since 8 June 1941, after the evacuation of Crete when, under orders from Churchill, Wavell had despatched an invasion force under General Sir Henry Maitland 'Jumbo' Wilson, GOC Palestine and Transjordan. British and Australian troops, with Free French forces alongside them, had advanced through the Lebanon, and an Indian division had attacked from Northern Iraq. A Palestine-based British horsed cavalry brigade of one regular and two yeomanry regiments was used as part of the invasion force, but this would be the last time that British mounted cavalry went on campaign. The invasion's aim was to counter the threat developing against the Allies and to protect regional Middle East oil supplies, for the Vichy French had started to allow the Germans use of their airfields.

Legally, the French status in the Levant (modern-day Lebanon and Syria) had been that of a mandate (similar to Britain's status in Palestine). In May 1941, following a pro-Axis coup in Iraq by Rashid Ali on 3 April, the Vichy French garrison of Syria and the Lebanon had provided equipment to Iraqi rebels besieging the RAF base at Habbaniya, and the *Luftwaffe* had been allowed to use Syrian airfields to bomb the British base. The Iraqi rebellion was quickly quashed and Rashid Ali had fled to Iran at the end of May. However, the Allies, under 'Jumbo' Wilson, found the Vichy French resistance in Syria, under General Dentz, much more spirited than anticipated. It was not until 14 July that the Allies were able to bring the Vichy French to heel.

Now, just over a year since the invasion of Syria, Wand-Tetley found himself with A Squadron in the Levant, on the Syrian-Turkish border. The task was to conduct reconnaissance and prepare for post-occupational schemes to provide 'stay behind' parties that would train and organize local guerrilla resistance if the Germans should break through at Stalingrad, swing south through the Caucasus and then overrun Turkey and Syria. However, over time, this would become increasingly less likely, particularly in light of the failure of the German offensive in the Caucasus in mid-1942, and their failure to take Stalingrad at the end of the year. Thereafter British and SOE focus would increasingly switch towards the Balkans.

For Wand-Tetley these months in the Levant, engaged in preparation for potential behind-the-lines work, would prove to be an invaluable experience given that he was destined to put all these skills to the test in the Peloponnese the following year. From August through to the end of October A Squadron based itself variously at Beirut, Banias and Mafraq, but ranged far over Syria and Iraq up to the Turkish border, particularly in the Aleppo region with its strategic airfields, and even embarking in HMS *Antwerp* to travel over to Cyprus to consider post-occupational schemes there before returning once again to the Levant.[54]

While Wand-Tetley was with A Squadron in Syria, another party from the SSR and SIG would be involved, along with L Detachment SAS, the Sudan Defence Force, and the LRDG in a number of concurrent operations in September 1942 to disrupt Rommel's supplies in preparation for Alexander's final offensive from El Alamein. Planning had started in earnest in August and involved concurrent attacks by the SSR and SIG party against Tobruk harbour in Operation AGREEMENT (a.k.a. DAFFODIL), by L Detachment SAS against Benghazi harbour in Operation BIGAMY (a.k.a. SNOWDROP), by the Sudan Defence Force against Jalo in Operation NICETY (a.k.a. TULIP), and a diversionary raid by the LRDG against Barce airfield in Operation CARAVAN (a.k.a. HYACINTH). However, only CARAVAN, the LRDG's raid on Barce airfield was successful.[55]

In the interim Montgomery had been awaiting his moment to push the enemy back on a broad front. He successfully repulsed Rommel's attack of 30 August in the second Battle of El Alamein, better known as the Battle of Alam el Halfa, and then launched his own offensive, the third Battle of El Alamein, on the night of 23 October. This was heralded by the largest artillery barrage since the end of the Great War, and Montgomery had also ensured that he had amassed an over-whelming superiority over the enemy. By 4 November Rommel was engaged in a fighting withdrawal, under pressure from Eighth Army;

this was a significant victory and a major turning point in the war for the Allies. Politically it was all that Churchill could have hoped for. With Anglo-American forces shortly due to land on the shores of North Africa, a clear victory such as this was essential in being able to hold his own in the Anglo-American alliance, where British influence would invariably be lost due to an imbalance of forces.

Following the raid on Tobruk, 1 SSR found itself well below operational effectiveness. A significant element of D Squadron along with the SIG had been destroyed at Tobruk, and C Squadron had already been split up and half of its manpower absorbed elsewhere within the regiment. This left just A and B Squadrons, which were still in the Levant focused on their role as stay-behind forces, to operate behind enemy lines in Turkey and Syria should these countries be overrun by the Germans. However, as has been related, following the failure of the enemy to take Stalingrad this scenario was becoming increasingly less likely as the second half of the year progressed.

Following an order issued by GHQ Middle East at the end of September, 1 SSR was disbanded at the end of October 1942. A number of its officers and men returned to their parent regiments, while some stayed on to operate with the SOE in the Balkans. However, Wand-Tetley, in common with a number of other officers and men, transferred direct to the SAS which was at the time undergoing rapid expansion.

Notes

1. NA Kew, WO 218/152, No. 3 SS Battalion War Diary, Nov 1940–Feb 1941; DEFE 2/45, No. 4 SS Battalion War Diary, Nov 1940–Feb 1941. Army Service Record (Army Form B199A) of P.M. Wand-Tetley.
2. NA Kew, WO 193/384, Independent Companies, June–Dec 1940 (Memorandum dated 13 Jun 1940).
3. NA Kew, CAB 44/152, Commandos and Special Service Troops in the Middle East and North Africa.
4. NA Kew, WO 218/152, No. 3 SS Battalion War Diary, Nov 1940–Feb 1941. DEFE 2/45, No. 4 SS Battalion War Diary Nov 1940–Feb 1941.
5. NA Kew, WO 218/152, No. 3 SS Battalion War Diary, Nov 1940–Feb 1941. WO 218/168, Layforce, A Battalion (No. 7 Commando) War Diary, Jan–May 1941.
6. Quoted in WO 218/166, HQ Z Force/Layforce War Diary, Jan–July 1941.
7. NA Kew, WO 218/168, Layforce, A Battalion (No. 7 Commando) War Diary, Jan–May 1941. WO 218/166, HQ Z Force/Layforce War Diary, Jan–July 1941.
8. NA Kew, WO 218/168, Layforce, A Battalion (No. 7 Commando) War Diary, Jan–May 1941.
9. Courtney, *SBS in World War Two: The Story of the Original Special Boat Section of the Army Commandos*. Chs. 1 and 7.
10. NA Kew, WO 218/168, Layforce, A Battalion (No. 7 Commando) War Diary Jan–May, 1941.
11. Moreman, *British Commandos 1940–46*. Ch. 2, Organization.
12. Messenger, *The Middle East Commandos*. Ch. 1.

13. NA Kew, WO 218/168, op cit. WO 218/166, op cit.
14. Quoted in Saunders, *The Green Beret: The Story of the Commandos 1940–1945*. Ch. 5.
15. NA Kew, WO 218/166, HQ Z Force/Layforce War Diary, op cit (Report on Raid on Bardia dated 20 Apr 41).
16. NA Kew, WO 218/168, op cit (Operation Order No. 2 dated 19 Apr 41). WO 218/166, op cit.
17. Saunders, op cit. Ch. 5.
18. NA Kew, WO 218/168, op cit. (Report on Raid on Bardia dated 20 Apr 41).
19. NA Kew, WO 218/168, op cit.
20. NA Kew, WO 218/166, op cit. Quoted in Laycock's letter to Maj Gen Arthur Smith at GHQ Middle East dated 6 May 41.
21. NA Kew, CAB 44/152, Commandos and Special Service Troops in the Middle East and North Africa.
22. NA Kew, WO 218/168, op cit.
23. Ibid. WO 218/166, op cit.
24. NA Kew, WO 218/168, op cit.
25. NA Kew, WO 218/168, op cit. WO 218/166, op cit.
26. Waugh, *The Diaries of Evelyn Waugh*. The Wartime Diary.
27. NA Kew, WO 218/168, op cit. WO 218/166, op cit.
28. NA Kew, WO 218/168, op cit.
29. NA Kew, WO 218/166, op cit. WO 218/168, op cit. WO 218/172, Layforce D Battalion (No. 52 (ME) Commando/A Battalion (No. 7 Commando)), Dec 1940–June 1941.
30. Quoted in Beevor, *Crete: The Battle and the Resistance*. Ch. 19.
31. NA Kew, WO 218/168, op cit. WO 218/166, op cit. WO 218/172, op cit.
32. Beevor, op cit. Ch. 19.
33. NA Kew, WO 218/166, op cit.
34. NA Kew, WO 218/172, op cit. WO 218/158, Middle East Commando Depot, Jan–Dec 1941.
35. NA Kew, WO 218/166, op cit. WO 218/172, op cit. WO 218/158, Middle East Commando Depot, Jan–Dec 1941.
36. Quoted in Churchill, *The Second World War*, Vol 3, Appendix G.
37. NA Kew, CAB 44/152, op cit.
38. This being the first of 8 VCs that would be earned by commandos by the end of the war, in addition to 37 DSOs with 9 Bars, 162 MCs with 13 Bars, 32 DCMs, and 218 MMs.
39. NA Kew, WO 218/158, op cit.
40. NA Kew, CAB 44/152, op cit.
41. NA Kew, WO 218/159, Middle East Commando War Diary, Jan–Jun 1942.
42. Ibid.
43. NA Kew, CAB 44/152, op cit.
44. Kennedy Shaw, *Long Range Desert Group: The Story of its Work in Libya 1940–1943*. Ch. 1.
45. Ibid.
46. Lloyd Owen, *Providence Their Guide: The Long Range Desert Group 1940–45*. Ch. 1.
47. Ibid, Ch 2.
48. NA Kew, WO 218/160, Middle East Commando A Sqn War Diary, May–Jun 1942.
49. Ibid, Patrol Report, dated June 1942.

50. A Squadron's War Diary report suggests that it was Lloyd Owen's LRDG Y1 Patrol that was encountered during this operation. However, Timpson's memoir, *In Rommel's Backyard*, and Lloyd Owen's memoir, *The Desert My Dwelling Place*, both corroborate that it was in fact Timpson's G1 Patrol, which had taken over duties on 8 June from Lloyd Owen's Y1 Patrol.
51. NA Kew, WO 218/160, op cit. Patrol Report, dated June 1942. It is also of note that Captain A. I. Guild's LRDG R1 Patrol, which was operating in the same area, also reports witnessing the destruction of A Squadron's transport on 14 June 1942.
52. NA Kew, WO 218/160, op cit. Patrol Report, dated June 1942.
53. NA Kew, WO218/149, 1 Special Service Regiment War Diary, Jul–Oct 1942. WO 218/150, 1 Special Service Regiment A Sqn War Diary, Aug–Oct 1942. WO 218/151, 1 Special Service Regiment B Sqn War Diary, Jun–Oct 1942.
54. NA Kew, WO 218/150, 1 Special Service Regiment A Sqn War Diary, Aug–Oct 1942. WO 218/151, 1 Special Service Regiment B Sqn War Diary, Jun–Oct 1942.
55. NA Kew, CAB 44/152, op cit.

Chapter 3

SAS Officer

1st SAS Regiment

The order to expand L Detachment SAS Brigade into 1st Special Air Service Regiment was issued by GHQ Middle East on 28 September 1942. This was concurrent with the disbandment of 1st Special Service Regiment at the end of October and Wand-Tetley's return from Syria, thus providing him with the opportunity for a direct transfer between units that would serve to keep him in special forces work.[1]

The expansion of the SAS had received the Prime Minister's blessing the previous month. Major David Stirling, along with one of his subalterns, Lieutenant Sir Hew Fitzroy Maclean, had been invited to dine with Churchill at the British Embassy in Cairo on 8 August by the Ambassador, Sir Miles Lampson. Also present were the CIGS, General Sir Alan Brooke, the new C-in-C Middle East, General Sir Harold Alexander, and Field Marshal Jan Smuts. After the meal Stirling took the opportunity to discuss his plans for the SAS with Churchill. He also expressed his serious reservations about the forthcoming Benghazi and Tobruk raids. Quite how Stirling came to be invited to dinner is somewhat unclear, but it is almost certainly the case that Randolph Churchill planted the idea in his father's mind.

Evidently Stirling was extremely persuasive, for the following morning he received a note from Churchill's private secretary asking him to put in writing his proposals and have them delivered to the Prime Minister that very day. This he did, suggesting in his note that the scope of L Detachment SAS should be expanded to cover all special service tasks, absorbing such special forces personnel as were required, and that other existing special service units should be duly disbanded. This was a far reaching suggestion but Stirling, ever conscious of the manoeuvrings of other military departments and fearful that his own unit might be at risk of coming under a less than satisfactory command arrangement, had therefore gone on the offensive with a strong counter-proposal of his own. Churchill was undoubtedly impressed with the proposal, for

Stirling was invited back to dine at the Embassy that evening to discuss the matter further.

With Churchill's support of Stirling clearly understood by the military hierarchy, Major General McCreery, Alexander's Chief of Staff, outlined a proposal in September to expand the SAS and raise it to the status of a full regiment within the British Army. The SAS would come under the Director of Military Operations (DMO), which by now had won its interdepartmental battle with the Director of Combined Operations (DCO) for control of all raiding forces. Control would be exercised through a new DMO department, General Staff (Raiding Forces), (G(RF)). Such an arrangement would also serve to restrain Stirling from bypassing intermediate command and going straight to the top of the military hierarchy.

The ill-fated Benghazi raid in mid-September, touched upon in the previous chapter, was the SAS's first unsuccessful operation since its first mission over twelve months before, but that did not serve to upset the planned expansion of the regiment or Stirling's future role. Indeed, no blame was attached to Stirling, who had been forced to abort the mission and beat a hasty retreat when it became clear that the enemy had been warned of the impending attack and that any element of surprise had already been lost.

The meeting on 28 September, chaired by Lieutenant Colonel Shan Hackett, now in charge of the new G(RF) branch, and with Stirling present, discussed the employment of 1 SAS and its part in Eighth Army's forthcoming El Alamein offensive, Operation LIGHTFOOT, planned for the night of 23/24 October. Stirling and Hackett immediately agreed, and this heralded the start of a good working relationship between the two. The twenty-six year old Stirling was promoted to lieutenant colonel to command the regiment, its headquarters location confirmed at Kabrit, fifteen miles north of Suez on the Canal.

First SAS Regiment was to emerge with an initial establishment of twenty-nine officers and 572 other ranks, made up of HQ Squadron (consisting of a depot troop, a signals troop, an intelligence troop, a parachute-training troop, and a repair section) and four fighting squadrons, A, B, C and D. In addition there were the Free French Squadron and the SBS, both of which would in due course increasingly become associated with C and D Squadrons respectively, but with the French maintaining a semi-autonomous integrity. Each of the four squadrons was established for three troops, each of three sections.[2]

One of Stirling's principal concerns was to find men of the right calibre to fill the expanded regimental establishment. His first port of call was 1 SSR, which was being disbanded, where he had his pick of the officers and men. Wand-Tetley duly applied for transfer, and was one of several officers selected, including two others from A Squadron, Knowles and

74

Barnby. Other officers included Lepine and Gurmin, with whom Wand-Tetley had patrolled the Suez Docks in the aftermath of Crete. Major R. V. Lea, a Gunner, who had latterly commanded B Squadron in Syria, Lieutenant J. E. Tonkin of the Royal Northumberland Fusiliers and T. C. D. Russell, Scots Guards, one of the two survivors from the Tobruk raid, were also accepted. A few who had already jumped ship to the SAS a few months earlier included Captain H. G. Chevalier, an Arabic-speaking Frenchman, and Lieutenants Gordon Alston, Royal Artillery, R. E. Galloway, Royal Scots, and R. P. Schott of the General List. All counted themselves fortunate to have caught Stirling's eye, for many others were deemed by him to be unsuitable for SAS training and were forced to find appointments elsewhere. It appears that Stirling first visited 1 SRR on 14 October, but he had been preceded by Major Mike Kealy of the SBS on 10 October, and by Major Peter Oldfield who had arrived on 24 September to interview other ranks, of whom some thirty were selected at that stage.[3]

Wand-Tetley was to serve no more than six months in C Squadron of the SAS, until April 1943, at which time the Regiment would undergo, as we shall see, another significant reorganization. Since this would also herald the end of the Desert War, with new decisions requiring to be made regarding his future, he would transfer to the SOE. The manuscript entry on his Army Service Record incorrectly states that Wand-Tetley joined the SAS, rather than the SOE, in April 1943, this no doubt being a clerical error. However, those responsible for maintaining records can perhaps be excused for being somewhat confused, given the number of different special forces organizations in existence, their seemingly constant title changes, and Wand-Tetley's relatively rapid moves between such units, all this exacerbated by SOE's secret nature.[4]

This six-month period of Wand-Tetley's service, and in particular the first three months of 1943, is somewhat frustrating for anyone researching early SAS history. The War Diaries provide relatively limited information besides that of routine training activity. The period encompasses Stirling's capture in late January, and no doubt the regiment was at that stage more concerned about its immediate future than with maintaining records, for Stirling had always played his cards very close to his chest and his fellow SAS officers knew little of what he had planned for the future. Major 'Paddy' Mayne, upon whom the responsibility might have fallen, was known for his aversion to paperwork at this stage of his career, although later as CO of 1 SAS he was to prove himself more than able in this regard. Stirling's exploits during this period are inextricably linked with those of A and B Squadrons and are well chronicled, although for the most part as a result of post-war memoirs and narratives. However, the activities of C Squadron, in which Wand-Tetley served, and of D Squadron are by comparison poorly documented. Wand-Tetley is easily enough placed, for he consistently appears in the 1 SAS monthly nominal roll of officers, but official detail is sparse regarding specific activities in which he and C Squadron were engaged during this six-month period. Nonetheless, after the war Wand-Tetley would reminisce on occasion about his SAS service, and this provides an insight.[5]

Still short of men having visited 1 SRR, Stirling and Hackett paid a visit to HQ Eighth Army, just ten miles behind the El Alamein Line, in early October. He briefed Montgomery on the SAS role and how his unit could best support him in the coming offensive. He went on to explain that he was after 150 high-calibre, experienced volunteers from amongst the regiments of Eighth Army. Stirling may have had the support of the Prime Minister but in Montgomery he certainly met his match, for the general explained in no uncertain terms that he would not relinquish his best officers and men to Stirling, for these very same soldiers were required by him if he were to succeed in driving Rommel back in the planned El Alamein offensive.

On showing them to the door Montgomery did, nonetheless, offer them lunch in his mess, even though he was unable to join them. Stirling and Hackett, both disappointed with their lack of headway, took some pleasure in ringing up a decent drinks' tab on the teetotal general's mess bill. However, before they left they met Montgomery's Chief of Staff, Brigadier Freddie de Guingand, who struck a more helpful chord than his superior and intimated that he would assist if he could. He also let slip news of the impending Allied invasion of North-West Africa in Operation TORCH. This set Stirling thinking, for he already had ambitions to expand the SAS yet further, and this might provide the justification to raise a second SAS battalion which, indeed, was borne out by subsequent events.

When Stirling received his rebuttal from Montgomery, the third Battle of El Alamein was only two weeks off and set for the night of 23/24 October. Montgomery's unwarranted comment made at the same time about the failure of the ill-fated Benghazi raid had also rankled Stirling. Although his relationship with Montgomery had got off to a bad start, he still enjoyed the backing of Alexander and the unequivocal support of Hackett. Nonetheless, Stirling felt the need to win over Montgomery in advance of the coming Eighth Army offensive so as not to lose any further ground. However, although the SAS now had regimental status, Stirling had yet to find the required numbers of recruits, and he still only had a squadron's worth of trained SAS soldiers. So he formed his existing troops, largely L Detachment men, into A Squadron, under Mayne, and sent them immediately to Kufra Oasis.

76

All of A Squadron had arrived in the desert oasis by 13 October. Here they set up their rear supply base. With Mayne were Captains Bill Fraser and Bill Cumper and several subalterns, Bill McDermott, a Gunner, J. W. Wiseman and J. A. Marsh, both from the Duke of Cornwall's Light Infantry, along with Raymond Shorten of the General List, Lord Charlesworth and D. S. Kennedy, another Gunner who would be killed in action during the following month.[6]

Then, guided by the LRDG, the squadron crossed the Great Sand Sea to set up a forward patrol base closer to the coast at Fort Maddalena, some 150 miles from the sea and 200 miles behind the German front line. The squadron formally came under command of Eighth Army on 16 October, and there were to be three phases to the SAS supporting operation. Phase One called for a number of raids against the Tobruk to Mersa Matruh stretch of the Western Desert Railway, and against the coast road and supply depots. Phase Two would allow for the squadron to reorganize and resupply itself. Phase Three, commencing on 23 October and concurrent with the main offensive, called for attacks against airfields and enemy vehicles withdrawing back down the coast road. A SBS party was also to land by sea in the region of El Daba to blow up supply depots and vehicle parks.

As planned the squadron divided itself into six parties, A to F, and in the last two weeks of October, leading up to and during the third Battle of El Alamein, Mayne's troops attacked and blew up the railway line at several locations from Tobruk in the west to Fuka in the east. The attacks occurred at Tobruk on the night of 14/15 October, although a similar attempt at Sidi Barrani was forestalled by the enemy and the Patrol Commander, Shorten, was killed when his jeep overturned in a chase across the desert. On 24 October the railway was blown up at three places again, at Fuka, at 'Piccadilly', and also a short way farther west. A further nine successful attacks were made on the night of 29/30 October north-west of Sidi Aziz, followed on 31 October by attacks at Niswel el Suf station. At this stage an order was despatched to Mayne to stop blowing the railway up any further, for Eighth Army was rapidly approaching and wanted the line intact for its own use. McDermott, a newcomer to the SAS, had got so frustrated when his charges had failed to detonate and blow up his target train, that he attacked and destroyed a railway station, capturing three Italians and two Germans, before withdrawing into the desert.[7]

One of the great SAS endurance marches took place in the aftermath of the attack by the enemy on Shorten's patrol at Sidi Barrani. David Sillito, the patrol navigator (a private at the time, but later commissioned), found himself separated and on foot after the firefight with the enemy. He had three choices: to give himself up, to lie up and hope the Eighth Army would arrive sooner rather than later, or march back to his patrol base in the Great Sand Sea – a distance of almost 200 miles. He chose the last option. He had on him just one water bottle, a compass and a pistol, but no food. By the end of the second day he had used up all his water, and thereafter was reduced to drinking his own urine. After eight days walking in the desert, and with his feet torn and bleeding, he reached the Hatiet Etla wadi, which his patrol had used as their last rendezvous and in which he knew there were concealed emergency rations and water. He had covered 150 miles, and did not need to march any farther for he was shortly afterwards picked up by a passing SAS patrol and taken to Kufra Oasis. Within two weeks he had recovered sufficiently to be back on active operations.

Stirling himself had stayed behind at Kabrit with a small recruiting and training team. He reckoned it would take a month to train experienced officers and men such as Wand-Tetley in SAS operating procedures, and two to three months to train inexperienced soldiers. During this period he finally succumbed to his desert sores and was laid up in hospital in Cairo for a short spell, but he merely moved his office there and continued to orchestrate events from his hospital bed. At this stage he heard that his brother Bill, also a former Commando officer, had been given the go-ahead to form a second SAS battalion in England. It was envisaged that 2 SAS would be used to support the Allied TORCH landings, set for 8 November in French North-West Africa. Stirling's plans to expand the SAS were gaining momentum, and some quipped that the regiment's title stood for 'Stirling and Stirling'.

The third Battle of El Alamein proved to be a resounding success and marked the beginning of the final phase of the Desert War. On 8 November, as planned, Anglo-American troops including the British First Army, under Lieutenant General Sir Kenneth Anderson, landed in North Africa at Algiers and Oran, and farther west at Casablanca.

In early November there were several follow-on SAS sabotage operations in the region, principally against fuel depots and motor transport. At El Daba the fuel dumps were successfully hit by Scratchley's patrol which, finding itself suddenly amongst retreating Germans, decided to drive east through British lines and back to Kabrit. The Gazala airfields were also attacked again, before Mayne took his raiders back through the Great Sand Sea to Kufra Oasis for a few days' rest in mid-November.

News of A Squadron's successful operations in the desert filtered back to Cairo, and Stirling and Hackett ensured that Alexander and Montgomery were kept well informed of developments. Montgomery could hardly fail to be impressed and, despite a somewhat shaky start, Stirling and he now began to develop a good working relationship and mutual respect. Indeed, Montgomery would with due reverence tell people that he thought 'the Boy Stirling' to be 'quite, quite mad', but that such madness had a place in war.

Within a month of A Squadron's deployment, Stirling and his team had recruited and trained a second squadron of men, and so B Squadron, under Major Vivian Street of the Devons, was able to leave Kabrit on 20 November to join A Squadron in the desert. Although B Squadron was not yet fully trained, Stirling felt it imperative that it was fielded as soon as possible. Accordingly he persuaded Hackett that the remainder of its training should be 'on the job'. By now out of hospital, Stirling, and his small tactical headquarters, accompanied the squadron on its nine-day journey across the desert to join Mayne and A Squadron. On the first part of the journey, from Alexandria to Agedabia, the coast-road was used as it was by that stage in British hands.

In his absence, Stirling appointed Jellicoe as second-in-command to remain at Kabrit and continue the task of recruiting and training. With Rommel now on the retreat, Mayne had moved from his patrol base at Kufra farther west to Bir Zalten, 160 miles south of Agheila, so as to be better placed to keep up the pressure on the retreating *Panzerarmee Afrika*. It was here on 29 November that Stirling and B Squadron, with its party of ninety-odd men, some thirty jeeps, and twelve 3-ton lorries, joined A Squadron.

In a wadi at Bir Zalten, just south-west of Jalo Oasis and 150 miles south of Agheila, Stirling briefed the two squadrons on their developing role in supporting Eighth Army's next push westward to Tripoli, scheduled for December. The aim was to keep ahead of the advancing Eighth Army and cause as much disruption to the retreating enemy as possible. The SAS would establish two main squadron bases from which sixteen jeep detachments, each of three to four jeeps would mount up to two raids each week along the 400 miles of coast road between Agheila and Tripoli. Under cover of darkness the raiders would focus on mining the road and harassing the enemy's lines of communications, thereby forcing the enemy to drive in daylight when they would become prey for RAF aircraft. All the raids would be planned to coincide with Eighth Army's advance, and also be synchronized to take account of the continuing LRDG 'Road Watch'. A Squadron was allocated the eastern sector of coastline from Agheila to Buerat, and B Squadron the western sector from Buerat to Tripoli. Their main supply base was by this stage at Benghazi, now also in Allied hands. The two squadrons then separated and headed for their respective sectors.

Close already to their area of operations, A Squadron were in action within two days but found the going for the jeeps particularly tough. Four of their jeeps and crews had to be left behind, with orders from Mayne to operate in the vicinity in which they had been left. In the event the squadron carried out relatively few raids, albeit successfully and with minimal casualties, as it would have been pointless to destroy the road immediately in front of Eighth Army, which soon advanced into their sector.

B Squadron on the other hand had more time before the Allies reached their sector, but found the area very difficult to operate in, being heavily populated with unfriendly Arabs and by an enemy who went to considerable lengths to curb their activities. Owing to the very difficult terrain, the squadron only just managed to get to their patrol base, Bir Fascia, 200 miles to the west of Bir Zalten, by 13 December, the day before Eighth Army's push. Stirling had decided to accompany this less experienced squadron to its area of operations, but upon arrival was compelled within a couple of days to return to HQ Eighth Army.

With Street in B Squadron were a few experienced officers, Lieutenants Alston and Carol Mather, and Martin of the Free French, but most were new and included Major Peter Oldfield, Royal Armoured Corps, and Major Wilfred Thesiger of the General List, later to become famous as an explorer. From the Rifle Brigade there was Captain The Hon. Pat Hore-Ruthven, Captain P. S. Morris-Keating and Lieutenant Andy Hough. Also present were Captain John O'Sullivan, King's Royal Rifle Corps, Lieutenants P. J. Maloney of the Royal Warwicks, and Brian Franks of the Middlesex Yeomanry.

At Bir Fascia there was a rainwater cistern dating from Roman times, as well as a number of wadis with thorn-scrub which provided a degree of camouflage. Here, as planned, the squadron divided into eight patrols, each of three jeeps, each being allotted separate sections of road. Raids were conducted over the next fortnight which resulted in a good deal of damage, forcing the enemy to divert large numbers of troops to counter their activities. However SAS casualties in B Squadron were particularly heavy, with many of the squadron killed or captured. Only four officers were to survive or avoid capture.

Mather's patrol was tracked down by Italian Carabinieri to a cave where they had been lying up. After a gun battle they managed to escape into the night, but were tracked down once again, captured, and after a mock execution were sent by submarine to Italy. The three patrols working in the region of Gheddahia to Misurata, under Street, Oldfield and Hore-Ruthven, found the enemy close on their heels a good deal of the time, which made their operations difficult in the extreme.

Hore-Ruthven's patrol left Stirling on 12 December at the Wadi Zazemat and headed for Bir Fascia. From there it drove up the Wadi Zem Zem and at Sedada combined forces with Street's patrol. Together they left Bir Gebira on the 15th and headed north-east. At Bir Dufan, some twenty miles from Misurata, the patrols came across some twenty trucks on the road. These they attacked at close quarters before planting bombs and leaving them in flames. Next they mined the road and cut the telephone wires before moving on. Coming across an enemy encampment at Tauorga on the 18th, some twenty-five miles south of Misurata, the patrol decided it was too well protected and so bypassed it. By the 20th the patrols were in the region south of Gioda, and here they mined the road again. Nearby, they then attacked six vehicles including two tanks, but the enemy returned heavy fire, seriously wounding Hore-Ruthven, who was later reported to have been killed, and forced the patrols to disperse.

The remnants of Hore-Ruthven's patrol withdrew back to the Wadi Sasu, north of Henscir el Gabu, which it reached on the 22nd. Then, heading back through Bir Gebira on the 25th, they came across the enemy, attacked a lorry, and headed straight on back to Bir Fascia, only to find the enemy there in some strength as well. Passing through the Wadi Zem-Zem on the 27th, they reached the Wadi Zazemet on the 30th, where they lay up for the next few days. Having had a close call here with the enemy on 4 January 1943, they eventually made it back to friendly lines on the 5th, only to hear that the patrols of Street and Oldfield were still missing.[8]

In fact, Street's patrol had been forced to abandon their jeeps for lack of petrol near their rendezvous at Bir Dufan. The location of their position was then given away by hostile Arabs to an Italian search party. The five men found themselves hopelessly outnumbered and were forced to surrender, but Street was soon to make a successful bid for freedom when the Italian submarine which was transferring him to Italy was attacked by the Allies with depth charges. Street, along with six other prisoners, was able to escape and was picked up by a British ship. He was back at the SAS base in Kabrit by February 1943.

The patrols of Mather and Hough were also captured and taken by submarine to Italy, although Mather would later escape from an Italian prisoner of war camp and be back in the fray for D Day.[9]

The patrols of Thesiger, Alston and Martin fared somewhat better, and all three managed to evade capture. Thesiger, who was not officially on the SAS strength but had been taken on attachment by Stirling only shortly before departing for the desert with B Squadron, had not had time to receive any training. Accordingly he was placed in a jeep with Alston, who had previous SAS operational experience, along with two signallers. Their patrol set off on 14 December from Bir Fascia and, having reached the road, they awaited a convoy before driving alongside it and raking it with their machine guns. Accelerating off into the darkness they laid some mines and cut some telephone lines farther along the road before driving into an enemy camp and attacking the tents with their machine guns. Returning to Bir Fascia before dawn, they laid up during the day before setting off once again under cover of darkness to wreak what havoc they could against supply columns and camps.[10]

This was a pattern they were to repeat over the next ten days until the enemy in armoured cars came looking for them at Bir Fascia. Alston and the signallers had gone for water at the cistern, so Thesiger was alone when he heard the enemy approach. Running off into the desert he hid in a slight depression under a blanket, covered with twigs and sand. He was undiscovered, as indeed was their well-camouflaged radio jeep, and so waited for the enemy patrol to move on and the return of Alston. Martin's patrol, which had been returning to Bir Fascia at the same time, was attacked by the departing enemy, but managed to escape into the desert and make it back to join Thesiger and Alston a few hours later. When the signallers got the radio working they and the remnants of the squadron were instructed to remain in the vicinity of Bir Fascia and await the return of Stirling, who had by now planned the next series of operations for January.[11]

Despite very heavy losses to B Squadron, the SAS caused the Germans significant headaches during December and tied up a considerable amount of manpower by their actions. Certainly Montgomery was pleased and had very evidently thawed towards the SAS, for at Christmas he sent every one of the raiders in the desert a bottle of whisky and 500 cigarettes. With his headquarters now in Sirte, he believed that since the third Battle of Alamein the SAS had done more to assist his push westwards than had any division.

In the interim Wand-Tetley and C Squadron 1 SAS had been training since November 1942 at Chekka, a small village on the Lebanese coast with which he was familiar from his time in 1 SSR. If Commando training had been hard, then for the new SAS parachutists it was a good deal harder. It was in many respects similar to Commando training, but taken to a higher plane. Long route marches across harsh terrain, carrying heavy packs, while navigating from maps with little or no detail, and with very limited food and water, became a regular feature. A sense of constant, total exhaustion was Wand-Tetley's abiding memory.

In fact, A and B Squadrons of the SSR had both remained in the Levant until the very end of October, the official date of 1 SSR's disbandment. Major R. V. Lea, Officer Commanding B Squadron, had visited Egypt between 9 and 21 October to discuss the future of these two SSR squadrons, and had called at the HQ of 1 SAS on the 19th, prior to returning to Beirut. A number of those selected for transfer to C Squadron 1 SAS had remained in the Levant without returning to Egypt. Nonetheless, there was also a good deal of coming and going, with Major W. A. Knowles, ex OC A Squadron 1 SSR, arriving at Kabrit, along with Captain J. P. Power and forty other ranks, in the second week of November. Eventually C Squadron 1 SAS in its entirety left Syria, arriving at the SAS base at Kabrit on 21 December. By this stage the regiment had grown to a strength of some fifty-six British officers and 570 other ranks, and the roll of regimental officers, the majority famous for their various exploits, is impressive indeed.[12]

On 5 January 1943 Wand-Tetley deployed with C Squadron, now 120-strong and under command of Lea, on operations in the Western Desert. Their principal role was to support Eighth Army's push westwards up the coast by providing advance guards and flank guards, and to cause as much disruption to the retreating enemy as possible. Having left Kabrit, Lea's squadron made good time, and reached the remnants of B Squadron in the vicinity of Bir Fascia on 19 January, where they were able to resupply Alston's and Thesiger's patrols with petrol and rations.[13]

Moving rapidly on and heading north-west up the coast, C Squadron then provided, with 11th Hussars, the advance guard to Eighth Army as it entered Tripoli on 23 January. Wand-Tetley remained with Lea and C Squadron in the desert, mining roads, and harassing the enemy's lines of communication to the front and flanks of the advancing Eighth Army, for some two and a half months before the last of the squadron's men finally returned to Kabrit on 18 March.

For transport Wand-Tetley's squadron was equipped with the American Willy Bantam General Purpose (GPs), or 'jeeps', with 3-ton Ford trucks for transporting heavy supplies. With excellent cross-country ability and a standard range of 200 miles, the SAS four-wheel-drive jeeps were modified with a radiator condenser, and fitted with brackets to carry additional petrol and water cans and steel sand-channels for extracting the vehicles when stuck in soft sand. Initially, pairs of Vickers K machine guns were mounted for the front passenger, with a further pair mounted in the rear of the vehicle. These .303-inch calibre guns, with a cyclic rate of fire of 1,000 rounds per minute and a 100-round magazine, came from obsolete biplane bombers. However, later the front pair of guns would often be replaced with the belt-fed, air-cooled .50-inch Browning M2 heavy machine guns.

The bomb that the SAS used, whether against enemy aircraft or transport, was the 'Lewes Bomb', an extremely simple but effective bomb invented by Jock Lewes, consisting of a mixture of one pound of plastic 808 explosive, a teacup of motor oil, and three ounces of phosphorus. The resulting mixture was placed in an army ration bag tied at the neck, and then a primer, a length of cordtex instantaneous fuse, and a delay time fuse with detonator were added. The bomb would be placed by hand, and the bomber would retire to a safe distance to watch the ensuing fireworks. The least reliable component of the bomb was the delay time fuse – a standard 'time pencil' which worked on the basis that acid in a glass phial, once broken, would eat its way through a metal wire and release a metal spring to the detonator.

Despite the pace of operations, there was often time to relax in the evenings. After the war Wand-Tetley would reminisce about nights out in the desert with C Squadron, after a hard day's patrolling, cleaning their weapons and cooking dinner over their petrol stoves, and of the strong sense of camaraderie, when often the men would sing; a firm favourite being 'Lili Marlene', the *Panzerarmee* anthem, appropriated by the SAS and set to their own lyrics, penned by Mayne.

> *There is a song we always used to hear,*
> *Out in the desert, romantic soft and clear.*
> *Over the ether came the strain, that lilting refrain,*
> *Each night again, of poor Lili Marlene, of poor Lili Marlene.*
>
> (Chorus)
> *Then back to Cairo we would steer,*
> *And drink our beer, with ne'er a tear,*
> *And poor Marlene's boyfriend will never see Marlene.*
>
> *Check your ammunition, see your guns are right,*
> *Wait until a convoy comes creeping through the night.*
> *Then you can have some fun, my son,*
> *And know the war is almost won,*
> *And poor Marlene's boyfriend will never see Marlene.*
>
> *Drive on to an airfield, thirty planes ahead,*
> *Belching ammunition and filling them with lead.*
> *A flamer for you, a grave for Fritz,*
> *Just like his planes, he's shot to bits,*
> *And poor Marlene's boyfriend will never see Marlene.*
>
> *Afrika Korps has sunk into the dust,*
> *Gone are his Stukas, his tanks have turned to rust.*
> *No more we'll hear the soft refrain,*
> *That lilting strain, it's night again,*
> *And poor Marlene's boyfriend will never see Marlene.*

Wand-Tetley would also recall the sense of pleasure upon returning from operations when a few days' leave would often be granted. After the stress of having been in the desert, days off and leave in Cairo were halcyon days indeed. By jeep the journey from Kabrit to Cairo took three hours, and Alexandria was a further three hours on from Cairo. Hot baths, cold beers, soft beds in which to sleep and clean clothes, after weeks living rough and sleeping on the sand out in the 'blue', were exquisite pleasures. By day one could eat lunch at Groppi's Restaurant near the Midan Suleiman Pasha, relax at the Turf Club or swim at the Gezira Sporting Club on its green island in the Nile. And just beyond the club's large pool were the polo grounds and racecourse. In the evening officers would frequent Shepheard's and enjoy cocktails served by Joe at the mahogany Long Bar. Indeed, such was the hotel's popularity with the GHQ staff officers that they were somewhat unkindly dubbed the 'Short Range Shepheard's Group' by Wand-Tetley and those who had just come in from the desert. The colonial-style Mena House Hotel with its view of the pyramids and its pool set in a garden of palm trees was another popular watering hole, as was the Continental-Savoy with its Roof Garden restaurant, where the infamous Hehmet Fahmy set pulses racing with her sinuous gyrating until she was caught out and arrested as a German spy. However, the queen of the Raa'sa, or belly-dance, was Carioca, at the Dugout Club, who would bewitch all with her amber eyes and lustrous ebony black hair as she shivered her hips in a spectacle that none who ever witnessed her would easily forget.

By night Allied and Commonwealth soldiers would pack the bars. There was no shortage of entertainment, nor of female company in the nightclubs with their belly-dancing cabarets. A dozen open-air cinemas would show the latest films and El Berka, the Cairene red light district, did a roaring trade. Decent dinners could be had in the restaurants for there was no scarcity of food in the shops. Beer was cheap at two piastres for the local brew, Stella. However, Arrack would leave a man with a wicked hangover. Prices increased as the war progressed, but there was little else for the troops to spend their money on. Of course, if a soldier were not too careful, the clap and 'Gyppy Tummy' were ever present occupational hazards of a night on the town.

Alexandria was also a popular city in which to unwind, possessing its own character from having been founded by a Greek; Wand-Tetley perceived it to have a noticeably more Western outlook than the Muslim city of Cairo. The wealthy businessmen of the 'Quartier Grec' still ran wartime Alexandria and greatly contributed to the lifestyle and ambience of the city. In the summer months the city was noticeably cooler than Cairo, which by comparison tended to be hot and stuffy, lacking the coastal sea breeze. Alexandria also had its own Sporting Club and pool, and the Cecil Hotel on the Corniche was a favourite haunt. Of course, the city also had the sea as a prime attraction and soldiers could swim off the beaches, such as the ever popular one at Sidi Bishr.

Inevitably off-duty fights would start and the Military Police would have their work cut out. Paddy Mayne, in particular, developed a certain notoriety, and stories endure of his drinking and fighting sprees on the town and of how many military police – anything up to six – it would take to subdue and restrain him. On one occasion a telephone call was required to spring him from his cell, it being fortunately recognized that he was more useful in the field with the SAS taking the fight to the enemy than languishing in military detention. Nor was Wand-Tetley immune from the attention of the 'red caps', for, in the latter half of February 1943, on a night off duty he was picked up in the Albergo Hotel, Garian in Tripolitania, some seventy-five miles south of Tripoli, and with due formality charged with conduct to the prejudice of good order and military discipline for all too evidently having had a few too many beers with fellow soldiers from C Squadron. In the event he was remanded for the Area Commander, somewhat ironically, by Mayne himself. However, the charge was quietly dropped when due process was seen to have been embarked upon and the Provost Marshal's attention had focused elsewhere. After all, there was a war to fight and Mayne no doubt felt uncomfortable in the role of poacher turned gamekeeper.[14]

While Wand-Tetley and C Squadron were deployed in the Western Desert, new recruits for the squadron, having arrived at Kabrit, would first undertake their Parachute Course. At this stage the course was a week long, with five jumps required to qualify the parachutist for his wings. Four of these jumps were conducted by day from a Lockheed Hudson and the final one was a night jump from a Wellington. Subsequently, but prior to deployment on operations, they would be taken out, under command of Lieutenant Peter Davis of the Queen's Royal Regiment, to undertake training schemes in the Sinai Desert.[15]

Stirling's quest for more men was therefore going well, and his recruiting and training team at Kabrit was doing excellent work. The regiment's ranks were swollen further on 1 January 1943, when Alexander allowed 121 officers and men of the Greek Sacred Squadron, the 'Hieros Lochos', to join 1 SAS. Founded by Christodoulos Tsigantes in the final week of September 1942, the Greek Sacred Squadron consisted of selected men from the Royal Hellenic Army who had made good their escape from occupied Greece. Heiros Lochos had been raised only twice before, and then only when the very heart of Greece itself was seriously threatened. The first occasion was in 370 BC when, in the defence of Thebes against the Spartans, every man died fighting; the second in similarly desperate circumstances in 1821 fighting the Turks. At the time of the German invasion of Greece Tsigantes had been in Rumania, from where he made his way to Ethiopia and then to Egypt. Fiercely patriotic and courageous, Tsigantes quickly become a potent focus for free Greeks and was an inspirational and gifted leader. The Greek Sacred Squadron based their fighting ethos on that of the ancient Thebans and the farewell of the wives to their warrior husbands, 'Return carrying your shield, or upon it'.

86

The Greek Sacred Squadron would significantly bolster the ranks of D Squadron, which formed up the day after C Squadron left Kabrit for the desert. Based around the core of the fifteen officers and forty other ranks of the SBS and volunteers from Ninth Army who had been stationed in Palestine and Transjordan, command of the squadron initially fell to Tommy Langton, Irish Guards, one of the few survivors of the Tobruk raid. However, George Earl Jellicoe assumed command soon afterwards upon returning from a period of convalescence in England following a knee operation. Part of the squadron under Sutherland, now a captain, went to Beirut on 20 January to conduct training, including boat familiarization with Greek caiques – local trading and fishing schooners often fitted with diesel engines. A further element of the squadron remained behind at Kabrit and would head out into the desert down the coast road with Jellicoe and Tsigantes on 25 January.

Meanwhile Fitzroy Maclean had been despatched to Iran to raise a detachment – M Detachment – of SAS parachutists there; an endeavour that would lead on to his next assignment, Operation PONGO, the abduction of General Zahedi, an Iranian officer suspected of conspiring with the Germans.

Having therefore, by early January 1943, recruited in excess of his regimental establishment, Stirling now began to give serious thought to how he might raise the SAS to brigade strength. Second SAS Regiment, under command of his brother Bill, was now in north-west Africa with First Army. It would not take much for the Free French, now at squadron size, to raise itself to full regimental strength in its own right, and with recruiting going as well as it was, the remainder of 1 SAS could be divided down the middle and built up to two regiments. This would provide a brigade force of four regiments able to support any operations after the Desert War, whether in the Eastern and Central Mediterranean, Italy, or a second European front.

Stirling was confident he could win over Churchill to this vision, and that he would have the support of Montgomery and the C-in-C. However, he realized that he also needed first to convince the Commander of the First Army, Lieutenant General Kenneth Anderson. He reasoned that if 1 SAS could provide the vital link up between the Eighth and First Armies this would favourably dispose Anderson towards the unit and any future plans for SAS expansion, as well as providing him with the opportunity to discuss his future plans with his brother, Bill. Therefore Stirling set about putting all this in motion.

It was anticipated by 'Jumbo' Wilson, GOC Ninth Army, that when the Desert War was over the SAS might be needed in Iran or Turkey or for operations in the Caucasian passes. For this reason Stirling decided to despatch A Squadron on a period of mountain warfare training in Lebanon. Accordingly, the squadron started to leave its desert camp on 4 January 1943, with Mayne arriving back at Kabrit three days later and the various patrols following him in over the next few days. A Squadron's return thus broadly coincided with Wand-Tetley's and C Squadron's deployment to the desert on 5 January. Alexander visited Kabrit on 14 January and was able to congratulate A Squadron on their recent operations. In turn he was entertained by the men of the squadron to an SAS firepower demonstration, which included the jeep-mounted machine guns and Lewes bombs. Before the squadron of some eighty all ranks, including several officers, departed on 24 January for ski training at the Middle East Ski School, located at the ancient Cedars of Lebanon, they were granted a short period of leave.

Thus by January 1943 the SAS had developed significantly since their inception some eighteen months previously and, at this stage, it is worth briefly casting back to their origins before returning to consider Stirling's capture, the last days of the Desert War, and Wand-Tetley's transfer from the SAS. The idea for the force had been drafted out in pencil in June and July of 1941 by Stirling, at the time a young Scots Guards' subaltern of No. 8 Commando, as he lay convalescing in the 15th Scottish Military Hospital following a parachuting accident.

Until this Stirling had led a remarkably undistinguished military career. He had relied largely on family connections and his natural charm to secure his place in the Scots Guards and thereafter in No. 8 Commando. Prior to Army service he had been sent down from Cambridge University for gambling. He then travelled to Paris with the intention of becoming an artist, but was informed by his tutor that he did not have the natural talent, so instead set his sights on being the first man to scale Everest but, with an expedition planned, war broke out. In Layforce he had gained a certain reputation for being somewhat less than conscientious and generally loafing about, for which he gained the nickname 'the great sloth'. All this was about to change though, for like his uncle, who had founded the Lovat Scouts during the Boer War, Stirling would achieve similar laurels.

With the Layforce Commandos facing disbandment, Stirling considered how best to develop the special raiding group role within the Middle East. He believed that smaller groups would prove more viable, and that for their insertion the parachute was the answer, with their subsequent extraction by the LRDG. He was able to discuss his thoughts with a number of visitors, including Orde Wingate who, at the time was coincidentally pressing GHQ Middle East to increase guerrilla activity behind enemy lines, and John 'Jock' Lewes, Welsh Guards, a brother subaltern from No. 8 Commando. He distilled his ideas into a memorandum, which he addressed to the C-in-C Middle East. The clear merit of the proposals, Churchill's preoccupation with the cause of the Commandos, and Auchinleck's interest in establishing parachute forces ensured that he was favourably disposed to giving Stirling, a subaltern of only twenty-five, a decent hearing. Stirling's timing was therefore extremely fortuitous.

The original memorandum was for a long time thought to have been lost, presumed to have been burnt in 1942 during 'The Flap', as it became known, when Rommel was knocking on the gates of Cairo, and GHQ Middle East set about burning all its classified papers. However, the memorandum has since come to light in the National Archives. In it Stirling outlines how he perceived his raiding force contributing to Auckinleck's November 1941 offensive, Operation CRUSADER. He proposed that, as a precursor to the main offensive, a number of small raiding parties composed of five-man sub-units should be dropped by parachute behind enemy lines to destroy aircraft parked on airfields. Extraction of the parties would then be by LRDG patrols from pre-arranged rendezvous in the desert.

Auchinleck was sold on the idea and, in the presence of Ritchie and Dudley Clarke (now a brigadier), Stirling was granted permission to recruit suitable men from Layforce to raise a parachute force of seven officers, including himself, and sixty other ranks to take part in CRUSADER. Additionally, allowance was made for a small administrative and support element. Clarke, in charge of A Force, a psychological operations and deception department, had created a fictitious SAS Brigade to confuse the enemy, and the formation of a real parachute detachment would certainly aid him in his endeavours to persuade the enemy that a brigade-sized parachute force existed in the Middle East. Accordingly, the new force was called L Detachment SAS Brigade, and Stirling was promoted to captain and placed in command of this new unit, which was formed officially on 28 August 1941.[16]

With just three months to go before CRUSADER, Stirling's first imperative was to recruit and train his new SAS unit, which he initially organized into two troops. No. 1 Troop was to be commanded by Lewes and No. 2 by Lieutenant Blair 'Paddy' Mayne, Royal Ulster Rifles, who, prior to transfer, had been commissioned in the Royal Artillery. Lewes, of course, was very well known by Stirling, who travelled to Tobruk, where Lewes was conducting raids against the enemy lines, to recruit him. Before the war Lewes had studied Modern Greats – philosophy, politics and economics – at Christ Church, Oxford, and had been President of the University Boat Club. As such, he was instrumental in the dramatic 1937 victory, halting a succession of thirteen Cambridge wins. By nature he was a determined, studious officer, and it was his capacity for original thought and ideas that Stirling particularly valued.

Mayne, of No. 11 Commando, was commended to Stirling by Laycock on account of his performance at the Litani river action in Syria, where he had been Mentioned in Despatches. A law graduate of Queen's

University, Belfast, Mayne had also been a pre-war sportsman of note. His extremely powerful physique, speed and courage suited him to boxing and in 1936 he won the Heavyweight Championship of the Irish Universities. He also enjoyed swimming and was a useful golfer, with a handicap of eight. However, Rugby Union was his great passion, and from 1937 until the outbreak of war he played as lock-forward at international level for Ireland, winning six caps, as well as for the British Lions in their successful 1938 tour of South Africa. An inspirational leader and an outstanding fighting soldier, Mayne would become a SAS legend, earning the DSO four times in as many theatres, the Croix de Guerre, and Légion d'Honneur, and would eventually become Commanding Officer of 1 SAS.

The initial officers selected by Stirling as Section Commanders included Lieutenant Eoin McGonigal, Royal Ulster Rifles, and Second Lieutenant Bill Fraser, Gordon Highlanders, both of whom were placed under Lewes. Lieutenant Charles Bonnington of the General List, (the future father of the mountaineer, Chris), and Major F. C. Thompson, whose role would be as an observer on the CRUSADER operation, were placed under Mayne. Captain Peter Warr of the East Surreys was selected as the unit parachute instructor. Having selected his officers, not surprisingly Stirling looked to the Commandos to recruit his first sixty or so SAS 'Originals'.[17]

It was about this time that the now world-famous cap-badge was first worn – the 'flaming sword Excalibur', often mistakenly thought to be a winged dagger, designed by Sergeant Bob Tait, with the motto at its base, 'Who Dares Wins', credited to Stirling, and 'inspired' by the motto, *Memento Audere Semper* (Remember Always to Dare) of the Decima Flottiglia MAS. The original white beret was quickly dispensed with, having proved itself to be an object of mirth to New Zealand and Australian soldiers and thus the cause of too many off-duty fights in downtown Cairo. It was replaced with a khaki forage cap and soon thereafter by the distinctive sand-coloured beret, which has since stood the test of time.

The design of the distinctive SAS parachute wings is attributed to Lewes, whose inspiration came from the fresco of an ancient Egyptian motif that he had noticed in the foyer of Shepheard's Hotel, Cairo. He substituted the body of the Scarab Beetle – often mistaken as the body of a Sacred Ibis – with a white parachute, and the dark and light blue within the wings reflect the colours of Oxford and Cambridge Universities, the Almae Matres of Lewes and Stirling respectively. In those early days the wings were worn on the chest like a medal rather than on the arm if the owner had conducted three operational raids behind enemy lines.

As touched upon in the previous chapter, participation in Operation SQUATTER in November 1941, the planned attack against enemy airfields in the Gazala and Tmimi region west of Tobruk, as a precursor to CRUSADER, proved to be a costly failure for the SAS. The five RAF Bristol Bombay aircraft carrying the raiders were blown off course by a savage electric storm, and many of the parachutists were scattered across the desert and injured seriously on landing, lost, or later captured. They had been unlucky enough to have experienced the worst storm to hit the North African coast in thirty years. Only twenty-one men of the fifty-four parachutists who set off that night came back, many of them badly injured as a result of the 40-mile-an-hour winds that were blowing across the desert's inhospitable and rocky surface.[18]

To some, the SAS concept may have appeared to have come unravelled on the very first operation. A lesser man might have been disheartened, but Stirling put a brave face on things. On the way back through the desert with the LRDG, Lloyd Owen put it to Stirling that, rather than using parachutes, which had proved conclusively to be a highly risky method of insertion, the SAS might instead use LRDG patrols for the insertion phase, as well as the extraction phase, of any future operation. This gave Stirling cause for some serious consideration. This was the genesis of an extremely successful partnership, with the SAS nicknaming the LRDG the 'Desert Taxi Service' and, until they had got to know them better, the LRDG referring to the SAS as the 'Parashites'.[19]

Stirling felt that his new unit had a great deal to prove, and decided that only a series of successful airfield raids along the Gulf of Sirte would serve to cement a firm enough reputation for the SAS. Accordingly, he planned raids on enemy airfields for the latter part of December 1941, all of which were extremely successful. Following the less than auspicious start a month earlier, the SAS had turned their fortunes around, completely vindicating Stirling's concept, with some sixty aircraft destroyed by a modest handful of twenty-five SAS soldiers. Further successful raids followed and in early January 1942 Stirling learnt that Mayne and he were to be awarded DSOs for their part in the raids. Furthermore, he was to be promoted to major, and Mayne to captain. There were some who quipped that they should have been awarded DFCs, for they had destroyed more enemy aircraft than any RAF fighter pilot. Auchinleck gave Stirling the go-ahead to recruit a further six officers and forty men, thus raising the fighting strength of the detachment to squadron size.

Having overcome certain diplomatic concerns, Stirling's depleted force was significantly bolstered by a group of some fifty Free French troops, under Commandant Georges Bergé, who had already received their parachute training at Ringway, in Cheshire. This group would become an integral part of the SAS, wearing British uniform and insignia. By July 1942 L Detachment SAS had increased to about a 100-strong squadron-sized force. They also now had a doctor with them, Captain Malcolm Pleydell, whose book *Born of the Desert* paints a wonderfully evocative picture of those early SAS days. Further SAS raids followed and by August 1942 Stirling's exploits had made enough of an impression on Rommel's soldiers that they had given him the nickname 'the Phantom Major' and by then, prior to expansion to regimental size, the SAS had destroyed some 150 aircraft on the ground.

Stirling's Capture and the Last Days of the Desert War

As related earlier, it was at the end of September 1942, following the Benghazi Raid, that the order to expand the SAS to regimental strength was issued, and when Wand-Tetley and others from 1 SSR, which was scheduled for disbandment at the end of October, transferred to the SAS fold.

By the end of 1942 it was clear that the days of the Desert War were numbered. In January 1943 Churchill and Roosevelt met at Casablanca in a conference, codenamed *Symbol*, which confirmed that the Allies would next deal with the Germans in Europe before turning their attention to the Japanese in the Pacific, and that Sicily would be the next Mediterranean Allied objective. Nonetheless the Desert War was not entirely over and the SAS still had a significant part to play. Montgomery's push in mid-December had proved successful, as was Eighth Army's January attack on Tripoli, from where it was planned to advance into Tunisia. Montgomery had let it be known that he wanted SAS assistance, particularly west of Tripoli where the main attack was due to be made, but also to provide intelligence on the Mareth Line, a fortified defensive link between Tripoli and Gabes built by the colonial French before the war as a precaution to keep the Italians out of Tunisia.

With A Squadron under Mayne preparing for its departure to the Middle East Ski School, and with C Squadron's men, including Wand-Tetley, under Lea, already committed to operations in the desert for the foreseeable future, Stirling set about putting in place a plan with HQ Eighth Army that satisfied these criteria. He formed a composite force of four components.

The first group, under Lieutenant Harry Poat, King's Own Scottish Borderers, a pre-war tomato farmer from Guernsey, would disrupt communications from Tripoli westwards as far as Mareth. A second group would reconnoitre the Mareth Line to see if the Germans were making use of the fortified anti-tank ditches and bunkers and, if so, whether it would be possible to outflank them to the south. A third, Free French, group under Jourdan would conduct raids on the coast road and railway from Gabes north to Sfax. The fourth group under Stirling would spy out the land in northern Tunisia, and aim to be the first Eighth Army troops to link up with the First Army.

Stirling's party of eight jeeps and twenty men included Lieutenant Bill McDermott, Mike Sadler and Johnny Cooper. Liaising with HQ Eighth Army at Buerat, and having commissioned both Sadler and Cooper in the field, Stirling headed for the Bir Guediffia rendezvous, where the rump of B Squadron, including Thesiger, Alston and Martin had remained since December. Travelling separately, and leaving Egypt at the beginning of January, the French group, in a dozen vehicles consisting of four patrols, commanded by Jourdan and Lieutenants Legrand, Harent, and Klein, reached the rendezvous with the other two groups on the 12th. At Bir Guediffia Poat's patrol left almost immediately for Tripoli. In line with Montgomery's request, the men set about mining the road and attacking enemy convoys to cause as much of a distraction as possible while the main Eighth Army attack went in.

Meanwhile other patrols from B Squadron complemented their activities. Captain R. E. Galloway's patrol of four officers and two other ranks operated in the region of Pisida, between Zouara and Ben Gardane. The target area was divided in two, Galloway and his vehicle gunner, Captain H. G. Chevalier, attacking vehicle convoys in the eastern sector, and Captain John O'Sullivan in the western sector. A larger patrol under Captain D. L. M. Murphy, of the Central Indian Horse, with eleven other ranks, operated similarly in the region of Nalut.[20]

Stirling and Jourdan's patrol left Bir Guediffia on 14 January and headed for Bir Soltane, near Kasr Ghilan Oasis, which was only some thirty miles from the Mareth Line (not to be confused with Bir Zalten, where A and B Squadrons had rendezvoused the previous November). Initially the patrols headed west towards Ghadames and from there turned north, through very slow-going country, past the eastern reaches of the Grand Ergh Sand Sea, and reached their destination several days later. It was at Bir Soltane, on 23 January, that Stirling heard by radio that Eighth Army, led by an advance guard of men from Wand-Tetley's C Squadron, and 11th Hussars, had entered Tripoli. There was now no time to waste, and if they were to achieve their mission the SAS would have to run the gauntlet of the narrow Gabes Gap, which was known to be thick with German and Italian troops, rather than going around it as initially planned.

Jourdan and his Free French group set off that same day for the Gap, no more than five miles wide at the narrowest point, created by the Mediterranean Sea on the east and the Lake Djerid salt marshes to the west. Compelled to change his plan, Stirling now intended to follow Jourdan's patrol through the Gap some twelve hours later, rather than passing south around the salt marshes. The intention now was to raid the harbour at Sousse before heading for Tunis. Alston and Thesiger were meanwhile to remain with a radio truck and use Bir Soltane as a base from which to reconnoitre the Mareth Line.

The Germans were by this stage providing strong escorts for their convoys, and had deployed a *Feldgendarmerie* special unit to Africa from Italy to hunt the SAS and LRDG. Despite the enemy numbers Jourdan's patrol, which now included Martin providing the rearguard, succeeded in making it through the Gap but not without incident, for at midnight they were caught in the headlights of an enemy convoy. The first six jeeps and the radio vehicle got past, but the seventh was machine-gunned by an armoured car travelling at the back of the enemy convoy. Martin's two rearguard vehicles drove off the road to escape and, although now separated from the main group, the patrol, soon down to one jeep, continued with its mission.

On the night of 24/25 January Martin and his team of four Frenchmen successfully mined the railway, machine-gunned several lorries, and attacked isolated Italian camps. However, while the team was resting during the following day, the enemy, guided by Arabs, closed in upon their position. Hearing the Germans approach the four Frenchmen were able to escape on foot. Marching for the best part of three days across the desert, on emergency rations of two litres of water each, chocolate and some dates, the team escaped through enemy lines to First Army lines at Zanouch railway station in the early hours of the 28th. Initially, they were thrown in prison, until at dawn they managed to persuade the American sentries of their true credentials.[21]

Following their initial encounter with the enemy, Jourdan's group of vehicles had driven on but soon saw the headlights of a smaller convoy of three enemy vehicles approaching them. Deciding to take no chances, they opened up first on the enemy vehicles with their machine guns. In the ensuing firefight they lost two vehicles, including a British-manned radio truck. Now with just four jeeps, they continued north. By dawn on the 24th they were through the Gap and had reached the Gabes-Sfax road and decided to lie up for the day. That evening they mined the road leading to Gafsa, and also carried out similar attacks the following night. However, on the way back to their patrol base in the El Hama hills on the 25th they encountered the enemy again and were forced to separate to make good their escape. On the 28th Jourdan, now separated from the rest of his men, was forced to surrender when he found himself cornered in a wadi by an entire Italian company. The remnants of the French patrol, with Legrand now in command, made it back on the 29th.

Close on the heels of Jourdan, and with the enemy now alert to SAS activities, Stirling's party of five jeeps and fourteen men, which included McDermott, also managed to make it through the Gap despite having been spotted by an enemy reconnaissance plane on the evening of the 23rd. However, at dawn on the morning of the 24th they came across a German armoured column parked on either side of the road having breakfast. Deciding to brazen it out, they accelerated and passed through the parked convoy receiving only quizzical looks while staring back with poker faces. Having travelled several miles farther down the road, which was now becoming busier with Axis traffic, they decided to lie up for the day some distance from the road, in a wadi in the foothills of Jebel Tebaga.

However, Stirling's legendary luck was about to run out finally. For that day the *Feldgendarmerie* special unit happened to be out on a training exercise and, by sheer chance, came across Stirling's party in the wadi resting from the exertions of the previous forty-eight hours. Sadler, Cooper and an Arabic-speaking Frenchman, Sergeant Freddie Taxis, managed to escape, but Stirling, McDermott and the other ten men were cornered and captured. Although Stirling and McDermott managed to escape from the Germans two nights later, Stirling was recaptured the following day having been betrayed by an Arab who had offered to lead him to water, but had instead led him straight to some Italian soldiers. He was taken under heavy guard to enemy head-quarters at Menzel and after a number of escape attempts from Italian prisoner-of-war camps he would end up being transferred to Colditz.[22]

Sadler, Cooper and Taxis, meanwhile, marched across the desert, heading west towards Free French-held Tozeur, which they reached on the 27th. From here they were collected by troops of the First Army, who transported them the 120 miles north to their headquarters at Tebessa. Thus Sadler's SAS team, followed a day later by Martin's Free French SAS, were the first Eighth Army troops to link up with First Army.

Wand-Tetley and the men of C Squadron were still out in the desert when official news of Stirling's capture was announced, some three weeks after the event, on 14 February. The following day command of the regiment fell initially to Vivian Street, now back in Kabrit after his escape from an Italian submarine following a short spell of captivity. However, in early March, command devolved upon Lieutenant Colonel Henry 'Kid' Cator, the former CO of No. 51 ME Commando. With news of Stirling's capture, and the Desert War now very much on the wane, GHQ Middle East considered what the future of 1 SAS should be in the coming European campaign. Stirling undoubtedly had had clear ideas of how the regiment might be used, but had never discussed these thoughts in any great detail with anyone. It transpired that it would be largely Mayne, who returned from Lebanon on 4 March, and Jellicoe who would ensure that 1 SAS would have a future fighting role in Europe.

On 8 March GHQ Middle East published a consultative document on the future of 1 SAS, upon which both Mayne and Jellicoe duly commented and made suggestions. A decision was reached quickly and by 19 March, by which stage the balance of C Squadron including Wand-Tetley had returned from the desert, it had been resolved that 1 SAS would be split into two large squadron-sized units, each of about 250 men. The first, commanded by Mayne, would be the Special Raiding Squadron (SRS). The second, under Jellicoe, would be the Special Boat Squadron, which would form around the core of the Special Boat Section component of D Squadron.

Both squadrons would come under a new HQ Raiding Forces, commanded by 'Kid' Cator. However his role was largely supervisory, and command and training of the two squadrons would remain very much in the hands of their respective commanders, Mayne and Jellicoe. The SRS would have three troops: 1, 2, and 3, commanded by Captains Fraser, Poat and Barnby, and its Advance Party would depart on 21 March for its new base at Azzib in Palestine. The SBS would have three detachments: L, M and S, named after their original commanders, Captains Langton, Maclean, and Sutherland, and depart for its new base at Athlit, just south of Haifa on the Palestine coast. Both squadrons would retain the sand-coloured beret and SAS insignia, and would officially be established on 1 April 1943. The Free French Squadron and the Greek Sacred Squadron of the SAS would both return to their respective armies. The SRS would, in January 1944, expand again to regimental strength and be redesignated 1 SAS. The SBS would remain independent and, operating from the Royal Navy's Levant Schooner Flotilla of converted caiques, it and the Greek Sacred Squadron would raid enemy-occupied islands and coastline around the Mediterranean, Aegean and Adriatic Seas, and in time would be renamed the Special Boat Service.

While the future of 1 SAS was being decided, Wand-Tetley did some serious thinking about his own future. He had been with the regiment for no more than six months, but already it was about to undergo fairly radical reorganization, and its future was far from clear. This echoed his general experience to date with special forces units which, besides often being misused, appeared to be subjected to a continual process of reorganization, disbandment or merger. It seemed that no sooner had he established himself within a particular unit than uncertainty over the organization's future would rear its ugly head. He was clear that he wanted to stay in special forces work, which he found challenging and fulfilling, but where would the newly proposed SRS and SBS lead, and how long before the next upheaval? First SAS Regiment had been halved in strength; would these new units survive, or wither on the vine? The answers were at this stage far from clear.

Wand-Tetley perceived that, as far as such units in the Middle East were concerned, the SOE had managed to endure and weather the storms remarkably well over the last few years. Having served in Syria while with 1 SSR, and having therefore been trained in SOE stay-behind guerrilla work, he was already familiar with its modus operandi. This seemed to be the solution; he would volunteer to serve with the SOE.

Technically, the end of the Desert War had been marked on 23 January with the surrender of the Vice Governor of Libya to Montgomery when Eighth Army's advance guard entered Tripoli. However, the enemy in North Africa was not yet beaten, although it now seemed only a matter of time. Montgomery continued with his advance from Tripoli and pursued Rommel from the east, while Anglo-American forces, under General Sir Harold Alexander, Commander 18 Army Group, moved in from the west.

Notwithstanding the continuing uncertainty and GHQ Middle East deliberations over the future of the SAS, the unit's assistance was still required in the desert, for following the fall of Tripoli the Eighth Army had come to the heavily defended Mareth Line. Montgomery intended to engage the enemy in a frontal attack, but he had alternative plans, if this should prove unsuccessful, to mount an outflanking manoeuvre which would involve sending the New Zealand Division westwards around the southern flank.

In the interim Montgomery wanted the SAS to conduct raiding operations behind the Mareth Line. With C Squadron including Wand-Tetley already otherwise employed on the flank of Eighth Army, a composite jeep-mounted SAS force under Fraser including elements of the Greek Sacred Squadron, Free French and British, left Tripoli for the Mareth Line. At this stage the Greek Sacred Squadron had Thesiger as their liaison officer. Arriving on 17 February, the SAS immediately set about creating what havoc they could. Having joined a Free French force that had made its way across the Sahara from French Equatorial Africa, on 10 March the SAS found themselves in a significant battle at Qasr Ghiliana, when their force was attacked by a strong enemy infantry battalion with artillery and air support. Fortuitously an RAF Spitfire squadron arrived at a pivotal moment in the engagement and was able to drive off the Luftwaffe and assist the SAS in beating back the attack. Nonetheless, by dismounting their Vickers guns from their jeeps and firing them from the ground, the Free French managed to account for four of the enemy aircraft. When the German infantry retired that evening, the Allies found that they had destroyed some fifty enemy vehicles.

Montgomery's frontal assault upon the Mareth Line on 20 March failed, but his subsequent outflanking manoeuvre succeeded in turning the enemy's flank and forced them to retire to their next defensive line at Wadi Akarit. On 9 March Rommel had been forced, through sickness, to leave Africa and hand over his command to von Arnim. At the subsequent battle of Akarit on 6 April, the Greek Sacred Squadron was deployed with Freyberg's New Zealand Division as it pushed its way through the Gabes Gap. On 22 April, SAS elements acted as an advance guard to the Allied offensive across the Tunisian plains to Enfidaville. At this stage the SAS contingent was recalled to Kabrit (shortly after the official formation of the SRS and SBS), although Fraser had actually returned to Kabrit earlier in March to take over 1 Troop of the SRS.

Subsequently the Allies would take Tunis and Bizerta on 7 May, trapping the remaining Axis forces in the Cape Bon peninsula. The enemy would capitulate on 13 May, with the Italian Field Marshal Giovanni Messe, Commander of Axis Forces in North Africa, formally surrendering to the Allies to mark the end of the Tunisian Campaign. Some 240,000 of the enemy would surrender to the Allies, a costly defeat and one as disastrous as Stalingrad to the Germans. It would therefore take almost exactly three years, but the Allies finally prevailed in North Africa, thus positioning themselves for the invasion of Europe.

In the later stages of the Desert War, between September 1942 and January 1943, the SAS conducted about forty-three successful raids behind enemy lines, and since their creation in 1941 they were credited with the destruction of 320 enemy aircraft. In a letter to his wife, after the capture of Stirling, Rommel made it clear that the SAS had caused him more damage than any other Allied unit of regimental size.

Notes

1. NA Kew, WO 201/743, Raiding Forces (GHQ Op Instruction No. 145, dated 28 Sep 42), Sep–Oct 1942.
2. Ibid.
3. NA Kew, WO 218/149, 1st Special Service Regiment War Diary, July–Oct 1942.
4. Army Service Record (Army Form B199A), P. M. Wand-Tetley. HS 9/1453/7, P. M. Wand-Tetley, 1939–1946. Wand-Tetley's SOE personnel file suggests that he served for twelve months with the SAS. However, given that he joined the SOE on 1 April 1943, at most he served six months with the SAS.
5. NA Kew, WO 218/96, 1 SAS War Diary (nominal roll of officers) Oct–Dec 1942. WO 218/97, 1 SAS War Diary (nominal roll of officers), Jan–Apr 1943.
6. Cowles, *The Phantom Major*, Appendix.
7. NA Kew, CAB 44/152, Commandos and Special Service Troops in the Middle East and North Africa. Sect. 8.
8. Ibid.
9. Mather, *When the Grass Stops Growing*, Ch. 28.
10. NA Kew, WO 218/97, op cit (Patrol report: Capt G. W. Alston).

11. Thesiger, *A Life of My Choice*, Ch. 26.
12. NA Kew, WO 218/150, 1 SSR A Sqn War Diary, Aug–Oct 1942. WO 218/151, 1 SSR B Sqn War Diary, Jun–Oct 1942. WO 218/96, op cit (nominal roll of officers, Dec 42).
13. NA Kew, WO 218/97, op cit (Patrol report: Capt. G. W. Alston).
14. Army Form B.252, 20/21 Feb 1943.
15. NA Kew, WO 218/97, op cit.
16. NA Kew, CAB 44/152, op cit, Sect. 6.
17. Ibid.
18. Ibid, Sect. 7.
19. Lloyd Owen, *Providence Their Guide*, Ch 6.
20. NA Kew, WO 218/97, op cit (Patrol reports: Capt. R. E. Galloway; Capt. J. C. O'Sullivan; Sgt E. A. Badger).
21. NA Kew, CAB 44/152, op cit, Sect. 8.
22. Cooper, *One of the Originals*, Ch. 5.

Chapter 4

SOE Agent

PART 1

Part 1 to this chapter sets the scene for the part played by Wand-Tetley in Operation TIBBENHAM, described in Part 2, which might otherwise assume too intimate a knowledge on the part of the reader of the Grecian wartime arena.

Set Europe Ablaze!

Wand-Tetley was posted formally to the strength of SOE Cairo on 1 April 1943, the same date that 1 SAS was divided and officially re-established as the SRS and SBS, specifically to MO4's East Mediterranean Group, and was allotted the symbol D/H 518. Later the same month he was despatched on a mission, Operation TIBBENHAM, that would see him parachute into enemy-held territory in the Peloponnese, the southern peninsula of Greece. He had no idea at the time that he would remain behind enemy lines for the next fourteen months.[1]

Wand-Tetley had joined SOE Cairo at a time when the organization was rapidly expanding its operations in the Balkans. At the Casablanca Conference, in January of that year, the decision had been taken to occupy Sicily as a precursor to eliminating Italy from the war. It was anticipated that this might serve to bring Turkey in on the Allied side, which would be essential if operations of a substantial nature in south-east Europe were to succeed. Thus 'Jumbo' Wilson, who in February had taken over as C-in-C Middle East following success in the North African campaign and in Tunisia, was now looking north. Given that the enemy garrisons in Greece and Yugoslavia were largely Italian, part of the strategy agreed upon would be to increase assistance to resistance movements in these two countries. The intention was to break Italy and stretch German forces to breaking point.

The invasion of Sicily, now being planned, called for a diversion to deceive the enemy into where the invasion would actually take place.

Operation MINCEMEAT – as outlined in Ewen Montagu's *The Man Who Never Was* – called for an elaborate scheme that involved planting a corpse, dressed as a British officer, on the Spanish coast with a briefcase containing misleading documents to suggest the target was Sardinia. This ruse worked and the Germans reinforced Sardinia. However, this was not the only major deception plan, and the Germans were also invited, by Operation ANIMALS, to believe that the invasion might be directed at Greece. By this scheme SOE Cairo, and the Balkan resistance activities they fuelled, undoubtedly served to further deceive the Germans. Whether, as suggested by Churchill, two German divisions were diverted to Greece which would otherwise have been sent to Sicily may be moot, but what appears clear is that in the period May to August 1943 the Germans increased their strength across the Balkans from eight to sixteen divisions.[2]

Wand-Tetley's fourteen months in the Peloponnese, from April 1943 to June 1944, thus covered a key period in Greece both militarily and politically. Arriving shortly after the commencement of SOE-inspired military operations, notably the destruction of the Gorgopotamos railway viaduct, he would play his part in deception operations in the run up to the Allied invasion of Sicily in July 1943. Thereafter he would be caught up in events as the country slid towards the chaos of civil war, and rival resistance movements fought it out amongst themselves for ascendancy and political control of the country.

SOE had been conceived at a Foreign Office meeting chaired by the Foreign Secretary, Lord Halifax, on 1 July 1940, in which it was agreed that a single, new and secret organization was required to take on the work of subversion, sabotage and 'black' (or secret, unacknowledgeable) propaganda against the enemy overseas. Churchill asked Neville Chamberlain, in his capacity as Lord President of the Council, to draft a paper setting out the terms of reference for the new body. This paper, which for the first time named the new organization as SOE and is considered as its founding charter, was circulated for comment in mid-July and formally approved by the War Cabinet on 22 July. Chamberlain died later that year but would no doubt have drawn comfort from the fact that, having earlier generated so much acrimony for his policy of appeasement, he was later instrumental in setting up an organization that would contribute significantly towards Hitler's downfall. Dr Hugh (later Lord) Dalton, Minister of Economic Warfare and a leading intellectual in the Labour Party, was charged with ministerial responsibility for SOE, which was formed by combining three existing bodies: Military Intelligence (Research) (MI(R)), Section D (D for destruction) of the Secret Intelligence Service (SIS), and Elektra House (EH), part of the Foreign Office. These bodies had, respectively, been broadly responsible for guerrilla warfare development, non-military means of attack, and black propaganda.[3]

Dalton appointed Sir Frank Nelson as SOE's first executive head, who took CD as his symbol. This symbology followed in similar vein to Colonel (later Major General Sir) Stewart Menzies, head of SIS (more often referred to as MI6), who was referred to as C, after the initial of SIS's founder Sir Mansfield Cumming.[4]

Dalton, as Ministerial head, took SO as his symbol, and he and CD divided the new organization into three branches: Special Operations 1 (SO1) responsible for propaganda, SO2 for active operations, and SO3 for planning. However, SO3 had withered on the vine by the autumn, and the following year SO1 was to become independent of SOE and assume a new title, the Political Warfare Executive (PWE), leaving SO2 as the future basis of SOE. Indeed, SOE's staff organization changed much during the war but developed broadly into two groups, those staff delivering facilities and those commanding operations, training being grouped with operations. On one matter Dalton was entirely clear, Churchill's intent for the SOE was to 'set Europe ablaze'.[5]

When Wand-Tetley joined SOE, Lord Selborne had replaced Dalton as SO and Sir Charles Hambro had succeeded Nelson as CD. Major General Sir Colin Gubbins, with a background in the Auxiliary Units of the British Resistance Organization, had initially been SOE's director of operations and training with the symbol M, but was at the time Hambro's deputy and would subsequently replace him as CD in the autumn of 1943. Initially SOE's very name was secret, and besides using the Ministry of Economic Warfare as a cover it also went by a number of aliases, including the Inter-Services Research Bureau (ISRB). The War Office referred to it as Military Operations 1 (Special Projects) (MO1 (SP)); the Admiralty as Naval Intelligence Department (Q) (NID(Q)), and the Air Ministry as Air Intelligence (10) (AI(10)). In October SOE moved from its initial site in Caxton Street to larger premises at 64 Baker Street, where it remained until it was wound up and its functions absorbed by the SIS soon after the end of the war. It therefore also came to be referred to as 'Baker Street'.[6]

Thus a further British secret service was set up, one which was quite separate from and independent of MI6, responsible for overseas intelligence, and the Security Service (otherwise known as MI5, which was responsible for home security), and which were, respectively, under control of the Foreign Office and Home Office. Nonetheless, all major SOE plans were required to be cleared with the Foreign Office, and the Chiefs of Staff – comprising the Chief of the Imperial General Staff, the First Sea Lord and the Chief of the Air Staff – were also to be informed so as to ensure that strategic objectives, whether pursued by regular or irregular means, were broadly in step. These three services and MI9, the escape service, were required often to work closely together and were therefore interdependent to a greater or lesser degree. Of course, the work of MI9 was not just about assisting prisoners of war to escape, important though this was; the military intelligence gleaned from debriefing such POWs was key.

Besides these four, there were five other wartime secret services. The London Controlling Section (LCS), otherwise known as the deception service, orchestrated strategic deception such as Operations MINCE-MEAT, ANIMALS and FORTITUDE, the latter to take one example persuading the Germans that the Normandy landings were only a feint and that the main force would land south of Boulogne. The work of the Government Code and Cipher School (GC&CS) at Bletchley Park in breaking the German Enigma code messages, the intelligence product of which was named 'Ultra' (after 'ultra-secret'), is now famous, but its deciphering of the *Geheimschreiber* messages is no less impressive. The Radio Security Service (RSS) was charged with responsibility for locating where unlicensed wireless transmissions emanated, both at home and overseas, such knowledge being critical in respect of both friendly and enemy transmissions. The PWE, an offshoot of SOE, has been covered earlier. Finally, there existed the Auxiliary Units of the British Resistance Organization, with a role as saboteurs within Britain should Germany invade.

Needless to say there existed a good deal of professional competition, not all of it healthy, particularly between SOE and MI6 but also between SOE and the Foreign Office. That said, relationships between the individual field agents of SOE and the Inter-Services Liaison Department (ISLD – a cover name for MI6 abroad) and those of MI9, were generally better than those between their respective headquarters staff.[7]

In London separate SOE sections were set up, each of which was responsible for looking after a country or region, with, if required for reasons of complexity, a number of sections each supporting a single region. In London there was a single section to oversee the work of its regional headquarters in Cairo, and this was headed by Colonel Jimmy Pearson at Baker Street for most of the war. Under him were Peter Boughey on the western Balkan desk and Major Eddie Boxshall on the eastern Balkan desk.

However, the situation at SOE's regional headquarters at GHQ Middle East, Cairo, which dealt with policy in parts of North Africa (including Egypt, Libya, Tunisia, Anglo-Egyptian Sudan and Italian East Africa), parts of the Near and Middle East (Turkey, Palestine, Syria, Transjordan, Iraq, Persia and Arabia), the Mediterranean (Crete and Cyprus), and parts of Europe (the Balkans and Hungary) was by no means as clear cut. Indeed SOE Cairo, which had a number of sub-stations across the Middle East including Istanbul, Baghdad, Tehran,

Beirut and Jerusalem, gained a certain reputation – very well deserved – for inter-service jealousy and animosity. Soon after the start of the war Section D's Cairo office had assumed the title MO4, after the organization that had existed in GHQ Cairo in the First World War and had lent support to T. E. Lawrence (of Arabia) in nurturing the Arab Revolt against the Turks. Meanwhile MI(R) had assumed the title G(R). So intense was the rivalry between MO4 and G(R), the former of which had assumed the SOE mantle, that despite the merger of their parent organizations in London they contrived to remain separate for a further two years until, in the autumn of 1942, they were finally merged by Lord Glenconner during his tenure as head of SOE Cairo. Notwithstanding this, SOE Cairo tenaciously retained a degree of control over propaganda, and only in March 1943 did it grudgingly hand over full responsibility to PWE. The fact that Glenconner was the sixth man to head SOE Cairo in the first two years of the war testifies to the acrimonious nature of the Cairene SOE environment. General Sir Archibald Wavell (previously C-in-C Middle East), subsequently C-in-C India, couched it succinctly to Brigadier Bill Slim, thus, 'SOE think they have taken over G(R), and G(R) think they have taken over SOE, so I suppose everybody is happy'.[8]

When 'Jumbo' Wilson took over as C-in-C Middle East in February 1943 he furthered the cause of service integration with SOE Cairo by including them in his daily conference. Coincidentally his personal secretary, the Countess Hermione Ranfurly, had worked for SOE Cairo as a secretary in the first half of 1941, and at the time had had such serious concerns with regard to the organization's security that she had felt compelled to apprise Anthony Eden of the matter when he was in Cairo visiting the British Embassy. As a result, following an internal appraisal, the department was investigated and action was taken. This would prove to be the first of a number of annual SOE Cairo purges that would take place, invariably in August, over the remaining years of the war.[9]

It should be mentioned though that Major Bickham Sweet-Escott, who had flown from Baker Street to Cairo with Sir Frank Nelson and Mr Terence Maxwell to conduct the 1941 investigation, believed the entire matter had been exaggerated out of all proportion by certain staff officers within GHQ Middle East who were gunning for SOE and had compiled an 'anti-SOE dossier'. Nonetheless, following discussions with Auchinleck, the C-in-C at the time, and with Mr Oliver Lyttleton, the Minister Resident, CD felt compelled to take action to ensure that SOE retained the confidence of the military. Accordingly, the high turn-over of SOE Cairo staff that occurred as a result of the investigation, which included its head Sir George Pollock, a barrister, was perceived by Sweet-Escott as being draconian under the circumstances, but politically necessary. It had initially been planned that Brigadier Taverner, an officer with a good deal of experience in both India and Africa, would assume command of SOE Cairo, but he had been shot down over the Bay of Biscay while flying out from England in the flying boat *Golden Fleece*. Therefore Maxwell, son-in-law of Chamberlain and a successful pre-war businessman and director of Glyn Mills Bank and Vickers, was directed to assume command, with Mr Ian Pirie and Major David Pawson heading the Greek Section. Maxwell set about reorganizing SOE and moved to new premises at Rustum Buildings, a block of flats in Garden City close to the Nile, where SOE headquarters would remain for the remainder of the war. However, his reorganization was relatively superficial, in that the fissure existing between MO4, headed by Colonel Tom Masterson, a distinguished First World War officer, and G(R), headed by Colonel Terence Airey, remained largely unresolved. Maxwell himself would last just twelve months in post until August 1942.[10]

He was succeeded by Lord Glenconner, a director of Hambro's Bank with SOE Balkan section experience, who finally merged MO4 and G(R) and took as his Chief of Staff Brigadier Mervyn 'Bolo' Keble, an enormously energetic and ambitious career officer of the Wiltshires who gained a formidable and fearsome reputation. Under Keble there were two officers who headed the operational side. Group Captain Patrick Domville supervised the Arab world and Persia as Director Special Operations (Arab World) (DSO(Arab World)), while Colonel Guy Tamplin, supervised the Balkans, as DSO(B). Under him, Colonel John Stevens looked after the Greek Section, which had the in-house title of B6 (the Yugoslav Section was B1 and the Albanian Section B8). It was this regime that Wand-Tetley joined in April 1943, although he concerned himself little with office politics, having the single objective, in which he was successful, of ensuring that he was deployed as quickly as possible as a field agent. Later, in November the same year SOE Cairo would undergo a further cover-name change from MO4 to Force 133, following Glenconner's replacement by Major General Billy Stawell, in an effort, no doubt, to keep the enemy as well as friendly forces guessing. However, this would not be the end of it for in Wand-Tetley's time, as we shall see, SOE Cairo would undergo further upheaval and changes to its organization.[11]

Axis Occupation of the Balkans
War in the Balkans had been precipitated by Italy's invasion of Greece in October 1940. Greece, like Yugoslavia and Albania, had been a monarchy up until 1939, and all three countries were destined to come under enemy occupation. Although all three kings were fortunate enough to escape, only those from Greece and Yugoslavia would take an

active part in leading their respective governments in exile. With strong communist elements at work, introduced by the Moscow Comintern, all three countries were also destined to endure civil war.

In March 1939 Mussolini had occupied Albania, a country in which Italy had had a presence for some years. After limited resistance King Zog fled to Greece and, with Albania now in Italian hands, it appeared that Greece would be Mussolini's next target. He launched an invasion of Greece from Albania on 28 October. Mussolini had anticipated an easy victory and had refused Hitler's offer of German troop assistance. However, under the extremely effective leadership of the German-trained General Ioannis Metaxas, who had assumed dictatorial power on 4 August 1936, the Greeks quickly drove the invading Italian forces from their country and pursued them deep into Albania. His finest hour secured for posterity, Metaxas was to die suddenly three months later.

In anticipation of a German invasion of Greece, British and Commonwealth troops had started to land there on 7 March 1941. This Allied W Force, under 'Jumbo' Wilson, would come to consist of a New Zealand division, two Australian divisions and a British armoured brigade. Following a coup on 27 March, Yugoslavia signed a non-aggression pact with the Soviet Union and made friendly overtures to Britain. This infuriated Hitler, who invaded on 6 April. The Yugoslav forces were in no position to resist the German onslaught and the occupation was complete by 27 April.

Hitler next turned his attention to Greece. There was little the Greek or British and Commonwealth forces could do against the German blitzkrieg tactics employed in Operation MARITA. The Greeks were overrun and the Allies were forced to evacuate to Crete and Egypt.

Following the Allied evacuation, Crete then entered a sustained period of resistance against German occupation, much of which was orchestrated and led by the SOE. The exploits of British agents, among them Paddy Leigh-Fermor, Xan Fielding, Billy Moss and Dennis Circlitira became legendary. Perhaps the most notorious was the capture in spring 1944 of Major General Karl Kreipe, commander of the German 22nd Division, by Leigh-Fermor and Moss, and his abduction from the island by submarine. This feat of derring-do was subsequently immortalized in Moss's book *Ill Met by Moonlight*, and in the film of the same name.[12]

In Greece the Germans established a puppet government under Tsolakoglou, the general who had betrayed his country by signing an armistice with the German and Italian high commands at Salonika on 23 April. The British Government continued to recognize and support the exiled King George II of the Hellenes and his monarchist, right-wing government, under Prime Minister Emmanouil Tsouderos.

Hitler's invasion of Greece had caught many, including SOE, somewhat wrong-footed, and only a little in the way of preparing for resistance had been planned. However, on the assumption that there was a danger that the right-wing Metaxas might at some stage have sided with the likes of Mussolini, SOE had made early overtures towards the Greek left, including influential Venizelists (liberal democrats, named after the First World War Prime Minister Eleftherios Venizelos, founder of the Liberal Party) and Greek communists. They had done this through members of the British and Greek business communities working under the 'Apostles' codename. However, a fulltime professional was required, so Ian Pirie had been despatched by London in May 1940 and shortly afterwards took over the reins of the organization.[13]

Another agent present in Athens was Nicholas Hammond, who had entered the country in March 1941. However, within a month of his arrival, and with the Germans at the gates of Athens, Hammond found himself with the rest of the SOE team beating a hasty retreat from the capital alongside the Allied army. Before doing so, Pirie and his team had hurriedly distributed their Wireless Telegraphy (W/T) set and sabotage equipment to their Greek agents. As they withdrew, the SOE agents carried out a number of pre-planned demolitions, including a less than successful attempt by Lieutenant Commander Mike Cumberlege RN to block the Corinth Canal.[14]

The most successful of British-run Greek agents would prove to be Ioannis Peltekis, codenamed 'Apollo', who contrived to run his organization, 'Yvonne', and remain free throughout the occupation. His team managed to sabotage more than 250 enemy ships and caiques, for which he would be awarded the DSO.[15]

SOE had also taken care to leave behind a W/T in good hands. The first communication that the British authorities had with occupied Athens was with their Greek agent, codenamed 'Prometheus', who was in fact Colonel Evripidis Bakirdzis, who had won a DSO in the First World War, and received a death sentence *in absentia* for his part in the 1935 anti-royalist revolution. Also known as the 'Red Colonel', his politics were in fact extreme republican rather than communist. However, Bakirdzis was forced to escape from Greece. Before he did so he handed his W/T over to 'Prometheus II'. This was Captain Koutsoyannopoulos, who was instrumental in organizing the first parachute drop of SOE agents into Greece. Six months ahead of Wand-Tetley's mission, these first British agents were parachuted into the mountains of Central Greece in October 1942.[16]

Operation HARLING

Under Colonel Eddie Myers this SOE twelve-man team had been entrusted with Operation HARLING, SOE Cairo's plan to blow up a viaduct on the only railway running between Salonica and the Athens port of Piraeus. The intention was to support Montgomery's forthcoming El Alamein offensive by cutting the German supply line that shipped supplies from Piraeus to Crete and thence to Benghazi and Tobruk. The most vulnerable part of this single-line railway, after it had crossed the Thessaly plains, was where it subsequently snaked through the steep Roumeli mountains. Here there were three large railway viaducts, the Gorgopotamos in the north, the Asopos in the centre, and the Papadia in the south. The first of these was selected as the target.[17]

SOE's concept for this operation was sound, but timing was extremely tight and this was to create significant challenges. The team were scheduled to be parachuted in on the night of 29 September, barely a week after Myers had been first approached.[18]

For the purpose of the parachute drop the team was divided into three groups of four men, and flown to their drop zones by three Liberator bombers. The first group included Myers, Captain Denys Hamson (an ex-commando, and Greek speaker), Captain Tom Barnes (Royal New Zealand Engineers), and Sergeant Len Wilmott (W/T operator). The second included Major The Hon. Chris 'Monty' Woodhouse (already an SOE agent with six months' behind-the-lines Cretan experience), Captain Arthur Edmonds (Royal New Zealand Engineers), Captain Nat Barker (an ex-commando, and Greek speaker), and Sergeant Mike Chittis (W/T operator). The third group consisted of Major John Cook (an ex-commando), Lieutenant Themie Marinos (a Greek), Lieutenant Inder Gill (Royal Engineers), and Sergeant Doug Phillips (W/T operator).[19]

The plan was that two of the groups, those led by Myers and Cook, would be dropped over Mount Giona to make contact with the resistance leader Alexis Seferiades, but they later learnt that he had been captured by the Italians a few days before the drop. However, Myers did make contact with the andartes of Ares Velouchiotis. The third group, under Woodhouse (who at the time of selection for this mission had been en route to join the SAS), would be dropped thirty miles farther north-west in the Valtos mountain region to make contact with the andartes of Colonel Napoleon Zervas.

The attack was set for the night of 25/26 November. Myers divided the force into seven groups and, once in position, these were launched on their specific objectives. When the southern end of the viaduct had been captured, he sent in the demolition group, with its 400lb of explosives initially packed on mules but later carried in by the men. The demolition group blew its charges and collapsed the bridge. With the bridge span now a heap of twisted metal in the river below, Myers and the andartes withdrew.[20]

The authorities were generous with awards for the Gorgopotamos operation. Myers and Woodhouse received the DSO; Captains Barnes, Hamson, Edmonds and Michalli (Zervas' Adjutant) the MC; Zervas and Ares the OBE; 'Barba Niko', a Greek guide who provided exceptional assistance throughout the entire operation, the MBE; Sergeant Michael Khouri (a Palestinian Arab) the MM; and Sergeant Len Wilmott, one of the W/T operators, the BEM. The Gorgopotamos operation proved to be one of the most dramatic guerrilla actions in Greece and, although too late to have an effect on El Alamein, succeeded in cutting the German lines of communication for several weeks. The operation would also prove notable for being the only occasion when the rival andarte bands, republican under Zervas and communist under Ares, cooperated![21]

Greek Resistance Movements

After the Gorgopotamos operation SOE stepped up its activities and infiltrated agents to liaise and support any resistance group, whether republican, monarchist or communist, which would take the fight to the common enemy. Over the coming months this was to create a good deal of political and diplomatic tension, for the Foreign Office pursued a doggedly pro-monarchist stance, while the military approach and that taken by SOE Cairo was to support those resistance groups that would prove most effective against the Axis occupation forces. Such groups in Greece proved to be the communist, anti-royalist forces, the basis of which had been created by the Moscow Comintern.

SOE's stance was, in part, supported by Churchill, who stressed that the primary concern should be winning the war rather than endeavouring to shape the political future of the Balkans after the war. Inevitably, in a desperate war, military considerations tended to prevail. However, the Prime Minister's position was not as straightforward as this, for he also strongly advocated the cause of the exiled King of the Hellenes, not least to retain British influence in Greece. However, this dual policy, of short-term military expediency and long-term political aspiration, would prove extremely difficult to balance, particularly for field agents at the sharp end, on the ground. Myers would come in for a good deal of unfair criticism from the Foreign Office, but proved to be remarkably astute in his advocacy of a compromise by which King George II should only be allowed to return to Greece after a plebiscite concerning the constitutional issue, in a free expression of the national will, had found in his favour.[22]

In common with most of the SOE British Liaison Officers (BLOs), Wand-Tetley had little knowledge of Greece, its people or the language before he parachuted into the country. Following the advent of Myers' twelve-man British Military Mission (BMM) in October 1942, the Mission in Greece would expand to a total of some eighty British officers and

400 men across the country by 1944. And, following the arrival in Greece in 1943 of officers of the American SOE equivalent, the Office of Strategic Services (OSS) and the forerunner of the CIA, the nomenclature for agents would change to Allied Liaison Officers (ALO), and the unit to the Allied Military Mission (AMM).

Following Axis occupation, resistance movements had sprung up across the Balkans in Greece, Yugoslavia and Albania, but in all three countries their effect was tempered by the bitter rivalry that existed between the communist and anti-communist groups; such rivalry would continue to have lasting effects long after the war was over. In Yugoslavia the two principal groups were Josip Tito's Communist Partisans and Draza Mihailoviæ's Četniks. Initially favouring the Četniks, the British eventually came to support Tito, while still maintaining contact with Mihailoviæ. In Albania the resistance groups at first combined after the Italian surrender, only to separate and start a virtual civil war when the communists under Enver Hoxha split from King Zog's supporters in the face of German reprisals against the population.

In Greece the resistance group of the extreme left was the communist National Liberation Front (EAM) with its military arm, the National People's Liberation Army (ELAS). Formed in September 1941, EAM/ELAS was created and controlled by the Communist Party of Greece, the KKE, the catalyst for its formation being the German invasion of Russia. With Nikos Zakhariadhis in German custody, the KKE was led throughout the period of the German occupation by Yiorgios Siantos as Secretary General. EAM/ELAS can be considered, apart from political and military function, the same organization in terms of stance and point of view. The military arm, ELAS, became operational a year after EAM and, under Athanasios Klaras (a.k.a. Ares Velouchiotis), took to the mountains in 1942. But it was far from clear to those joining EAM/ELAS, particularly the rank and file, that they were in fact joining a front for the KKE. Indeed, it was only during Woodhouse's visit to Athens that the BMM perceived that KKE were controlling EAM, for it was Siantos and Andreas Tzimas, both communists, who were clearly in control. Ruthlessly suppressed by Metaxas prior to the war, the KKE was adept at masking its activities and communist credentials. Indeed, faced with certain arrest by Metaxas, the KKE had been forced underground and established secret cells throughout the towns and many of the larger villages of Greece. Thus those in EAM/ELAS – many of whom were democrats by inclination and had joined for essentially patriotic reasons to take the fight to the Axis powers – were not communist, although their leadership was firmly controlled by communists. Throughout the occupation EAM/ELAS contrived ruthlessly

110

to monopolize and integrate the entire resistance movement, by force of arms if necessary.[23]

Three independent republican andarte organizations existed which, collectively, represented a threat to EAM/ELAS, not just in terms of recruiting competition, but by offering republican-minded people a viable political alternative to communism after the war. The military arm of the National Democratic Greek League (EDES) under Zervas took to the mountains of southern Epirus in 1942. The political component of EDES, which shared the same name, had been formed a little earlier in Athens by Zervas and another prewar republican officer, Stylianos Gonatas, both of whom looked to General Nicolaos Plastiras, exiled in France by Metaxas in 1936, for their political leadership. To distinguish the two functions, Zervas later adopted the military title National Bands of Greek Guerillas (EOEA), although this name was short-lived. The initial anti-monarchist stance of EDES was transformed by Zervas, who later declared himself for the King without consulting the EDES political arm in Athens. This had the result of increasing the popularity of EDES which expanded to rival EAM/ELAS in many regions, including the Peloponnese. The other two republican groups were of less consequence. The military arm of the National and Social Liberation (EKKA) under Colonel Dimitrios Psaros, with a political stance some-where between EAM/ELAS and EDES, took to the field relatively late in March 1943 and attracted particularly strong support in Roumeli in the area of Mount Parnassos. The Liberation Struggle Leadership (AAA) headed by Colonel Stephanos Sarafis, with Venizelist sympathies, had taken to the field earlier, at the end of 1942, in Thessaly but was not destined to last long.

Other republican andarte organizations existed but offered little in the way of competition to EAM/ELAS, and the National Organization of Magnetes (EOM), operating out of Volos, was soon liquidated by them. In Macedonia a Republican-Venizelist orientated League of Officers of the Reserve existed in Salonica, but more successful in the region were the right-wing Defenders of Northern Greece (YVE), later to change their name to the Panhellenic Liberation Organization (PAO), which at least gained some national recognition but was destroyed by EAM/ELAS in the summer of 1943.

When Wand-Tetley arrived in the Peloponnese two other minor resistance movements existed on the peninsula, the National Organization of Officers (EOA) and its military arm with the grandiose title of the 'Greek Army' (ES). In fact the former was not only political in nature and by the summer of 1943 both EOA and ES had fielded andarte units in the mountains. Regular Greek officers formed the basis of its leadership, including Colonels Yannakopoulos, Karakhalios and

Papadhongonas. By nature EOA and ES were nationalist and recognized the King of the Hellenes and his government in exile.

EOA and ES represented competition to EAM/ELAS in the Peloponnese, but this was relatively minor compared to the wider potential threat posed to the communists by the three republican andarte organizations, the AAA, EKKA and EDES. In March 1943 Sarafis and his headquarters was captured by EAM/ELAS and his force dissipated, although he was able to save his skin by switching sides and accepting the role of C-in-C of ELAS. EKKA suffered a similar fate in May 1943 and, although Psaros was able to quickly rebuild his force, he was attacked once again by EAM/ELAS the following month. However, the communists did not find EDES, under Zervas, quite such an easy target, not least because SOE was actively supporting Zervas with arms, ammunition and money in the shape of gold sovereigns.[24]

In July 1943 Myers managed to intervene sufficiently to bring the three main belligerents to the negotiating table and secure their agreement to a truce. The National Bands Agreement recognized EKKA, in common with EAM/ELAS and EDES, as the three foremost resistance movements and placed them under command of GHQ Middle East. A Joint General Headquarters (JGHQ) was established in Greece with representatives from the BMM under Myers and from all three resistance groups. By now andarte forces had multiplied rapidly. EAM/ELAS had some 16,000 under arms with the same number of self-armed village reservists. EDES had in the region of 5,000 with a similar number of village reservists. EKKA, by comparison, never had more than 1,000 andartes under arms. At this stage EAM/ELAS controlled some 80 per cent of the available mountain territory on mainland Greece. Under JGHQ arrangements payment to the andarte organizations was also standardized, it being decided by the British authorities to pay one gold sovereign per month for each andarte member permanently under arms.[25]

For the present it made sense for the BMM to support all the resistance groups, a decision based upon military rather than political considerations, for no single resistance group could be relied upon by the British, and the BMM was keen to avoid EAM/ELAS hegemony, which would have been the likely result but for their presence and control. It was the intention that new andarte groups could take to the field against the Germans without being molested by EAM/ELAS, or any other groups for that matter. Cooperation and good relations were underpinned by the promises of increases of British supplies and gold. None of the resistance movements wished to be the only one not on the receiving end of British support, for this would weaken it vis-à-vis its rivals.

Frederick Tatham, Boer War 1900, Peter Wand-Tetley's maternal grandfather. (Family collection)

Tatham ended the Boer War with six clasps to his campaign medal and was twice Mentioned in Despatches. A decade earlier, in the Basuto War of 1880, he had enlisted at the age of fifteen in Willoughby's Horse. In the First World War he was awarded the DSO and twice Mentioned in Despatches.

Cécile Tatham, First World War, Peter Wand-Tetley's mother. (Family collection)

Cécile was born in Natal, South Africa, in 1894 and was educated at Priorsfield, in England. She was descended from the branch of the Tathams that established itself in County Durham during the sixteenth century.

Marlborough College Shooting VIII, 1935, winners of the Ashburton Shield, Bisley. *Back row left to right*: E. H. Dowdell Esq, C. A. G. Walker, L. F. H. Merton, K. Coxon, J. G. C. Jameson, P.M. Wand-Tetley, RSM Lawrence; *front row left to right*: G. A. Neligan, J. C. James, T. A. Davison, C. Aveling, M. C. Camell. (Marlborough College collection)

Peter Wand-Tetley excelled himself, securing the highest individual score and establishing himself as the best shot in the school at the age of just fifteen.

Thomas Wand-Tetley, Peter Wand-Tetley's father, Second World War. (Family collection)

Wand-Tetley is acknowledged as the founder of the modern Royal Army Physical Training Corps. In his youth he competed at the Olympic Games in the fencing and modern pentathlon in 1920, in the fencing in 1928, and as a judge of fencing in 1936.

HMS *Glengyle*, in which Peter Wand-Tetley sailed in January 1941 with No. 7 Commando from Arran as part of Z Force (later retitled Layforce) to Suez. (IWM FL 22266)

The German airborne invasion of Crete in May 1941, in which Peter Wand-Tetley with No. 7 Commando provided the Layforce rearguard during the Allied evacuation of the island. (IWM A 4154)

Peter Wand-Tetley, Cairo, Second World War, early 1942. (Family collection)

Wand-Tetley is wearing the cap-badge of the Royal Wiltshire Regiment. Commandos initially wore the insignia of their parent regiments. The introduction of the Commando green beret later in 1942, along with common unit insignia, eventually introduced uniformity.

An LRDG patrol leaving its headquarters at Siwa Oasis in May 1942, the month in which Peter Wand-Tetley with A Squadron Middle East Commando first deployed to the oasis to undertake operations with the LRDG. (IWM E12375)

LRDG Chevrolet trucks in the Western Desert in May 1942, the period in which Peter Wand-Tetley with A Squadron Middle East Commando operated under LRDG command and conducted raids behind enemy lines in Cyrenaica. (IWM E 12385)

The officers' lines at Sidi Bishr Camp on the eastern outskirts of Alexandria early in the war. Sidi Bishr was one of a series of locations in the Alexandria area in which Wand-Tetley's A Squadron 1st Special Service Regiment was located in July 1942. (Major (Retd) A. W. Hogg ERD)

Peter Wand-Tetley, Cairo, Second World War, mid 1942. (Family collection)

The rigours of operating in the Western Desert have clearly had an effect in shaping Wand-Tetley's lean physical condition. It is evident from the wings sported on his right arm that by this stage he had undertaken parachute training with the Middle East Commando.

LRDG Chevrolet trucks travelling through a pass in the Western Desert in May 1942, the period during which Wand-Tetley as a Troop Leader in A Squadron Middle East Commando acquired LRDG desert skills and learnt the arcane art of desert navigation. (IWM E 12384)

Peter Wand-Tetley's commanding officer, Lieutenant Colonel David Stirling, photographed standing next to a SAS jeep patrol shortly before his capture in January 1943. (IWM E 21338)

A Halifax heavy bomber of No. 148 (Special Duties) Squadron RAF, of the type from which Peter Wand-Tetley was parachuted as an SOE agent into the Peloponnese in April 1943, dropping parachute canisters of supplies over a drop zone in the Balkans. (IWM CNA 3243)

Soldiers of Peter Wand-Tetley's 7th (LI) Parachute Battalion take cover from Indonesian nationalist snipers in Batavia (now Jakarta), Java in December 1945. (IWM SE 6092)

Men of 7th (LI) Parachute Battalion search 'bashas' for Indonesian nationalist snipers in Batavia (now Jakarta), Java in December 1945. (IWM SE 6091)

7th (LI) Parachute Battalion march past the Commander-in-Chief during the Rhine Crossing Anniversary Parade by 5 Parachute Brigade at Semarang, Java on 24 March 1946. Peter Wand-Tetley is marching behind his commanding officer, Lieutenant Colonel Geoffrey Pine-Coffin. (IWM SE 7104)

Joan Wand-Tetley (née Engelbach), Peter Wand-Tetley's first wife. (Family collection)

Wand-Tetley married Joan, an artist, in England in 1946. Joan had been born in Egypt, the daughter of the celebrated Egyptologist and Chief Keeper of the Cairo Museum, Reginald (Rex) Engelbach who, among many archaeological achievements, orchestrated the opening of Tutankhamun's tomb by the British archaeologist Howard Carter.

Peter Wand-Tetley (*far left*), addressing villagers, Northern Nigeria, 1948. (Family collection)

Wand-Tetley was to spend his first four years as an Assistant District Officer in Minna. Wide expanses separated the many tribes, some of which had yet to see white men.

Felicia Wand-Tetley (née Bloxham), Peter Wand-Tetley's second wife. (Family collection)

It was in Kaduna that Wand-Tetley met and married, in 1960, Felicia. A history graduate of Bristol University, 'Flick' had come out to Nigeria in 1957 to assume her appointment with the Government of Northern Nigeria through the Crown Agents.

Peter Wand-Tetley in the Northern Nigeria Colonial Service, in ceremonial 'tropical whites', with his pointer, Flanagan, in Kaduna, 1962. (Family collection)

With self-government came a change in the design of the 'tropical whites' to accommodate Muslim leaders who wished to adopt the uniform; the jackets were lengthened and an astrakhan side-cap replaced the Victorian helmet.

Kenya Rifle Shooting VIII, Bisley 1968, Peter Wand-Tetley is sitting in the front row on the right of the photograph, with Dave Drummond, who as a member of special forces had played a leading role in pioneering covert operations against the Mau Mau Rebellion, standing behind his left shoulder as the last man on the right. (Family collection)

Seychelles delegation visit to State House, Mombasa, Kenya, 1972. *Front row left to right*: David Joubert, Mr Koinage, President Jomo Kenyatta, Chief Minister (later President) James Mancham; *back row left to right*: Peter Wand-Tetley, Dr. Mungai. (Family collection)

Wand-Tetley conducted a short-term assignment as Salaries Review Commissioner in Seychelles in 1969, but returned in 1970 for five years as Secretary to the Chief Minister (later President) James Mancham.

Seychelles, record 528 lb black marlin caught by Peter Wand-Tetley on 23 July 1972. (Family collection)

The fight lasted an exhausting three hours and twenty minutes before Wand-Tetley finally brought the black marlin to the gaff; a new Seychelles record for a billfish caught on rod and line.

The first JGHQ meeting took place on 18 July at Myers' new headquarters at Pertouli, Western Thessaly, in the middle of the Pindus Mountains. Myers also used the occasion to invite his BLO area commanders, some of whom had not yet met him or all their colleagues. This was the first time, for instance, that Myers and Hammond met in Greece, although upon meeting both realized that they had been undergraduates at Cambridge together. The conference was extremely valuable and enabled the BMM to compare and contrast views on the resistance firsthand, for their W/T messages were necessarily sent direct to SOE Cairo and not between one another. Also present at the conference was a Foreign Office representative, David Wallace, holding the temporary rank of major, who had been parachuted in to make a political assessment of the various andarte bands. Fluent in Greek and with a sound understanding of the country's politics, Wallace had served from 1939 to 1941 as the Press Attaché in the British Embassy, Athens and had even spent his honeymoon in the Peloponnese studying Frankish castles.[26]

The JGHQ was not a joint headquarters in the true sense, for its andarte parties only accepted and carried out orders that suited them. It was an uneasy relationship but in the short term it suited all members. No party wanted to be left out for fear that those in the JGHQ would gain an advantage over them, particularly in terms of British patronage. EAM/ELAS had by this stage managed to neutralize the AAA and this period, while the National Bands Agreement lasted, was to represent a pause before the communists once again went on the offensive with the intention of snuffing out their rivals. EAM/ELAS were, effectively, to remain in a state of civil war with the remaining rival resistance groups.

Operation ANIMALS

Meanwhile, Operation ANIMALS had been launched on 21 June and was to last until 14 July, by which time Allied landings in Sicily had been established successfully. Already Allied Force Headquarters (AFHQ) in Algiers was starting to plan the subsequent operations that were to take place in Italy. However, Eisenhower's command stretched only as far east as Italy, so the Balkans still came under command of C-in-C Middle East, 'Jumbo' Wilson. The orders that Myers had received earlier in January and February had laid out the general concept for ANIMALS as an SOE deception operation designed to convince the enemy that an Allied assault on the west coast of Greece was at hand.

The comprehensive plan of sabotage that Myers initially developed with SOE Cairo called for the country's mountains to be divided into four regions, each being placed under a lieutenant colonel of the BMM. The four commanders selected were Tom Barnes in Epirus, Arthur

Edmonds in Roumeli, Rufus Sheppard in Olympus, and Nick Hammond in Macedonia. Hammond and Sheppard had, respectively, parachuted into Greece with small four-man teams in January and February. Following his earlier evacuation from Greece, Hammond had been engaged in the Cretan campaign and subsequently as a demolitions instructor at the SOE Special Training School at Mount Carmel, Haifa, otherwise known as Military Establishment (ME) 102. SOE Cairo undertook to take direct responsibility for the Peloponnese, for Myers was too distant to control events in that region effectively. Nonetheless, Myers initially put forward Denys Hamson's name as a possible commander for the area, but in the event he was diverted to the Pindus region.[27]

At this stage Colonel John Stevens, head of SOE Cairo's Greek Section, parachuted in to visit Myers's headquarters before touring the northern region to assess for himself the situation on the ground. His main purpose was to form a view on the widely differing reports on the andartes that were being despatched to Cairo from the BLOs. Sheppard in Olympus, for instance, was full of nothing but praise for EAM/ELAS, whilst Myers insisted – correctly as it transpired – that they should be treated with extreme caution. With his tour completed he was evacuated by boat from the east coast to Turkey. Stevens would shortly return to Greece, this time to assume responsibility for the Peloponnese, but not before Wand-Tetley's Mission had established itself in the region.[28]

In February, SOE Cairo had put in place a plan to support ANIMALS and step up its supplies of equipment to Greece. Starting with eight sorties in March, these were built up to twelve in April, sixteen in May, and twenty-four in June and in the following months. At the beginning of the year SOE Cairo had only four Liberators available – one of which was invariably being serviced – with which to supply its missions in both Greece and Yugoslavia. These four bombers of the RAF special duties X Flight were initially the only aircraft available that had the necessary range to do the round trip from the Nile Delta to the Balkans and back. However, in March 1943 X Flight was reformed as No. 148 Squadron at Gambut in Libya and reinforced with ten Halifax Mk II bombers to be sent over from England, although not all ten of them would be available until July. Moreover, following the Allied advance west from the Nile Delta, No. 148 Squadron, which had also been flying out of Tokra, was able from May to fly out of Derna in Libya, thereby greatly reducing the distance to Greece.[29]

At the very end of May Myers received a top secret signal from SOE Cairo informing him that the invasion of Sicily would take place in the second week of July and instructing him to launch ANIMALS in the last week of June, putting into action the widespread sabotage that had

114

been planned in the previous few months. Moreover, he was instructed to continue with the operation until it had been confirmed that Sicily was in Allied hands.

The destruction of the Asopos railway viaduct heralded the start of ANIMALS in a spectacular fashion. Planning for its destruction had started in February 1943, and it was not initially intended that the attack on the viaduct should necessarily be linked to the deception operation. However, the fact that the viaduct's destruction was delayed until the night of 20/21 June meant that it could not have been better timed. To assist, in early May SOE Cairo parachuted in three new officers from the Royal Engineers, Majors Pat Wingate and 'Scottie' Scott, and Captain Henry McIntyre.

Following a reconnaissance by the two commando-trained officers, Major Geoffrey Gordon-Creed and Captain Donald Stott, a New Zealander, a plan was conceived that called for a covert act of sabotage using a small team. This plan called for a stealthy approach down the river gorge, with the team in gym shoes, carrying only pre-prepared waterproofed explosive charges, rope, and rubber coshes as weapons. German soldiers had by now replaced the Italians on guard duty and, if spotted in the narrow gorge below, the team would have no chance of escape.

In mid-June a six-man team set off for the viaduct. Present were Gordon-Creed, Stott, Scott, McIntyre, Lance Corporal Charlie Mutch (an escaped British prisoner of war) and Sergeant Michael Khouri (who had taken part in the Gorgopotamos operation). Having worked their way down the gorge, they reached the viaduct a few days later. The team set off for their final approach on the night of 20/21 June. Some time after midnight, and having set the timers for ninety minutes, the team finally ignited the fuses and carefully withdrew up the gorge. The viaduct and the railway were out of action for the next four months. Churchill was delighted when he heard of the success of the operation and sent the team his personal congratulations. All were decorated: Gordon-Creed and Stott with the DSO; Scott and McIntyre with the MC; and Mutch and Khouri with the MM.

Northern Greece proved to be a saboteur's paradise, and the enemy was hard-pushed to protect their lines of communication. Road and rail links were channelled by the mountainous terrain through the valleys and gorges or confined to the coastal plain. If the Allies were to land on Greece they would be most likely to do it on the western coast, so Myers built this into the deception plan.

In the Peloponnese the control and development of resistance was a far more challenging task for SOE Cairo than in northern Greece. Following the Axis defeat in North Africa, the southern Peloponnese had effectively come to represent a front line and accordingly more enemy troops were garrisoned here than in northern Greece. Also, a better network of roads existed across the central Peloponnese mountains. This made the andarte bands more vulnerable to enemy sweeps than was the case for their northern counterparts, who had the advantage of being able to withdraw to inaccessible mountain strongholds. However, regardless of the difficulties, SOE Cairo was all too conscious that it could not ignore the Peloponnese.

Subsequent to Myers' suggestion that Hamson be sent to make initial inroads into organizing the Peloponnese resistance, Zervas recommended that contact should be made with a leader there that he had heard controlled some 1,000 andartes. Accordingly, Zacharius Minis (a.k.a. Simos), a Greek agent, was despatched by Myers. Having marched south to the Gulf of Patras, Minis and his guide then crossed to the Peloponnese. Here he discovered that the leader suggested by Zervas was ineffective and no match for the local andarte bands of EAM/ELAS and EOA. Minis then endeavoured to contact SOE Cairo to arrange for a parachute drop of SOE agents into the Peloponnese. However, because he had been unable to bring a W/T set on his journey south from northern Greece, his only means of contacting Cairo was through Athens. His efforts to do so were overtaken by events.

PART 2

Part 2 to this chapter focuses upon Wand-Tetley's SOE mission to the Peloponnese.[30]

Mission to the Peloponnese – Operation TIBBENHAM

SOE Cairo decided that, in the light of the forthcoming invasion of Sicily and the ANIMALS imperative, it could wait no longer and took the decision to parachute a team in 'blind', without the benefit of signal fires on the ground to guide the agents or of an andarte reception party to secure the drop zone and receive them. This three-man mission, consisting of Major Bill Reid, Wand-Tetley and a Greek W/T operator, Second Lieutenant Theodoros 'Yannis' Yannopoulos, was dropped by parachute on the night of 21 April into the central prong of the Peloponnesian trident under the codename Operation TIBBENHAM. SOE Cairo was unable to provide the team with any information of substance on the Peloponnese, as no other mission had been established there successfully, nor, at that time, had anything been heard from two Greeks agents, Lieutenant G. Tavernarakis and Sergeant A. Gardhelis, who had been infiltrated by submarine into Eastern Laconia in the previous month.

Shortly after Wand-Tetley's drop, a small party comprising two Greeks, Second Lieutenant Panayotopoulos and Corporal Kamilos, parachuted in over Strezova to act as an advance party to that region, but nothing more was heard from them. Panayotopoulos had in fact been captured by the Italians, but Kamilos had managed to escape to Athens, from where he was later evacuated. Another party that met with similarly poor luck in north Peloponnese was a British sabotage team, working under the codename of Operation LOCKSMITH. Led by Lieutenant Commander Mike Cumberlege RN, the team also included Warrant Officer (CSM) J. C. S. Steele, Corporal F. Handley and a Czech. Their task was to attempt, again, to block the Corinth Canal, but they were all captured.

Having been dropped in Northern Arkadia, Reid and Wand-Tetley's mission would soon come to establish itself in Western Messinia. Tavernarakis and Gardhelis would eventually manage to contact SOE Cairo, and in early May a four-man mission, comprising Major John Harington, Flight Lieutenant C. P. Drakoulis, Warrant Officer (BSM) F. J. Richmond and Corporal A. Robertson would be dropped to them on Mount Parnon in eastern Lakonia. Tragically, due to high winds Drakoulis and Richmond would both die of injuries sustained while landing.

With SOE BLOs now in south Peloponnese, missions would next be established in the north. Two advance parties, one of three Greeks, the other of two, would drop to Harington in late May, and having been briefed by him would head northwards to Akhaia and Korinthia. In July Major Antony Andrewes, a pre-war Professor of Ancient History at Pembroke College, Oxford, would drop with his W/T operator, Corporal W. A. Hill, to the advance party in Akhaia. They would be followed by a three-man team dropped to Taigetos, comprising Captain P. M. Fraser, Corporal K. H. W. Death and a Greek W/T operator, D. Gyftopoulos. However, a mission comprising two Greeks who had been infiltrated by caique to the Monemvasia region never succeeded, for Captain D. Argitis was killed, although his W/T operator, Sergeant N. Hamberis, managed to escape and was later evacuated.

Thus five SOE missions would be established in the Peloponnesse by the end of July. Three of these would be in the south, with Reid and Wand-Tetley in Western Messenia, Fraser in Taigetos, and Harington on Mount Parnon in East Lakonia. In the north at this stage there would be just the one British mission led by Andrewes at Akhaia in the north-west, but with a Greek reception party also established at Korinthia. The next step would be to establish an overall headquarters in the Peloponnnese and, with this in mind, Lieutenant Colonel Peter McMullen would be dropped to Andrewes in August. A further four British agents would follow shortly afterwards, Major D. L. Campbell to establish a presence at Elis, Major H. M. James at Argolido-Korinthia and Captain E. W. Gray and his W/T operator, Corporal E. A. Scarlett, to the Patras area. In the summer civil war broke out between the ELAS and the EOA andartes in the Western Messenia and Taigetos areas, and it quickly became apparent to Reid and Wand-Tetley that any hope that there might have been of establishing a viable joint headquarters with the andarte bands had quickly disappeared. Thereafter their work concentrated for the most part on the collection of intelligence, the distribution of relief, and the carrying out of specific acts of sabotage as directed by GHQ Middle East. In September Colonel John Stevens was to drop to Akhaia to assume command of the overall mission in the Peloponnese. Having toured Thessaly and Macedonia earlier in the year he was under no illusions about the difficulties he would encounter in the months ahead.

In the week before Reid and Wand-Tetley had parachuted over Nasia, an advance party to their mission consisting of two Greeks, Second Lieutenant Koukoutas and Sergeant Kokkinos, had dropped on 16 April with a W/T set near the village of Dyrakion, but nothing had been heard of them. This led to the decision, on 21 April, by the mission's other three members to jump 'blind'. Wand-Tetley would later learn that their advance party had been betrayed by a schoolmaster and that Koukoutas had been captured by the Italians. However, dressed as a woman, Kokkinos had managed to escape and then took great satisfaction in sending the traitorous schoolmaster to an early grave, before managing to contact Reid and Wand-Tetley. They heard later that Koukoutas had resisted efforts by the Italians to persuade him to talk before being taken to Xylokastron to await execution, although it would be the Germans who would finally shoot him, and not until after the surrender.

At the outbreak of war Bill Reid was thirty-two, married with two very young daughters, and had been working for Shell Oil in Greece for five years, during which time he had developed a good grasp of the language. Having joined the Officers Emergency Reserve, he was then commissioned into the Cyprus Regiment before moving to Egypt and transferring to the Royal Army Service Corps. Naturally very fit and of slim, athletic build, sporting an RAF moustache, he was a tenacious, intelligent and shrewd man. Given his knowledge of Greece and its language, SOE saw in him a clear asset for clandestine work after that country had been invaded by the Germans. He transferred to SOE in 1943 and completed his parachute training only a month before his operational jump in the Peloponnese. Reid had selected the village of Nasia for their drop on the basis that he thought it unlikely to be garrisoned by the enemy and that the territory was reasonably well known to Yannis. Wand Tetley recalls:

The drop was remarkable only for the precision with which Wing Comdr Blackburn deposited us on the spot chosen. We found each other with little difficulty, concealed ourselves from the bright moonlight in the shade of a tree and awaited developments. It was not long before we heard footsteps and saw two shadowy figures approaching. We drew our revolvers and Yannis ordered them to halt. There followed identification, tears and kisses. The men told us that the whole village had witnessed our descent as the Easter celebrations were then in progress, and that we were fortunate in that an Italian patrol had left the village the previous day. A few minutes later other villagers arrived, assisted us to dispose of our equipment under cover on the hillside and helped themselves to my parachute.

It was not until the following day that the three agents were able to examine their equipment. They were horrified to discover that the tuning dial for their W/T set was broken. Not only that, but a particularly valuable container had smashed in the drop, and one of their three W/T batteries was wrecked and another badly damaged. They would therefore have to rely on a single battery and a hand-charger. Although the transmitter was undamaged, their chances of hearing SOE Cairo with a broken tuner were exceedingly slim. Spare parts for the W/T set were of such importance that Reid decided to take the risk that the mission's presence had not been reported to the nearby Italian garrison, only some thirty minutes away, and to send 'blind' messages to SOE Cairo requesting that the necessary spares be dropped at the same point before the end of the moon period precluded further flying.

The mission therefore remained in the same hide for the next five days, hoping and waiting for the requested drop, but the spares did not come. Their chances of discovery were high, particularly given that the local villagers could not contain their curiosity and flocked to visit Wand-Tetley and his two comrades. Nonetheless the professional classes in the villages – doctors, priests and army officers – had the good sense to stay away and not to draw unnecessary attention to either themselves or the three agents. Despite the number of visitors, none were able to provide any information concerning andartes or resistance movements.

At the end of the moon period there was no sense in staying any longer. They had been fortunate not to have come to the notice of the Italians. Disappointed that they had not secured any spares for the W/T set, it was nonetheless with a great sense of relief that they were able to set off south towards Taigetos with the intention of establishing contact with the two members of their advance party and with andartes, if indeed any existed. However, it was with some difficulty that they managed to secure guides and mules for their journey, for despite the villagers having previously professed their commitment and willingness to shed their blood for the cause and their country, none seemed so keen to assist when finally put to the test. However, with the promise of gold sovereigns by way of recompense, two guides and three mules were eventually secured. Wand-Tetley:

> We had five Beretta sub-machine guns with which we offered to arm anyone willing to accompany us, but they all with one consent began to make excuses. Of two youths who accepted our offer one turned back after thirty-six hours saying that he was not getting enough to eat. The other stayed with us for a month, then stole two-hundred sovereigns and fled to Athens. In this he acted wisely, as had he returned to his village I should have had much pleasure in appointing myself his executioner.

The three SOE agents journeyed south for several days with their mules, moving by night and lying up during the day. They travelled cross-country by minor paths, avoiding the villages and main tracks which were used by the Italian carabinieri.

Despite assurances from their guides and muleteers that they knew the country like the backs of their hands, occasionally they would lose their way. Nonetheless the first stage of their journey went largely without incident, although their stamina was severely tested due to a lack of food arising from the requirement to avoid the villages. East of Megalopolis they came across a railway line and here they paused while they considered how best to cross it. Wand-Tetley:

> The line was reputedly well guarded and at the only crossing considered possible with loaded mules was an Italian guard of about twelve men. Here we met an old man who offered to guide us across, guarded by five volunteers whom we armed with the sub-machine guns. At the crossing we found a hut in which were sleeping, so we were told, the Italian guard. All went well until the last mule slipped its load and a drum of 9 mm ammunition fell with a crash on to the line, but the Ities were either too frightened or too fast asleep to investigate and the crossing was successful.

The following dawn the tired agents lay down to sleep in a copse, but were soon awoken by one of the muleteers who pointed out to them what appeared to be a well-trodden track only some twenty yards away. He went on to explain that the carabinieri were accustomed to patrolling the path regularly, so the men quickly roused themselves, pulled on their packs, and headed up the hillside to find a safer place. Then, looking up, they noticed their guide trying to make himself scarce against the rock face, while at the same time gesturing back down towards the track below them. Wand-Tetley:

I was astounded to see the two carabinieri; their rifles slung, walking unconcernedly along it. From their position it would seem that they had been immediately behind and not twenty yards away from me for several minutes while Bill and I, in full view, wearing battledress and armed to the teeth, had been exchanging pleasantries about the state of our feet and the emptiness of our stomachs. There can be no explanation for this incident other than the Ities, who must have both seen and heard us, had been doing their uneventful patrol for so long that they could not assimilate the astonishing fact of our existence!

They remained in hiding south of the railway line for the next two days, enquiring of the locals whether there had been any recent signs of andartes operating in the region, and endeavouring to raise SOE Cairo on their broken W/T set. However, all they managed to ascertain was that several Italian troops had, at the time that the advance party dropped, conducted a drive of the region surrounding Dyrakion. On the third day a mysterious man appeared and asked the agents a number of probing questions, but refused to be drawn on any questions himself. He then disappeared, only to return the next day to instruct the three agents to follow him to his headquarters, the location of which he refused to reveal. Nonetheless, by estimating time and distance and noting the position of the Pole Star, Wand-Tetley surmised that they were approaching Megalopolis, which was somewhat disconcerting given that they knew there were 5,000 Italians garrisoned there.

They reached a copse and, with dawn approaching, the men shrugged off their packs and settled down to lie up for the day. Their guide said he would depart to fetch some food, but would be back shortly and then, almost as an afterthought, warned the three of them to stay hidden as they were only 400 yards from the Italian garrison. This seemingly casual snippet of information served to focus their attention, and was confirmed when they heard bugles blowing reveille and the noise of a military band striking up. It seemed that the Italians were preparing to engage in some early morning square-bashing. Their guide was back soon with some food, and some civilian clothes so that the agents could disguise themselves. Wand-Tetley:

> He arrived none too soon, for as he did so an Italian soldier elected to graze his sheep in our patch of cover. In full view we lumbered across a ploughed field with exterior confidence but interior trepidation and settled ourselves under a hedge overlooking the road, feeling conspicuous.

Their guide then disappeared again, telling the agents not to move from the location and so the three of them settled down to await his return. They were all disguised in civilian overcoats pulled over their battledress with cloth caps pulled down over their eyes, and Wand-Tetley had been persuaded to wear a dark pair of spectacles which, the guide had insisted somewhat unconvincingly, would help disguise his fair beard. An hour later they were somewhat unnerved when they heard the sound of a rifle shot behind them. Despite it being a sunny May morning, the disguise of unseasonably heavy clothing evidently worked. Wand-Tetley:

A number of Italians, out for their morning exercise in white shorts and singlets, trotted through a gap in the hedge thirty yards away. At any rate we were left in comparative peace until our guide rejoined us during the afternoon with the information that the shot which had caused us so much concern was only our friend the military shepherd improving his marksmanship on a tin can.

They then set off with the guide, arriving at a ruined church on the outskirts of Megalopolis at nightfall. Here the agents met five of the guide's comrades who, working through an interpreter who had introduced himself as the local scoutmaster, satisfied themselves by means of a general knowledge quiz on British history that the agents were indeed who they said they were. Wand-Tetley:

He proceeded to ask us who was the first Prime Minister of England and what was the composition of the Union Jack. I disgraced myself, when asked who was the English Foreign Minister during the war of 1821, by enquiring, 'What war of 1821?' When the inquisition was over they beamed happily at us, thinking, I suppose, that such bloody fools must be British.

When asked, the five Greeks confirmed they represented EAM but that no ELAS andartes were currently operating in the Taigetos region, for there had recently been a large Italian drive and they had been forced to quit the area. When pressed, the five somewhat grudgingly admitted that there was another andarte group composed of Greek officers – EOA – also operating in the Peloponnese, but dismissed them as being of no consequence. The support of the local civilian population was dismissed in similar derisory fashion, and it was suggested that the three SOE agents should therefore place their safety in the hands of EAM.

The agents were then escorted to a derelict house in a nearby village, where they were told to wait for two days while certain arrangements were made. In the interim they were told that EAM would endeavour to repair the broken W/T tuning dial. Here they were fed twice a day, but the two days soon stretched into a week and the strain on the men increased due to the Italian forage patrols that regularly visited the village and the ever present danger of discovery.

Just when Reid had declared to Wand-Tetley that they would, regardless, depart the following day, their recently discovered EAM acquaintances returned from Megalopolis. They brought with them an exact replica of the W/T tuning dial, skilfully carved in wood. The three SOE agents set off that same evening south-west towards Ano Melpia, which they reached two days later, and finally made contact with Greek guerrillas. Wand-Tetley:

> Here we met our first Andartes, a band of fifteen cut-throats in civilian clothes armed with an astonishing variety of weapons. They did not impress me then as having taken to the mountains from the purest of patriotic motives and after a short acquaintance I was left in no doubt that their single aim had been to extort from the villagers contributions to their own welfare. Their avowed purpose was to make the land fit for heroes to live in by judicious elimination of 'traitors'. They expressed their confidence that the British would supply them with the arms and equipment necessary to drive the enemy from their native land. They included three Cypriots.

All this time Reid, Wand-Tetley and Yannis had endeavoured to make contact with SOE Cairo, but had had no response. One night they heard the sound of a low-flying plane which, from the familiar note of its Rolls-Royce engines, they judged to be a Halifax Mk II. Quickly grabbing a torch, they signalled 'TB' in morse, indicating their operational code-name, TIBBENHAM. Much to their surprise and satisfaction they were rewarded with an answering flash from the bomber. Assuming that upon their return the crew reported the contact, SOE Cairo would now be aware that at least one of their TIBBENHAM agents was alive.

The following day Minis, the Greek agent despatched to the Peloponnese in March by Myers and Woodhouse, turned up at their headquarters. This was good news indeed. Furthermore, it transpired that he was a gifted amateur mechanic, and almost immediately he set about repairing their damaged W/T set. When Wand-Tetley saw the set strewn around their headquarters in pieces he wondered about the wisdom of allowing Minis loose on it, but by this stage the mission had little to lose, for the set had by then proved itself to be all but useless. A little while later, Minis announced that he had detected the fault and to the mission's delight he was then able to get the set going. The battery was too weak, but this was overcome by attaching the charger directly to the set and while one of the team wound in the power directly, another would send the message. Although this technique burnt fuse after fuse, they were able to tap out two morse messages in quick succession. The first informed SOE Cairo about the TIBBENHAM advance party, and the next that German troops had arrived in Kalamata.

Shortly afterwards Yannis Frangos, the Secretary of the EAM of Kalamata, appeared unannounced in the small hours at their head-quarters, or what passed as their headquarters at the time, for it was in fact a hut, the previous occupants of which had been a small flock of sheep. Wand-Tetley:

> In appearance he was undersized, with a large close-cropped head and features which gave him an unmistakable resemblance to a monkey. In spite of this he possessed a certain dignity, enhanced by a clear, soft voice in which he spoke in an almost unemotional tone – a contrast to the conversational technique of most Greeks. His manners were perfect and his smile charming, but his almost colourless eyes never altered their expression.

Having established his credentials, Reid explained to Frangos that the mission's business was to train and arm andarte groups regardless of their political persuasion, and to provide strategic military direction from GHQ Middle East. For his part Frangos informed the mission that there were only some 150 andartes in the Peloponnese, and that they were poorly armed and equipped. He also gave them his assurance that they could count on him and EAM to support the mission's endeavours, and that he supported the mission's non-partisan approach to advising and arming all andarte groups, regardless of creed, that would take the fight to the common enemy.

SOE Cairo was immediately informed of the meeting with Frangos and this was followed up with a request for a drop of rifles and boots with which to equip and arm the guerrillas. Having received confirma-tion from SOE Cairo that they would send a sortie to a drop-point near Avlon, one of a number of pre-selected points, Wand-Tetley changed into civilian clothes and shaved off his beard in an unsuccessful attempt to pass unnoticed by the locals, and set off to receive the sortie.

However, events did not unfold as smoothly as they might have done. By the time Wand-Tetley arrived at the sortie point he had been joined by an andarte group led by a young regular officer, more professional-looking than the first group the mission had come across. Together they awaited the drop, and were disappointed that boots were not amongst the items. However, forty Italian rifles were dropped although they were not in a fit state for immediate action, for it would take some effort to rid them of their grease. Grenades, clothing and tinned rations were also received, although unfortunately one container broke up upon impact, scattering bacon and sugar across the hillside.

The Italians, their suspicions aroused by the sound of the aircraft, despatched a patrol to investigate first thing the following morning, but this had been anticipated and Wand-Tetley and the andartes had worked through the night to clear away the evidence of the sortie and hide their newly-acquired stores before themselves going to ground. The enemy patrol passed close to their hiding place, but without noticing Wand-Tetley or the andartes.

Reid arrived on the scene two days later, bringing the W/T set with him. They established their headquarters on the top of a hill, close to the village of Platania. Frangos departed at this stage, promising to return if he was called upon, but before doing so he had been persuaded, under some pressure from Reid, to introduce the mission to the overall ELAS commander of the area, Major Vassilis Strategis. Wand-Tetley:

> Strategis was an old man with a kind heart, very little brain and a reputation for courage in action. In spite of his stupidity and a tendency to heroics both Bill and I developed a curious affection for him and were genuinely sorry when, after being relieved of his command by ELAS, he and his son were arrested by the Germans and shot as hostages in Tripolis.

Shortly after establishing their base at Platania, the mission became increasingly aware of the political rivalry between the various andarte groups. It became evident that, despite his assurances to the contrary, Frangos had every intention of denying other andarte groups access to the mission. When Reid discovered that Strategis had prevented a delegation of EOA officers from approaching their headquarters, he threatened to relocate to Taigetos.

After heated debate Strategis eventually climbed down, assuring Reid that it would not happen again although insisting, for security reasons, upon the right to prevent 'dangerous elements' from approaching the mission. Nonetheless, they learnt later that EAM/ELAS had contrived to block the majority of delegations apart from their own, although at a far greater distance so that the mission would not come to hear of it. When the mission did meet the local EOA/ES commander they were not impressed. Wand-Tetley:

> Captain Harahalias was weak and vacillating and his political out-look was as narrow as that of his opponents. His case, omitting his general abuse of the 'Communists' was that his organization, while not as highly organized as EAM/ELAS, was strongly supported in the neighbourhood. He insisted that his andartes, if we formed them, would act solely under our orders and independently of any political organization.

When Reid requested SOE Cairo to confirm the policy with regard to the support of different andarte factions, he was informed that the mission's task was a military one and that they should act impartially and without regard to political colour. Accordingly, Reid announced his decision to arm equal numbers of andartes on both sides of the political divide. This appeared acceptable to the hierarchy of both EOA and EAM/ELAS, and an agreement was drawn up which was signed by the respective commanders.

The Peloponnese agreement was established in advance of the National Bands Agreement drawn up in July by Myers (known by Wand-Tetley's mission as the Agreement of the North), but in all respects the two agreements were essentially the same. A joint headquarters was established, presided over by the mission, which was under the command of GHQ Middle East. Prospective guerrillas were to be allowed to choose freely within which andarte faction to enlist, and the mission undertook to contribute one gold sovereign per month towards the cost of food for every andarte on the ration roll. With all in agreement, the mission hoped that it would be relatively plain sailing thereafter. They were to be disappointed.

While the agreement was being brokered, Colonel Giorgiou, a representative of EDES, presented himself at the mission headquarters. He had with him a letter of introduction purporting to be from Woodhouse requesting that he be afforded every assistance. Giorgiou explained that his remit in the Peloponnese was to organize EDES andarte units. With this in mind he had already commenced the evacuation of the families of his officers from the towns. This he had initially financed with money supplied by Minis, but he went on to explain that, in order to complete the operation and pay the evacuated families suitable allowances, he would require considerably more funds. When asked to confirm the suspiciously generous allowance scales, SOE Cairo did not corroborate Giorgiou's story, so the mission cheerfully sent the colonel on his way to try his luck elsewhere.

With the Peloponnese agreement signed, the mission set about organizing and equipping their andarte units. The aim was to establish twelve bands, six of EAM/ELAS and six of EOA, each band consisting of one officer with two sections of twelve men, thus producing a total of 300 men. The bands were to be armed initially with light machine guns (LMGs), sub-machine guns (SMGs) and rifles, but it was hoped that, later, they would expand the establishment to include specialists in demolitions, visual signalling and mortars. The mission was impatient to proceed with this work. Wand-Tetley:

> In our enthusiasm the allowance of one or two sorties a month seemed pathetically inadequate and we criticized bitterly the quality of the weapons sent in to us. Demanding Mauser rifles, Beretta sub-machine guns and German MG 15s we were disappointed to receive Italian rifles, Stens and Breda LMGs. At the time we felt

strongly that in view of the small number of sorties possible the equipment should be of the highest quality and exactly balanced to fit our establishment: later we remembered with satisfaction the amount of bloodshed averted by the failure to meet our requests.

Wand-Tetley supervised the reception of the sorties, but was powerless to prevent the pilfering of stores by the andartes. Initially, the mission had been somewhat perplexed that the theft continued when the andarte commanders had made it clear to their men to desist under pain of death. However, it became clear that such orders were purely for the benefit of the BLOs, and that their men had secretly been ordered to continue with the pilfering. Although Wand-Tetley had reassured the commanders of both EAM/ELAS and EOA/ES that they would benefit equally from the sorties, each endeavoured to gain an advantage over the other. EAM/ELAS appeared to be in the lead by squirrelling away routinely 25 per cent of the stores, until EOA/ES were able to come from behind and even things up by securing 80 per cent of the stores on the final sortie.

For some time Reid had endeavoured to secure the services of a senior Greek officer to assume overall command of the various andarte groups, so as to leave him and his BLOs to focus on the business of liaison with GHQ Middle East. It seemed that this might have been achieved with the arrival of Colonel Papadopoulos, a much-respected officer devoid of political ambition, who had secured an enviable reputation during his tenure in command of a Cretan battalion in Albania. However, despite his best efforts, he was unable to achieve any degree of accord between the andarte groups, and one morning the mission found Papadopoulos gone. He had left a note saying that his task was an impossible one, that conflict was unavoidable, and he had no desire to remain and see the inevitable bloodletting.

One evening as Reid and Wand-Tetley were looking out over the village of Pavlitsa from the vantage point on their escarpment they heard an aircraft approach. To their astonishment they saw a number of beacon fires being lit in the vicinity of the village. Wand-Tetley immediately set off with a group of ELAS andartes to investigate. They tracked down the three men responsible for lighting the fires to the house of the local priest, and then marched them back to their headquarters on the escarpment to be questioned. The leader of the three was Captain Theodopoulos, who maintained that he represented EKKA and had come from Athens to receive sorties pre-arranged by Cairo. Reid hauled him over the coals for endeavouring to receive sorties without having the courtesy of first checking in with his mission, then signalled SOE Cairo to verify the story, which appeared to the mission to be particularly dubious. Their suspicions were confirmed. However, despite this it appeared to the mission that Theodopoulos had, un-wittingly perhaps, acted in good faith. Wand-Tetley:

> Further light was thrown on this incident when Theodopoulos was later murdered by ELAS and a document found on his body, addressed to Major Reid and signed by the Chief of Staff of EKKA, was delivered without comment by Strategis. The letter began, 'In obedience to repeated urgent instructions from GHQ Cairo we specify the following areas in Peloponnese as suitable for secret sortie of arms'. This was an example, one of many, of the way in which all right wing organizations did their best to compromise us with EAM/ELAS, and also gives an indication of their careless assumption that BLOs had been charged with the duty of arming them against 'the Communists'.

In the interim Reid warned Theodopoulos that under no circum-stances was he to attempt to receive any further sorties, but that the mission would consider the matter of arming EKKA andartes following discussion with his immediate commander, Major Kokkonis. By this stage the mission had established a guard of thirty Cretans to protect their headquarters, the W/T set, and the dropping zone. With this security in place, andarte bands were despatched to reconnoitre possible lines-of-communications targets, railway lines and roads. However, the respective bands used the opportunity to visit the local villages, and both sides engaged in an unbridled exhibition of rabble-rousing and provocative speechmaking in an attempt to win the villagers over to their respective causes. Meanwhile the mission was entertained on a daily basis with the accusations and exaggerations of both sides concerning the unacceptable behaviour of the other. Wand-Tetley:

> Finally a clash occurred involving a fatal casualty. There ensued a violent quarrel between Harahalias and Strategis, the former drawing his revolver while the latter bared his breast to receive the bullet. The combined headquarters was disrupted, ELAS moving to Avlon while the EOA remained at Platania. The Mission, apprehensive of a German drive developing from the South and not wishing to establish itself in either camp withdrew across the Neda to the village of Stomion.

One day, on returning to his headquarters from investigating the latest clash between ELAS and EOA andarte bands, Wand-Tetley found Reid in civilian clothes preparing for a trip. At this stage, notwithstanding the continuing clashes, the mission was hopeful that oil might be poured on troubled waters, for EAM/ELAS and EOA had both signified their willingness to sign the Agreement of the North. It was hoped that this would serve to reinforce the earlier Peloponnese

Agreement, which was in danger of breaking down altogether. The text of the agreement had yet to arrive, but Reid had received an urgent summons from Major John Harington and was planning on travelling alone, leaving Wand-Tetley to manage the headquarters and W/T set assisted by the guard of thirty Cretans.

Having heard disturbing rumours of trouble brewing, Wand-Tetley called a conference at the mission's headquarters at Platania for 6 August, but after waiting some time it became clear that neither Strategis nor Kokkonis, who had shifted allegiance and was now in command of EOA, intended to turn up. He was then informed that a strong force of ELAS were crossing the Neda gorge to the south and that EOA had taken up a defensive position on the high ground above Platania. Wand-Tetley estimated that each side had in the region of 250 men under arms, although he was also aware that ELAS also had a number of undeclared andartes that they had endeavoured to conceal from the mission.

After weighing up the situation Wand-Tetley set off, accompanied by an interpreter, in a final bid to call a truce between the two opposing factions. However, his party lost time in following poor directions from a villager and, before they were able to close with the andartes, he heard the sound of heavy firing. Although his first thought was to hurry on and attempt to impose a ceasefire, he realized this would probably prove futile, and knew that his first responsibility was the defence of the headquarters and W/T set, so he quickly retraced his steps and upon his arrival hastily organized the Cretans into defensive positions, ready to protect the headquarters from attack and capture.

The fighting continued throughout the afternoon and as night was falling Kokkonis and a small band of EOA andartes arrived at the headquarters. Kokkonis confirmed that ELAS had marched upon their positions and attacked them, and that now he had come to make his final stand at the mission headquarters. While Wand-Tetley was dressing Kokonnis's wounded arm he firmly disabused him of any such notion, making it clear that although the Cretans and he had every intention of defending his headquarters he could not take sides with either faction in their political dispute. Although the EOA wounded could stay and seek protection, on no account were EOA to take any part in the defence of his headquarters. Kokkonis did not take this well, and hung around despondent for an hour before disappearing with his men. He was not seen again until some eight months later, when he came to light as a commander of a Security Battalion in Pyrgos.

That evening Wand-Tetley reassessed his position for he realized that he was significantly outnumbered and his tactical position was parlous in the extreme. Wand-Tetley:

The O.C. Cretan band was confident that ELAS would raid us during the night or early the following morning, and the air was full of rumours of their intention to seize the [W/T] set and massacre every member of the headquarters. I came to the conclusion that to retain the band would not serve any useful purpose and might only result in useless bloodshed. I therefore instructed them to make for Major Harington's HQ at Dyrakion and to place themselves under his orders. At the same time I sent Yannis, with the W/T set and the gold, into hiding some distance away.

The anticipated attack by ELAS did not come, but the following day a stream of refugees flowed into the headquarters professing to be victims of the earlier clash. Strategis finally arrived at the mission the next day and attempted to persuade Wand-Tetley that EOA had fired upon him and his andartes while they had been walking harmlessly up a hill. It did not wash. Strategis then attempted to convince Reid, who had just returned, theatrically throwing his dagger at his feet as a token of acquiescence. Reid was unmoved and told Strategis that he'd better pick it up quickly otherwise one of his own andartes would be sure to pilfer it.

Of much more concern to the Mission was the unsavoury character accompanying Strategis, a certain 'Orion', whom SOE Cairo had warned was likely to arrive on the scene. This man professed to have been sent to the Peloponnese by ELAS headquarters on the mainland, although he could produce no identification and it appeared his only military qualification was that of reserve second lieutenant. Wand-Tetley:

> This man, bearded and dressed like a brigand in a comic opera, had apparently taken over command from Strategis. He made no secret of his intention to move the whole force, supplemented by others armed with the recently captured weapons, to attack Col Yannacopoulos [of EOA/ES] with Major Harington at Dyrakion. He showed little interest when Bill, in the name of humanity, commonsense and GHQ Middle East, ordered him to desist. Strategis, refusing to accompany him, remained behind with fifty men.

It was clear that EAM/ELAS were intent upon snuffing out all opposition, and that Reid and Wand-Tetley's efforts to mediate were falling increasingly on deaf ears. For the next few days they remained at Stomion and waited to hear news of the anticipated clash at Dyrakion. While waiting, a pre-war friend of Reid during his time in Athens, George Photiades, arrived at their headquarters. He had received word of the mission's presence from EAM, whom Reid had asked to pass a message announcing the mission's presence. Photiades was lucky to be alive, for Megalopolis EAM had mistaken his name with one of their hierarchy and, in a message of their own, had referred to him as 'one of us'. EOA had intercepted the message and had despatched an assassin to deal with him. Fortunately Photiades arrived at the mission a day ahead of his assassin; the two later became firm friends. Photiades was to prove himself not only a true and loyal friend to Reid and Wand-Tetley, but also to become a highly valued and politically impartial member of the mission. Wand-Tetley:

> His personality, organizing ability, knowledge of languages and considerable intellectual gifts became an invaluable asset to us during the difficult and dangerous period which followed the civil war and the suppression of freedom by EAM.

Although the arrival of Photiades was most welcome, the recent andarte clashes had not gone unobserved by the enemy and had drawn dangerous attention to the mission. Wand-Tetley:

> On the day of his [Photiades] arrival the Germans, hearing news of our troubles, sent a thousand men on a punitive expedition to Platania and Avlon. We accordingly moved north to Minthi, the highest feature in the area, and set up our headquarters on the Campus Milias.

The andartes had still not reappeared by September and the mission realized that there was now little hope of achieving their original aim as the andarte factions were totally engrossed in eliminating one another rather than taking the fight to the common and occupying enemy. Reid and Wand-Tetley recognized that a different approach was required, that direct military action must be replaced by diplomacy, and the various missions across Greece would need to take particular care to be consistent in their approach lest they were played off against each other by the differing factions. Under the circumstances it made little sense to continue with the sorties to arm and equip the andartes.

They sought SOE Cairo's guidance and also requested updates on events in Taigetos but, much to their frustration, they received little in the way of direction and received the distinct impression that Cairo was even in some way disappointed in their failure to prevent civil war. Morale was further undermined when they caught malaria. Their frustration was compounded by their inability to bring andarte military action to bear to undermine further Italian morale, which was now on the wane. Instead they assisted the poorest of the villagers affected by recent andarte clashes. By this stage EAM/ELAS had declared martial law, enforced by executions and floggings, but attempted to justify their actions to the mission with increasingly less convincing stories of the actions of their 'traitorous' opponents.

When, one day, Wand-Tetley and Reid were sitting on their mountain top at Campus Milias they received news from a runner that Strategis was making his way towards their headquarters. When he arrived he was in good heart and with a flourish produced a piece of paper – the Agreement of Dyrakion – which he went on to explain was a peace treaty between the Peloponnese andarte factions. He then produced a second piece of paper, this being a letter signed by Yannacopoulos, of EOA/ES but purporting to be commander of all andartes in southern Peloponnese, requesting that Cairo commence regular sorties once again. The list of arms and stores was optimistic in the extreme and included requests for mountain artillery pieces (suitable for mule transportation) and a number of field telephone exchanges.

Upon brief examination it was obvious that the Agreement of Dyrakion had been signed under duress. Wand-Tetley:

> Before he had read half the new agreement Bill was bristling with indignation. By the time he had absorbed the significance of a clause briefly stating 'the duty of a British Liaison Officer is to liaise' I began to fear that a sudden stroke would rob the Mission of its leader.

The agreement stipulated that andartes could from now on only be recruited by ELAS and that although ES could continue temporarily, in due course it must be absorbed by ELAS, at which stage its members would be vetted to purge any 'Fascist' elements. It went on to suggest that Yannacopoulos would have military command of andartes in southern Peloponnese, but that he was answerable to an EAM-appointed commander, political officer and supplies officer. Wand-Tetley:

> We were by this time well acquainted with the ELAS technique of 'persuading' trained officers to join their ranks. This policy had its origin partly in an attempt to support their contention of national support, partly in an honest endeavour to fill their desperate need for competent military leadership and partly in a firm resolve to draw the teeth of any prospective opposition. In practice no attempt was made to conceal the fact that the military commander was subordinate to the political officer, who received his orders from sources he was seldom willing to disclose.

Reid then took the wind out of the sails of Strategis by reminding him that they were all still bound by the Agreement of the North, and since the Agreement of Dyrakion clearly contravened the democratically espoused principles in respect of all andarte groups, the new agreement could not be recognized. He went on to stress that under the circumstances he could not recommend that sorties recommence and the matter would be referred to Cairo for consideration.

The mission was applying the letter of the law as far as SOE instructions were concerned, which stipulated that only andartes working to the Agreement of the North would be supported by GHQ Middle East by receiving payment of gold sovereigns and equipment. Expecting to receive encouragement and endorsement of their firm stance on the matter, they were disappointed to receive little in the way of acknowledgement of their situation. Indeed, Cairo authorized an additional payment of sovereigns for the purchase of winter food. Their position was made all the more difficult when it became clear that sorties were continuing to be flown to northern Peloponnese, and EAM accused the mission of intransigence motivated by BLO political prejudices.

Strategis departed the mission headquarters frustrated and convinced of BLO duplicity, taking with him all his andartes. Although this left the mission vulnerable to attack it also provided them with freedom of movement, of which they were quick to take advantage. Over the space of a week Photiades had visited all the villages in the region and set in place the fundamentals of an intelligence network, which in itself provided security for the mission. By similar token those who wished to visit the BLO headquarters could now do so without hindrance from EAM/ELAS.

The villagers were puzzled as to why the andartes had departed leaving the BLO headquarters without a guard, and were initially unable to reconcile the mission's version of events with that of EAM/ELAS. Accordingly, Reid and Wand-Tetley made available the copies of the two conflicting agreements and invited the locals to come to their own conclusions. The evidence was inescapable. The villagers then implored the mission to raise and lead its own band of andartes, to which Reid and Wand-Tetley had to explain that they did not have GHQ Middle East authority to do so.

In late September the mission's intelligence network brought word that the Germans had been busy on the road to the north of the mission. Trucks had been spotted with radio direction finding (RDF) equipment, and although Reid and Wand-Tetley suspected that their headquarters was the focus of the enemy's attention they felt quietly confident of being able to elude any German drive to capture them. However, the threat was to present itself in a slightly different guise. Wand-Tetley:

A day or two later a Henschel recce plane circled over the area for two hours during our contact with Cairo, but to our eternal shame we disregarded this final warning. The following day as if in answer to Yannis's call sign, it appeared again flying low over the hilltop and opened fire on our solitary hut. The only casualty was a hen wounded in the leg but the damage to our morale was considerable. As soon as dusk fell we loaded our mules and beat an undignified retreat to Garditsa.

Having established themselves at Garditsa it was not long before the BLOs heard news of attempts to create independent andarte bands in Elia. This was reported to SOE Cairo, and Wand-Tetley was despatched to visit Colonel Pareskevopoulos in the vicinity of Olympia. He immediately set off for the village of Platanos, taking with him Petros, a Greek W/T set operator. Conscious that EAM/ELAS would attempt to thwart any attempt to make contact with rival andarte group-ings Wand-Tetley explained, whenever asked, that he was travelling to meet another BLO to discuss the matter of andarte supplies. After a long march he thus reached Platanos where he met Major Harahalias, who had with him in the region of 100 andartes, and was just about to set off to Monastiraki. Without resting, Wand-Tetley and Petros set off on another long march north with the andartes. By the time they reached the hill overlooking Monastiraki both men were weak with fatigue.

Here they met Captain Vretakos, commander of the Taigetos EOA/ES bands, who had with him a further 250 andartes. Wand-Tetley was now brought up to date with the situation. Harahalias had succeeded Pareskevopoulos, who had had second thoughts about the life of a guerrilla and had returned home. Yannacopoulos, the ES commander, whom Frangos had placed in command of all andartes in southern Peloponnese at the time of the signing of the Agreement of Dyrakion, had now disappeared under suspicious circumstances. Thus Vretakos, fearing a similar fate, had moved quickly into Elia territory, where he and his andartes hoped to receive sufficient British assistance to establish a defence strong enough to fight off any ELAS attempt to snuff them out.

Wand-Tetley and Petros were still at Monastiraki the following night. They sat shivering in the cold rain, wondering when they would next benefit from a decent meal, a luxury they had not enjoyed since departing Gardista on their forced march a couple of days previously. The arrival of Major Antony Andrewes and Lance Corporal W. A. Hill with W/T set 'Scimitar' interrupted their deliberations on the emptiness of their stomachs. They learnt that Colonel Stevens' advice that these bands be supported had been received favourably by SOE Cairo, and that four loads of equipment and arms would be despatched if Vretakos and his andartes were attacked by ELAS.

The sound of rifle-fire the next day heralded this eventuality. ELAS had moved close to the ES camp and engaged in sporadic skirmishes and sniping throughout the day. The decision was taken to move south-east to Pirgaki with all possible speed, and the BLOs arranged with SOE

Cairo to send the emergency consignments to that destination. During the forced march to Pirgaki an event occurred which ELAS would later use as the basis to assert through propaganda that Vretakos was in fact a collaborator. Wand-Tetley:

Our route lay close to a German W/T Station guarded by about twenty-five men. By altering our course we could have avoided this point but in view of the exhausted condition of the men and the necessity for speed in reaching the dropping area it was agreed to continue along the main road. Vretakos visited the Station, according to ELAS, for the purpose of communicating with German HQ in Tripolis. By his own account he went to invite their surrender and when they refused he considered that the certainty of reprisals made the use of force inadvisable. We therefore marched past while the Germans watched our progress from the balcony of their house. It was a strange experience.

Having arrived at their destination, for the next two days they remained at Pirgaki, bad weather making it unfeasible for sorties from Cairo to deliver the much-needed equipment to the mission and their EOA/ES bands. Then, very early on the morning of the third day, an andarte ran into their room proclaiming excitedly that a force of Germans had just entered the village. Wand-Tetley:

Andrewes and I dashed to the window to see a dozen German trucks drawn up on the road which, though it is not shown on the map, runs two hundred feet below Pirgaki. We moved, hastily and indecorously, carrying our wireless and leaving the rest of our equipment to be concealed by villagers. We suffered no casualties though a few bullets whistled round our posteriors before we finally reached the safety of a large pine forest south of the village.

Wand-Tetley and Andrewes remained in hiding close to Pirgaki until early afternoon, at which stage the Germans left the village having discovered nothing of interest. The villagers then came out to return their equipment to them, which they had had the presence of mind to hide in a beehive. A couple of hours later the two SOE agents were holding a council of war with Harahalias and Vretakos when they were abruptly interrupted. Wand-Tetley:

Suddenly, without warning, a mortar bomb landed uncomfortably close. It was followed immediately by others. A moment later our mules were bucking and rearing and shedding their loads, and we were beating our second retreat of the day with whatever we could salvage in the general disorder. Our first impression, of course,

135

was that the Hun was trying to blast us out of the forest, but this was soon corrected by a report that a force of fifteen hundred ELAS Andartes was hard on our tail.

The men were on the march all night. By dawn they had reached the southern edge of a vast forest and, taking account of the speed at which they had made good their escape, they felt quietly confident that they had a few hours' lead on the pursuing ELAS andartes. Andrewes decided that it was worth going back alone to parley with Stasinopoulos, the ELAS leader they believed to be leading the pursuit, in an effort to call a truce and avert any unnecessary bloodshed. He also wished to see if he could find the W/T operator, Hill, who had become separated during the hasty withdrawal of the previous day.

Wand-Tetley remained with the main force of ES andartes and had in his care the W/T set 'Scimitar'. They had with them two batteries which Petros had managed to rescue at the start of their retreat, not without considerable risk to his own safety. However, the charging engine was no longer with them, the mule in whose panniers it had resided having stampeded when the first of the mortar-bombs had landed amongst them the previous day. Wand-Tetley estimated that they would only have contact with Cairo for a further three or four days unless it could be tracked down.

In discussion with Wand-Tetley, Vretakos proposed that they should make for Petrina in south Taigetos. Given that this was his home territory he felt confident that they stood a good chance of making it, fighting their way through if necessary, and then standing their ground at Petrina until emergency supplies arrived. Accordingly SOE Cairo was signalled and requested to divert the sorties to the new drop-zone. They made it without significant drama, by which stage the andartes had been on their feet marching for a fortnight; their boots had mostly worn through and rations and sleep had been scarce in the extreme, yet their morale was still high.

Their belief in the EOA/ES cause was unwavering. Furthermore they had every confidence that the British would soon deliver the promised supplies and that they would shortly be in a position to fend off any attack by ELAS. Thus it was with a sense of complete despair that they heard an 'all stations call' from SOE Cairo that all sorties had been suspended on account of civil war breaking out on the mainland. Wand-Tetley maintained a degree of hope that Cairo would continue to treat them as an exception, given that sorties had been suspended for some time on the Peloponnese and they were due to receive emergency supplies. Regardless, Wand-Tetley's last W/T battery was now as good as dead, and he knew that he must maintain contact with SOE Cairo if there was to be any hope of achieving this, so he and Petros ran the gauntlet of travelling to Harington's headquarters, hoping that their former good relations with Frangos would see them safely through.

Having safely reached Harington and discussed the situation with him, they decided to pay a visit to Frangos, whose headquarters was some thirty minutes away. Both were well received, Frangos being unaware that Wand-Tetley had recently been consorting with the 'enemy', as he would have perceived it. Frangos then proceeded to read out loud a report from one of his 'trusted agents' working in the Pirgaki region. In essence the account maintained that Vretakos had captured a BLO and had subsequently held a lengthy meeting over dinner with a senior German commander, after which he had received a significant cache of arms and ammunition. At the end of the narration Wand-Tetley declared the account to be largely a work of fiction, declaring that the BLO in question was undoubtedly Andrewes or himself and that since he had, on orders of GHQ Middle East, accompanied Vretakos ever since Elia he could vouch that the 'trusted agent' was a long way wide of the mark.

Frangos maintained his composure remarkably well under the circumstances and stated that although he trusted Wand-Tetley, Vretakos was nonetheless a malevolent force who was clearly in league with the Germans, and was furthermore also guilty of leading Harahalias astray. Keen to clear Vretakos's name, Wand-Tetley then put it to Frangos that he should allow Vretakos the opportunity of conducting a fighting operation against the Germans. If Vretakos was really in collaboration with the Germans then he would no doubt find an excuse to avoid such an action, but if he were innocent of treachery then there should be no reason for him not to take the fight to the Germans, in the process of which he would inevitably risk his own neck and those of his andartes. He went on to stress that this would almost certainly leave ES weaker in both men and equipment, and so could in no way damage ELAS. However, Frangos was not going to allow Vretakos the benefit of the doubt, for after a few minutes' consideration he rejected the proposal and declared that, in order to guarantee their safety, the ES bands must hand over their weapons to ELAS. Wand-Tetley:

> I had no doubt what such a guarantee, from the author of the Agreement of Dyrakion, was worth. In that moment I understood something of the quality of the man whose assurances of support Bill and I had accepted with such good faith six months before. I realized, too, how under the mask of friendship he had plotted step by step the downfall of our ambitions. How he must have laughed to himself at our childish enthusiasm! Here was the most dangerous type of fanatic; a man who looked on their present suffering as merely a line in the history of his people; a man who could order

137

the destruction of thousands of his own countrymen without the faintest sensation of pity, anger or even sadistic pleasure; a man whose motives are best left to the judgement of posterity.

Wand-Tetley realized that further discussion would achieve nothing, and so he departed for Petrina assuring Frangos that he would pass on the ultimatum to Vretakos as soon as possible. Much to his surprise he was thanked for his help and assured of safe passage. The following day at Vretakos' headquarters he recounted his meeting and also broke the bad news that in his and Harington's opinion it seemed certain that GHQ Middle East would conduct no further sorties.

This was a blow of the cruellest kind, and Harahalias vented his frustration in a fervent tirade concerning the duplicitous nature of the British, but Vretakos quietly calmed him and then proceeded to thank Wand-Tetley for his endeavours to do the right thing by them, before magnanimously surmising that if GHQ Middle East had taken such a decision then it would no doubt prove the right one and to be in the long-term interests of Greece. Wand-Tetley:

> A moment later the rattle of machine guns and the whine of bullets about our ears told us that ELAS had arrived for the slaughter. In the battle that followed the two leaders [Vretakos and Harahalias] and their men fought with inspired courage. One unit, recovering quickly from its surprise, drove the attackers from a point of vantage above the village. Another, armed mainly with antiquated Mannlichers, came out to meet the advancing ELAS in a charge. Vretakos cantered everywhere on a white horse, encouraging his men. Within an hour the ELAS were retreating in confusion leaving fourteen dead, and a number of wounded out of a total of about two-hundred-and-fifty. The ES, now reduced to the same number, had lost two men killed.

With the battle over they discussed their next move. Vretakos decided he would exploit success by taking a force of andartes and attacking Frangos' headquarters at Dyrakion, before proceeding to Manhi in southern Taigetos. Harahalias, whose leg had been wounded during the battle, decided he would make for Elia with a small force. Wand-Tetley set off in advance of both of them to apprise Harington of the plan. At Neohori Vretakos learnt that ELAS forces had for the most part already fled from Dyrakion, and by the time his andartes arrived there even Frangos' rearguard had departed.

While at Dyrakion Wand-Tetley considered the options open to him. He still had no working W/T set of his own. In view of the manner that Vretakos had been let down by the cancellation of British sorties, he felt obliged to provide what moral support he could, but if he were to accompany Vretakos he would be without communication. Harington then received a communication from SOE Cairo which settled the matter. Wand-Tetley:

A message from Cairo informing us of Hubbard's[31] murder had been followed by another [message] instructing us to 'sit on the fence and smile at all insults'. Harington's comment on this signal was typical of the patience and humour of one who had suffered more indignities than most in the cause of Andarte unity: 'I have sat on the fence for so long that the iron has entered into my soul and my smile is therefore somewhat ironic'. Harington considered that this [second signal] should definitely be interpreted as an order not to proceed.

When Wand-Tetley discussed the matter with Vretakos, the latter made it clear that he would not have countenanced the BLO accompanying him in any case, which served finally to put his mind at rest. This did not make the parting any easier. When Vretakos quietly and modestly took his leave, nobody was under any illusions about what likely fate faced him. Wand-Tetley:

As he shook hands and saluted for the last time we knew we were watching the departure of a man whose best hope was a quick death and we reflected bitterly on our share in the responsibility for it.

Several weeks later Wand-Tetley received reports that confirmed their fears. Vretakos and his andartes never reached their destination of Manhi in southern Taigetos. A significantly superior ELAS force contrived to block their way. Vretakos chose to make his last stand just east of Kalamata. Most of his men died in battle, but apart from a very few who contrived to escape, the remainder were executed by ELAS immediately afterwards. Vretakos himself was wounded in the chest during the battle, taken prisoner and died under torture, refusing to speak or look his persecutors in the eyes.

Harahalias met a similar unpleasant fate. En route to Elia his men had come across an ELAS reserve unit. Disguising themselves with ELAS berets they managed to enter their lines before opening fire upon them, killing twelve in the process, but Harahalias was later caught, and Frangos decided to put him on a show trial. This rapidly descended to farce, particularly when the key witness, having recounted Harahalias' instructions to his ES andartes, was then incapable of pointing him out in court. The court was adjourned, but in the interim Harahalias was knifed while in custody. The lawyer who had travelled from Megalopolis to defend him was similarly executed.

Wand-Tetley remained troubled by SOE Cairo's policy with regard to the Vretakos episode. Having been encouraged to form a counter-weight to ELAS hegemony, Vretakos was left high and dry in his moment of greatest need. It is moot whether his ES andarte force could have held its own against ELAS indefinitely, but if GHQ Middle East had continued with their sorties it is entirely likely that reinforcements would have been recruited and, with equipment and arms forth-coming, some semblance of balance of power achieved. Wand-Tetley:

> It is impossible to understand the allowance of four sorties: Vretakos should have been supported fully or not at all. Of one thing I am certain. If the movement had failed in spite of sorties more than one BLO would have paid for it with his life.

When Frangos and his men returned to Dyrakion they were incensed to learn the extent to which the villagers had played host to the ES andartes. Their fury was not restricted to the villagers, and it was debated hotly that the mission members should be taken prisoner and their headquarters burnt to the ground. This course was discarded, but ELAS subjected all to an intimidating programme of political indoctrination that included Wand-Tetley and Petros within the target audience. ELAS andartes forced their way into the mission headquarters, confiscated arms and ammunition and threatened the severest of sanctions against anyone who stepped out of line. Wand-Tetley:

> Frangos refused to consider my departure for Garditsa and advised me with venomous politeness, 'in the interests of my own safety' not to leave the Headquarters. As we were still bound by Cairo's wish to avoid incidents involving casualties to BLOs there was no choice but to obey.

Relations remained very fraught for the next week, with Wand-Tetley kept under armed house arrest. He then received a signal from Stevens telling him to return to Reid regardless of EAM/ELAS permission. Sensing the situation had by now calmed sufficiently to comply with this directive, he and Petros set off for Garditsa. Here they found EAM, assuming their deaths to have been a forgone conclusion, in the process of issuing propaganda reports of their demise and of their 'collabora-tion with the Germans'.

On his arrival at Garditsa Wand-Tetley was informed by Reid that he had just blown the Neda Bridge. By this stage sorties delivering clothing and explosives had once again commenced, so Reid had had no qualms in requesting that ELAS provide him with a covering guard of twenty-five men for the operation. The promised men had duly arrived at his headquarters on the day of the sabotage. Much to his indignation he discovered that eighteen of them were Italian deserters, whom he dismissed immediately. He then departed with the remaining six andartes, laid his charges, successfully blew the bridge, and managed to destroy a railway engine and a number of coaches which crashed into the river following the explosion.

ELAS was suitably impressed by the damage and decided to form a sabotage section of its own. The Germans, working flat out around the clock, managed to repair the bridge in eighteen days, so ELAS decided they would go back and endeavour to repeat Reid's success. However, they failed to seek Reid's professional expertise. The result was that instead of carefully positioning the explosive where it would have maximum cutting effect, they piled it up in the middle of the tracks. The result was an impressive enough explosion but little damage was caused to the bridge itself. Nonetheless, the Germans were far from amused and a senior commander was despatched to investigate. He pronounced that while the first explosion was obviously the work of professional military saboteurs, the second attempt must have been the work of local villagers given the amateurish approach. Thus ELAS were responsible for the several villages that the Germans then burnt by way of reprisal.

Reid and Wand-Tetley discussed what further might be done besides intelligence collection, given that their original task of persuading the andartes to fight the Germans had been thwarted by internal Greek politics. Following this debate, Reid set in place an extensive 'hearts and minds' operation[32] focused upon the nursing mothers and young children of the local villages. In this work, which was designed to bring relief to the daily hardship of their lives, he was assisted most ably by Photiades. Nonetheless, they encountered unforeseen frustrations, for even this charitable work was subjected to EAM sabotage. Having failed to secure control of the relief programme, for which they hoped to gain the credit, they then attempted to undermine it and to discredit the mission. This was compounded by the persistent quarrelling of the village committees that had been set up to help distribute the aid. It was with some satisfaction, therefore, for the BLOs to hear that in one village the women had attacked an EAM official who had attempted to denigrate their work.

While Reid and Photiades focused on the relief work, Wand-Tetley, accompanied by Petros, set off in November to visit Stevens at Demestika and meet Lieutenant Colonel Peter McMullen, who had been dropped in Akhaia some months previously. Wand-Tetley:

> To save time we changed into civilian clothes and chartered a bus at Andritsana to take us as far as Dara. I think neither of us enjoyed that journey very much, particularly when we were deposited on the road in sight of a German garrison while the bus went into

141

Megalopolis to get petrol, but we arrived intact in spite of the usual series of mechanical breakdowns.

Despite the dangers, the change of scene and chance to meet again with other BLOs was welcome. Stevens was able to inform him that, given the opportunity offered by the capture of the Taranto naval base, it was likely that sea operations would commence shortly from the west coast of Reid and Wand-Tetley's area. He confirmed that their policy of 'distant politeness' to ELAS should continue, and he also endorsed Reid's proposal that a 'bribe for ELAS' should be paid for every sortie of stores otherwise intended exclusively for the mission's relief work. With their visit complete they returned to Garditsa, but found ELAS up to their usual tricks. Wand-Tetley:

> On our way back we were arrested by two members of Col Stevens' 'guard' who knew very well who we were. We were taken to ELAS HQ at Skepaston (I.6. 9261) before being released by Mikhos, after I had caused a scene by refusing to accept ELAS passes (on orders from Col Stevens) and instructing Petros not to answer any questions put to him by the ELAS committee. We returned to Dara to find our bus in one of its obstinate moods and were compelled to make half the journey with a man sitting on one of the mudguards feeding petrol into the engine from a tin held between his knees.

Upon his return Wand-Tetley discussed his visit with Reid. It was decided that while Reid and Photiades focused upon the 'hearts and minds' relief scheme, Wand-Tetley would concentrate his efforts upon the forthcoming sea operations. The first of these was to be the evacuation by submarine of McMullen and ten others, due to occur at the end of December. Accordingly Wand-Tetley set off for Zakharo, the coastal embarkation point, to conduct a reconnaissance. Here he met Athenassy Carambotsos who became an indispensable assistant to the mission. Wand-Tetley:

> We were successful in our task of nursing, feeding billeting and finally evacuating large parties of many nationalities. Athenassy can be said to have been very largely responsible. He unfailingly produced food, quarters, mules or runners in every circumstance of difficulty and every degree of danger. There is good reason to believe that for his many services to the Allied cause ELAS eventually cut his throat.

The winter weather conspired against the success of the first sea operation in late December. Although in the first few days the conditions were reasonable enough, the submarine was forced by engine trouble to return to port. By the time it returned on its second attempt a north-westerly gale had blown up. Wand-Tetley lit the signal fires and the submarine, which turned out to be an Italian 'co-belligerent', answered appropriately. On that stretch of coast there were no suitable small Greek boats available for use and so the submarine's rubber dinghies had to be used. On board there were two British officers and one of these, Sub-Lieutenant Roberts RN, attempted to come ashore in one of the dinghies. Almost immediately after leaving the submarine he very nearly drowned when his dinghy capsized in the heavy swell, but he managed to swim ashore some two miles farther down the coastline.

When Roberts met Wand-Tetley they decided that, given the ferocity of the storm, it would be best to delay the operation until the following night, but before they could make this intention known to the submarine a morse signal was flashed to them that it had gone aground. This was followed by a second signal that the crew would have to abandon ship. A further rubber dinghy was launched and this one, with Lieutenant Jeffrey RN and an Italian officer aboard, managed to make the shore. They brought news that the submarine had stuck fast on a sandbank. Under cover of darkness half of the crew of forty-five managed to make it ashore in the submarine's remaining rubber dinghies. However, it was impossible to make the outward journey against the driving swell of the waves against the shore, and come the dawn half the crew was still on the submarine. Wand-Tetley despatched those who had already come ashore up into the mountains with a guide, while he and Koukoulakos remained behind to encourage those still on board to swim ashore. There was still a very heavy swell, and it became clear that they preferred to run the risk of capture by the Germans than to take their chances swimming ashore. However, by mid-morning the storm had blown itself out, and all finally took the plunge and swam ashore safely. Fortunately the Germans failed to notice the submarine for several days, despite a plane flying over the scene at no more than 2,000 feet. Wand-Tetley:

> We therefore had time to salvage a few of the small important articles, such as the chronometer, the sextant and a jar of rum.

Wand-Tetley now had the awkward task of ensuring that the submarine could not be floated off the sandbank by the Germans. The Italian captain showed him where in the magazine the explosive was kept, but would not let him light the fuse for fear that they would not reach the shore before the submarine blew up. So Wand-Tetley went back later and placed the 50lbs of explosive against the control room hull but was thwarted when, in attempting to ignite the explosive with two time pencils[33], the flash would not ignite the slow-burning fuse. His next attempt proved successful. Wand-Tetley:

Later, as all the dinghies had been damaged by EAM attempts to salvage the heavier armament, Eric and I swam out with time pencils, Bickfords detonators and a small charge of '808' sealed in strips torn from an anti-gas cape[34]. This ignited the heavier charge, which blew a hole in the double hull and flooded the submarine.

Wand-Tetley then directed the local authorities to protect themselves from later reprisals by informing the Germans of the submarine's existence, suggesting that they should relate that the storm had blown it ashore during what they presumed to be a routine shore patrol.

The coastal village of Marathopolis was chosen as the location for the next sea operation. This had the advantage of providing access to numerous fishing boats as well as being afforded a degree of protection from the worst of the winter weather by the offshore island of Proti. However, it was not without risk, for nearby at Filiatra there was an enemy Radio Direction Finding (RDF) station and the village could also be approached by road, thus enabling the Germans to arrive on the scene quickly if their suspicions were aroused. The evacuation by destroyer of the original party as well as the crew of the submarine went without incident, but as Wand-Tetley and his team were leaving the village by lorry with their stores they saw ahead of them a convoy of German troops. Fortunately their quick-witted driver saw the Germans first and swerved off the road onto a side track and out of sight before being noticed. The German trucks they had seen were carrying an advance guard, for Filiatra was occupied a few days later. There the enemy learned of the evacuation operation, and Wand-Tetley therefore returned to Kaiafa.

By early 1944 Reid and Wand-Tetley were having increasingly less to do with EAM/ELAS. Although ELAS had by now organized itself into battalions and brigades, it was evident to the mission that the andartes would provide little by way of military support to the Allied cause, and they communicated this assessment to SOE Cairo. Wand-Tetley:

> This was plainly shown in their [ELAS] disinclination to assist in any operation against the Germans, and it was sometimes even admitted, in moments of confidence, that their real mission was to oppose the return of a reactionary government. On the few occasions when they had ambushed a convoy or fired at a patrol it was obvious that their intention was merely to secure arms and ammunition, and perhaps to invite reprisals against the villages on the theory that suffering induces a revolutionary spirit amongst the people.

Nonetheless, at this stage the mission had under its command a small band of twenty-five ELAS andartes. Reid had insisted upon an officer of moderate political views to command the band and for the most part there was little trouble, although pilfering remained a habitual pastime. On one occasion the andarte supplies officer broke into their stores, having been refused the key by Reid, and made away with the equipment and clothing intended for Wand-Tetley's evacuees. For his troubles he was tried and sentenced to two years' imprisonment.

EAM maintained outwardly civil relations with the mission, although they never ceased their covert attempts to undermine BLO endeavours. Nor did they let up on their efforts to persuade the mission to supply them with arms and ammunition. To this end they employed the ruse of coercing village committees to appeal, in person and with seemingly official documents, to the mission, requesting sorties from GHQ Middle East in the interests of liberating their country. The village committees, once formed, invariably contained the village priest to lend an air of authority and an EAM member, often ill-disguised, to ensure the committee carried out its purpose. Although generally wearisome, such deputations occasionally had a lighter side. Wand-Tetley:

> Comic relief was sometimes provided when a member, having made a long emotional speech on this theme, drew George [Photiades] aside and hurriedly whispered 'for God's sake don't give them anything'. The strain was intense, but the EAM finally had to abandon the scheme when after three weeks Bill's nerve had outlasted the number of villages.

In February Wand-Tetley was on the coast at Xirohori, this time to evacuate twenty American airmen who had been involved in a flying accident over northern Peloponnese, but had survived the crash landing. It was evident that they were all badly shaken by their ordeal, especially the rear gunner who, isolated from the remainder of the crew, had rapidly dropped 20,000 feet in the aircraft's tail – a disconcerting experience he had not anticipated walking away from. Having reached the mission headquarters, the BLOs had not found the aircrew to be the easiest of guests, so it was with some relief that they were now finally being despatched. Arriving early at the embarkation point, they were in turns taking the opportunity to catch up on some sleep before their destroyer's arrival, but were interrupted. Wand-Tetley:

> I was awoken by the sound of heavy gunfire. From the hillside I could see a furious naval battle in progress so close inshore that some of the shells were landing in the woods behind our pin point. When four ships were set on fire and began exploding violently I decided to send the American party farther away from the pin point, in view of the probability that a German patrol would be sent down the coast to look for survivors.

Fortunately the Germans did not react as anticipated and the survivors from the naval conflict came ashore farther south, close to the Neda Bridge, so the precaution proved unwarranted. In spite of the naval battle and to their relief, the destroyer arrived the following night as originally planned. Wand-Tetley went down to the beach to liaise with the Italian captain, who was astonished to hear of the previous night's battle over the very spot where his destroyer now lay. A little while later, in bright moonlight and therefore not without considerable risk, the captain evacuated the American airmen.

For the most part the evacuation operations continued smoothly. Photiades was evacuated in the early spring, for it became clear to the mission that he would otherwise become a victim of his own success – quite literally – for owing to his growing influence in the area he had become a thorn in the side of EAM, and it increasingly became evident that he was soon going to meet with an 'accident'. On occasion traffic occurred both ways; thus Captain E. C. Dunne and Second Lieutenant K. Harding were infiltrated on one operation. Wand-Tetley:

> Dunne and Harding had a cheering welcome to Greece when the Hun attacked Garditsa the day after their arrival there. The Huns' marksmanship was poor, however, for they missed everyone at a hundred yards. Only Koukoulakos – a little man with great courage – was wounded, and he escaped.

In their frustration, the Germans proceeded to put Garditsa to the torch, and made it quite clear that the villagers should hold the British agents responsible for the reprisals. The enemy then stepped up their efforts to capture the SOE agents. Wand-Tetley:

> During April and May German drives kept us very much on the hop. These invariably had our pin point as their ultimate goal, but never seemed quite to coincide with our operations. In the end we became a little contemptuous of their efforts to catch us and would sit watching them from the hillside while they occupied the village below. We acquired confidence in the inherent skill of the Greek villager in supplying the enemy with misleading information and we knew that members of the Security Battalions who accompanied these drives considered themselves our allies.

At one stage Wand-Tetley had on his hands sixty Russian POWs waiting to be evacuated. All had previously served with ELAS but held andarte fighting qualities in contempt. Twelve of these men had been serving in an ELAS company when attacked by Germans one night. The Russians soon found themselves to be the only ones in the fight, for the andartes had all fled, but the twelve Russians were nonetheless able to drive off the Germans and only fell back themselves when strong

146

German reinforcements were called up. The Russians never let the andartes forget this incident, and Wand-Tetley took a degree of pleasure in quartering them in a village known to be sympathetic towards EAM, where the POWs quarrelled vociferously with everyone.

In the late spring of 1944 Reid's three-man team left the Peloponnese for Italy. Wand-Tetley:

> In May I handed over to Captain [H.] Pickering and was sent to Major [D. L.] Campbell's HQ to become liaison officer to a party of OSS after the proposed evacuation of the majority of the missions in June. At the last moment it was decided to evacuate the OSS as well and that I was to leave with them. Bill, Yannis and I therefore returned together, exactly fourteen months after we had startled the village of Nasia by our unexpected descent.

On 4 July 1943, shortly after they first established communications with Cairo, Wand-Tetley and Reid were both recommended by SOE for Immediate MCs. Given SOE's covert nature and the fact that the mission was still in the field operating behind enemy lines, the citations, which were signed by SOE Cairo's Chief of Staff, Keble, were annotated 'Most Secret'. Gazetted the following month, on 26 August, Wand-Tetley's citation was released only after the end of the war. By the end of 1943, following a strong recommendation by Reid, he had also been promoted to captain.

PART 3

Part 3 to this chapter focuses primarily upon the Greek Civil War, but also covers Wand-Tetley's assignment in Turkey.

Descent to Greek Civil War

Following the large-scale departure of SOE and OSS agents from the Peloponnese in June 1944, just a few BLOs remained, each assisted by a Greek agent and W/T operator. Major A. Andrewes based his party at Akhaia, Captain E. W. Gray at Patras, Captain D. J. Gibson at Kalamata, while Captain H. Pickering remained in the south-west and continued the naval reception work which Wand-Tetley had initiated.[35]

For the most part their work continued to concentrate on the collection of intelligence, while Andrewes also continued with the subversion of the two Fortress Battalions, work that Campbell had initiated at the beginning of that year. This task was conducted through the auspices of an Austrian communist deserter, and was made possible after the BLOs discovered that a strong anti-Nazi organization existed in two of the battalions of the 41st Fortress Division.[36]

The experience of the British missions in the Peloponnese had not been a happy one. The BLOs there had been treated by EAM/ELAS with a vicious opposition unparalleled in the somewhat pleasanter atmosphere of northern Greece. Nonetheless their experience, as with the missions in the north, was largely characterized by the remorseless slide into civil war that had commenced a year earlier and that had resonated throughout the entire country. By the summer of 1943 SOE Cairo had successfully expanded throughout Greece and, besides the missions in the Peloponnese, had established headquarters in West Thessaly, Mount Olympus, Macedonia, West Roumeli, East Roumeli, and Parnassus, as well as two in Epirus.

Prior to the SOE presence in the Peloponnese, EAM/ELAS had considered it a relative backwater and treated it accordingly, but as soon as British field agents had arrived on the ground and they had become aware of Allied interest, EAM/ELAS had set about rapidly expanding their operations. With the determined approach already demonstrated in northern Greece they increased their presence in the Peloponnese. To speed the process Ares had despatched from northern Greece one of his most trusted and ruthless lieutenants with a force of 100 andartes. Arriving in July 1943 he and his band had immediately set about orchestrating the systematic takeover of the EOA and ES competition, by force of arms where necessary.[37]

Nonetheless, the countrywide wave of sabotage and chaos inflicted against the enemy's lines of communications throughout Greece in Operation ANIMALS during June and July of 1943 was entirely success-ful. Forty-four significant operations were conducted against the road and rail communications of Greece, of which thirty-two were against main roads. Ambushes were sprung against enemy convoys and trains, bridges blown, telephone lines cut, and a good many miscellaneous acts of sabotage took place across the country. In the Piraeus docks a five-day transport workers' strike was also staged. The majority of this destruction occurred in northern Greece, for in the Peloponnese, and to a lesser extent in Eastern Roumeli, EAM/ELAS were more interested in liquidating rival andarte bands than fighting the common enemy. Sabotage continued until 11 July, when Myers was directed by SOE Cairo to cease activities, for Sicily had been invaded successfully the previous day. The operational aim was achieved and the enemy deceived into believing an Allied attack against the Balkans was imminent. Furthermore, the secret had been well kept, for the andartes were also similarly convinced. The operation undoubtedly contributed to the success of the invasion and capture of Sicily, and even after the Sicily landings Hitler was certain that the Allies were planning an invasion of Western Greece and the Peloponnese. Between May and August 1943 the Germans increased their strength across the Balkans from eight to sixteen divisions.[38]

The situation on the wider Mediterranean stage had developed rapidly. The Allies had landed in Sicily on 10 July 1943 in Operation HUSKY. By 17 August all Axis forces had left the island for mainland Italy and the Allies entered Messina. Faced with defeat, the Italian Fascist Grand Council arrested Mussolini and a new government under Marshal Badoglio began to make friendly overtures to the Allies. Sensing this might happen the Germans moved troops to northern Italy under the command of Rommel to shore up their defences, Kesselring remaining as Commander-in-Chief South at Rome. The subsequent main landing on Italy was at Salerno on 9 September, complemented by a subsidiary landing at Taranto on the same day, although Eighth Army had landed at Reggio on 3 September. The Italian armistice with the Allies was signed on 8 September.

Meanwhile in Greece on 9 August, shortly after formation of the JGHQ, Myers and six delegates from the National Bands, accompanied by Wallace from the Foreign Office, had flown to Cairo from a newly-constructed airstrip to meet the King of the Hellenes and his government-in-exile. Hamson also departed Greece with this very first flight – a Dakota with long-range tanks fitted – carrying Myers and the delegation to Cairo. Four of the delegates were from EAM/ELAS (Andreas Tzimas, Petros Roussos, Costas Despotopoulos and Ilias Tsirimokos), and one each from EDES (Komninos Pyromaglou) and EKKA (George Kartalis). The communists had a different vision for the future of Greece than did the republicans. Nonetheless, regardless of differences, all six of them felt that they represented better the political future of Greece than the King of the Hellenes and his government-in-exile, with whom they were due to meet. From the outset the conference was ill-fated.[39]

Antipathy between SOE Cairo and the Foreign Office reached an all-time low during the delegation to Cairo and Reginald 'Rex' Leeper, Ambassador to the Greek government-in-exile in Cairo, became quite vitriolic concerning Myers, whom he considered to be meddling in political affairs. It would not be the first, nor the last, time that the bearer of an unpopular intelligence assessment suffered as a consequence. The situation had been exacerbated by the rapid expansion of missions in Greece, Yugoslavia and Albania, for MO4 had found itself in an uphill struggle to maintain the required numbers of Cairo support staff.

In fact Leeper represented an extreme Foreign Office view, but nonetheless was instrumental in ensuring that Myers did not return to Greece. Myers found himself in an invidious position and was forced to depart for London to clarify the situation with his SOE superiors and Churchill and, with relations becoming increasingly fractious, King George II of the Hellenes also insisted that Myers was not to be

149

allowed to return to Greece. Accordingly, Myers' second-in-command, Woodhouse, took his place. However, at this stage there was at least some good news for Myers because Sweet-Escott's sister, Lutie, who worked as secretary to Guy Tamplin in SOE Cairo, accepted his marriage proposal.

It was perhaps not surprising that SOE Cairo would inevitably become the scapegoat in trying to balance the conflicting short-term military imperatives of GHQ Middle East and the long-term political imperatives of the Foreign Office. The shock waves created by the andarte delegation did not stop there though. Leeper ensured that, in future, SOE Cairo referred any matter that might have political ramifications to the Foreign Office, and instigated a further purge in SOE Cairo that appeared now to have become an annual August event. Lord Glenconner, head of SOE Cairo, felt compelled to resign and was replaced by Major General Billy Stawell, a Sapper and former Deputy Director of Military Intelligence at the War Office, with Brigadier Karl Barker-Benfield, highly decorated in the First World War with a DSO and Bar and MC, being placed in charge of the Balkans, which in turn was placed formally under the military control of 'Jumbo' Wilson. The formidable chief of staff, Keble, was removed finally from post and reassigned to regular army duties and Tamplin, also due to be removed, died of a heart attack. Moreover, in Baker Street, the replacement of Sir Charles Hambro with Major General Sir Colin Gubbins as CD in September was not entirely unconnected with events in Cairo.[40]

A month later than scheduled – on the night of 16/17 September – the delegates flew back in a Dakota to their airstrip in Greece, having achieved little but disharmony. Also on board were Peltekis (a.k.a. Apollo), Colonel Bakirdzis (the 'Red Colonel'), and the first two American OSS agents, Captain Winston Ehrgott and Lieutenant Bob Ford, their presence heralding the change in nomenclature for the mission from BMM to AMM. In fact, events over the summer months had convinced EAM/ELAS that now was the time to make a concerted bid for power and eliminate their rivals once and for all. The civil war that had been simmering came rapidly to the boil in October. Until this point the communists had kept up steady military pressure against their rivals – EOA and ES had been attacked in the Peloponnese following the invasion of Sicily, and PAO had been liquidated in Macedonia – but now they launched a general civil war across the country.[41]

At the end of the first week of October EAM/ELAS launched attacks against EDES in Thessaly, and in the Peloponnese attacks against EOA and ES were stepped up. By the end of the second week attacks by the communists against rival guerrilla groups had spread right across Greece although EKKA managed to maintain its neutrality. In the chaos

Lieutenant Arthur Hubbard, a New Zealand SOE officer, was shot by EAM/ELAS andartes as they were clearing the village of Triklinos of Zervas's men – an event that led to questions in the House of Commons. Rival members of JGHQ were arrested and, apart from the AMM component, the JGHQ became one and the same as the ELAS GHQ. By 13 October, the day that Italy declared war on Germany, there was no doubt that the communists were more intent upon destroying their andarte rivals than they were the Germans. Despite this, the National Bands Agreement was never dissolved formally, nor did EAM/ELAS ever suggest that they were not working under the direction of GHQ Middle East. In the Peloponnese EOA and ES had sided with EDES and EKKA in August when EAM/ELAS had initiated their takeover bid. However, the result was inevitable and in October the communists secured control. Nevertheless, EAM/ELAS and their KKE masters had miscalculated the intent of the Germans, who were quick to take advantage of the civil war and the divided country. Just as it had seemed to them that the Germans would leave Greece, the *Heer* turned upon the communist forces and, in the face of a professional regular force, EAM/ELAS were mauled and chased back into their mountain retreats. The Germans then proceeded to fill the positions that the Italians had previously held and systematically began to reoccupy the Aegean Islands.[42]

In the chaos of this 'First Round' of the Greek Civil War the Security Battalions, which had been formed in the summer of 1943 by the third of Greece's collaborating Prime Ministers, Ioannis Rallis, gained in respectability. Deployed to quell the civil war, they were active and particularly popular in the Peloponnese, where their anti-communist stance earned them many recruits. Given the political leanings of the majority of those in the Peloponnese, EAM/ELAS had engaged in a more ruthless regime of arrests and murders than in northern Greece. It is perhaps not surprising that the first Security Battalion raised there came under the command of Vretakos, the brother of the leader of the EOA/ES bands, whom EAM had murdered. Vengeance was no doubt a consideration, and the Security Battalions were soon to become numerically superior to ELAS in the Peloponnese, growing to a strength of 10,000 soldiers by August 1943. To many Greeks concern over being ostensibly a collaborator appeared the lesser of evils compared with the threat of communist hegemony. And to many enrolment in a Security Battalion appeared a more effective means of fighting communism than taking to the mountains and joining a rival andarte band.

When the civil war had started in October, SOE Cairo had considered pulling the AMM out of Greece, but the area commanders had advised that their position was still tenable despite the very obvious risk to its agents of liquidation. The civil war had stirred up a hornets' nest and the ALOs frequently found themselves on the run, the risk to their lives posed by the andartes being probably greater than that from the Germans. Nonetheless they pointed out that if they were evacuated there would be no means left to maintain contact with, or supply, any resistance movement, and that the risks were therefore worth taking. EAM/ELAS had shown their true communist colours and failed in their objective, although they would not acknowledge this until December. By coming close to destroying their rivals they had also now weakened Greece's potential for resistance against German occupation, and the communists were denounced by increasing numbers of their fellow countrymen and by the Allies. Such discredit also served to play into the hands of King George II and his government-in-exile. The BMM's approach of supporting all andarte resistance groups was vindicated. Without such counterbalances in place the KKE-backed EAM/ELAS would undoubtedly have succeeded in absorbing or destroying all rival political and andarte groups. The BMM had by now stopped supplying EAM/ELAS with arms, although given their cache of Italian weaponry this had had limited effect. A small pocket of EDES under Zervas, supported by British air supply drops, had managed to survive in Epirus, and EKKA had managed to survive by maintaining its neutrality. EAM/ELAS had little choice but to ask for a truce and under the circumstances the BMM had to appeal for unity and refocus the resistance movements against the German occupation.

Thus, in the six critical months between the spring and autumn of 1943, the BMM's policy with regards to supporting andarte groups – based on a pragmatic assessment of military rather than political considerations – experienced a pendulum-like swing. In the spring Zervas and EDES were held in clear favour by Myers. By the summer EAM/ELAS had achieved relative balance with EDES. However, by autumn the communists had shot their bolt well and truly, and the pendulum had swung back to its starting position with EDES once again held in clear favour. SOE Cairo's approach was nothing if not consistent and impartial, for during the same period in Yugoslavia the military potential of Tito's communist partisans had, from late May, been recognized and nurtured by Captain Bill Deakin, whose Rumanian wife Pussy Nasta also worked for SOE, and, from September, by Brigadier Fitzroy Maclean. SOE thus reversed its policy, and now favoured Tito and his National Liberation Army over Mihailoviæ and his Četniks. This meant that by the autumn of 1943, within the same Balkan theatre, the Allies favoured the Yugoslav communists, but not their comrades in Greece. From a strategic perspective Churchill was also clear that, with the Sicily landings over, Yugoslavia was now more important than Greece, and this was reflected in his personal selection of and interest in Maclean – his man on the ground in Yugoslavia – who had enjoyed a meteoric rise from lieutenant to brigadier in the space of two years.[43]

Operation NOAH'S ARK

Meanwhile in January 1944, with Eisenhower and Montgomery now back in Britain to prepare for the invasion of Normandy, the Allies resumed their efforts to advance in Italy. As a result, by the beginning of 1944 SOE was able to acquire an airfield at Brindisi, in the heel of Italy, which in terms of distance was an improvement over the Protville airfield outside Tunis which they had been given by AFHQ in the summer of 1943. However, the position was not as straightforward as it might have seemed for agents destined for the Balkans still required to be briefed by the respective Country Section staff in Rustum Buildings, Cairo. They would then fly on to Italy where they would be equipped by Force 333, the SOE supplies base south of Bari, before travelling down the coast to Brindisi, from where they would fly out on their various missions.

Stawell, who had recently succeeded Glenconner at SOE Cairo, which had been operating under the cover name of Force 133 since the previous November, had only limited previous experience of special operations. To assist him in interpreting the myriad of relationships existing between the various secret organizations in the Middle East, and the political machinations of Baker Street, Sweet-Escott was appointed as his liaison officer. By this stage a replacement for John Stevens as head of the Greek Section had been found in the shape of a Grenadier Guardsman, Colonel Vincent Budge. SOE was now firmly on the map and well known to the authorities in every theatre of war, and it had some eighty distinct missions operating across the Balkans alone.[44]

In Greece much of January 1944 was taken up by efforts on the part of the AMM and the exiled Greek Government to persuade the rival andarte groups to come to the negotiating table. EAM/ELAS and EDES both prevaricated and manoeuvred for position. The civil war had, effectively, put paid to the National Bands Agreement and to the JGHQ. It was also clear that, although for the time being EAM/ELAS had been thwarted, their ambition for political and military hegemony remained. In this respect it is of note that a month earlier EAM had suggested to Zervas that he should swap sides and offered him the appointment of C-in-C of ELAS. Unlike Sarafis he declined. In February the rival groups, represented by Sarafis for EAM/ELAS, Pyromaglou for EDES and Psaros and Kartalis for EKKA, came to an armistice conference at Plaka Bridge – an elegant Turkish span over the River Arakhthos – in Epirus. Woodhouse, who had succeeded Myers, and Major Gerry Wines, his American OSS second-in-command, had trouble focusing Greek minds on fighting the German occupation and on Operation

NOAH'S ARK – the andarte attacks being planned against German forces during their anticipated withdrawal from Greece, for all parties were more concerned with the political ramifications of any agreement reached. Little was therefore agreed at the conference, which came to a conclusion at the end of February, but the 'Plaka Agreement' did at least serve to prolong the armistice, with EAM/ELAS agreeing that if Zervas confined his andartes to the southern Pindus they would leave him unmolested. The agreement marked the end of the 'First Round' of the Greek Civil War.[45]

In their violent bid for power KKE had well and truly unmasked EAM/ELAS, and the true nature of the communist threat was clear to all Greek political players at the beginning of 1944, if it had not been before. It became increasingly apparent to the population, both at home and in exile, that the old political choice between Monarchist and Republican had been replaced with the stark choice of either supporting communism or not. Increasingly, Greek republican democrats were swayed more by the fear of communist rule than they were by the King's return. Such a choice was reinforced by the spread of communism and communist-inspired revolution across the Balkans, in Albania, Yugoslavia and Bulgaria. Indeed, a Soviet Republic of Macedonia was a real enough aspiration for Russia but could only be achieved by sacrificing the national territories of Greece, Yugoslavia and, in some part, Albania and Bulgaria.

With an increasingly wary Greek population, the KKE still had the two tools of political infiltration and armed violence available to further the communist cause. Although ELAS's old andarte adversaries had been neutralized or diminished in size, those that had survived had become tougher, and the Security Battalions still presented them with a considerable military threat. It was also clear that EAM was a spent political force, and a new political front was required by the communists. This was launched at the end of March in the shape of the Political Committee of Greek Resistance (PEEA). Timing was all important, the intention being to profit from the political vacuum created by the anticipated withdrawal in April of the Germans and liberation by the Allies. However, the liberation did not materialize as expected, and the assessment proved premature. Destined to fail, it nonetheless provoked instability and more bloodshed. Tsouderos' resignation was demanded by a group of republican Greek naval officers, culminating in a mutiny on 6 April within the Greek armed forces in the Middle East. This served to force the King's hand and, having arrived in Cairo from London on 11 April, he declared that the constitutional issue would be shelved until after the liberation of Greece. Two days later Tsouderos resigned and was replaced by Sophocles Venizelos, son of the First World War Prime Minister.

In mid-April a conference had been called by Woodhouse and Wines at Koutsaina, Thessaly, in an attempt to placate the rival andarte groups. Uppermost was the desire to persuade the andarte rivals to cooperate with one another, and with groups of the British Raiding Support Regiment (RSR) – a commando unit armed with heavy weapons – which was due to make landings during NOAH'S ARK, with the aim of stiffening the andartes and harassing the retreating German forces. However, the conference proved too late to prevent EAM/ELAS from destroying EKKA. On 17 April Psaros and 400 of his andartes were surrounded, captured and disarmed. Immediately afterwards Ares and his andarte death squads conducted a mass execution of their EKKA rivals by machine gun. At Koutsaina the only point agreed upon by the andartes was to allow the RSR Groups a free hand during NOAH'S ARK. Given the deteriorating situation, SOE Cairo once again asked Woodhouse and Wines whether the AMM should be evacuated, for Churchill was concerned that the AMM members might be taken as andarte hostages. Once again Woodhouse responded that the missions should remain, stressing that the situation would deteriorate further if the missions departed and left EAM/ELAS an entirely free hand.[46]

Nonetheless, following the Koutsaina Conference Woodhouse and Wines were withdrawn and replaced by Hammond and a new American on the scene, Colonel West. Meanwhile, at the end of April, George Papandreou succeeded Venizelos, who had assumed the reins from Tsouderos for only two weeks, and at the Lebanon Conference of 17 to 20 May restored a semblance of unity in the Greek Government, all the pre-war political parties being represented. However, it was clear that PEEA, and EAM/ELAS were still set on their original track, for they had refused to participate at the conference.[47]

By mid-April 1944 a new forward headquarters called Special Operations Mediterranean (SOM) had been set up at Bari, an old Crusader port, following a decision earlier in the year by the Chiefs of Staff in London to place SOE Yugoslavian and Albanian operations under command of AFHQ Algiers. Stawell was appointed Commander SOM, and the SOE Yugoslavian and Albanian country sections were moved from Cairo to Bari as Force 266 (later Force 299). For technical reasons, concerning the 'skip' phenomenon by which W/T short-wave morse code messages bounced between earth and ionosphere creating zones of good and poor reception, the SOE main wireless station headquarters remained in Cairo, and messages regarding Yugoslavia and Albania were relayed through Cairo to Bari. The location of SOM also proved to be convenient and closer to 'Jumbo' Wilson, who had succeeded Eisenhower as Allied Supreme Commander Mediterranean, and who had moved the AFHQ from Algiers to Caserta Palace, near Naples. It was now also possible for SOE couriers to operate out of Bari

155

by submarine and boat to the west coast of northern Greece and the Peloponnese. Moreover, in January No. 148 Squadron had moved from Derna in Libya to Brindisi in Italy, where it operated alongside the other special duties squadrons, No. 624 Squadron and the Polish 1586 Flight, thus greatly reducing the flying distance to Greece. With Stawell now in Italy, Brigadier K. V. Barker-Benfield assumed command of Force 133 and its Greek Section, which remained in Rustum Buildings, Cairo, along with the Arab world and Persia section and, for the time being, the country sections for Bulgaria, Hungary and Rumania. This suited General Sir Bernard Paget, the new C-in-C Middle East, who was keen to retain at least some influence in SOE operations. Needless to say at this stage Force 133 was to find its life becoming increasingly complex, for before making any decision it now had to satisfy an increasing number of masters including AFHQ Caserta, SOM Bari and GHQ Middle East in Cairo, as well as London.[48]

From May 1944 Hammond and West focused primarily upon ensuring that the andarte bands would honour their agreement of facilitating free passage and assistance to the RSR Groups, which would have to be infiltrated through both EDES and EAM/ELAS territory. The Peloponnese continued to be problematic from an AMM command and control perspective, and for the most part Stevens and his successor McMullen, remained independent and were forced to continue to deal direct with SOE Cairo. Shortly after conducting the EKKA massacre, Ares had crossed to the Peloponnese and he and his andartes placed the missions there under considerable pressure and in an increasingly precarious position. So much effort was expended in negotiating and endeavouring to keep EAM/ELAS on track – for its sole aim was in liquidating its rivals and the Security Battalions – that it became almost impossible for the Peloponnese missions to achieve the primary objective of taking the fight to the enemy. Consequently, as highlighted previously, Wand-Tetley's team found that intelligence gathering (ordinarily the remit of MI6) had become increasingly its primary function.

Assignment in Turkey
Having been evacuated from the Peloponnese to Italy in June 1944 and following his debriefing, Wand-Tetley took some very well-earned leave. On the larger world stage this was also a most auspicious month, for in Italy on 5 June Rome was liberated by the Allies, and in France on 6 June British, Canadian and American armies launched the greatest amphibious landing ever, in Operation OVERLORD, the battle for Normandy and the liberation of Europe. A month or so later Wand-Tetley was despatched on his next SOE assignment and was infiltrated by caique to Smyrna, on the west coast of Turkey. Arriving in August, he was to remain there for the next three months.[49]

156

SOE operations in Turkey were coordinated by Gardyne de Chastelain, a leading light in pre-war Rumania, from his offices within the old British Embassy in Istanbul; the British Ambassador, Sir Hughe Knatchbull-Hugessen, being housed in the new embassy in the capital Ankara. Churchill, in particular, maintained a very close interest in neutral Turkey and never gave up hope that she would eventually come in to the war on the Allied side. The British were acutely conscious of Germany's economic interests in the country, particularly chrome, but while Turkey remained neutral, and as long as Germany did not invade, the Foreign Office remained adamant that SOE should refrain from sabotage. Apart from a couple of 'unauthorized' operations, SOE's focus was therefore primarily with the infiltration of agents into and out of the Balkan countries, and with schemes for sabotage of Axis equipment within Turkey in the event that Germany did invade the country. For many of its maritime activities SOE used the 'Shipping Department' as a front and in particular the Goeland Shipping Company, and, although the company was eventually penetrated by German intelligence, SOE escaped detection and overall proved successful in its many enterprises.

Smyrna, the port to which Wand-Tetley was despatched, featured significantly in operations, and SOE had maintained a presence there ever since the fall of Greece. It was to this port on the west coast of Turkey that a steady flow of Allied escaped prisoners of war were evacuated from the east coast of Greece. Once in Smyrna the evacuees would be disembarked and rested before being moved on yet again, often to Cairo via Cyprus. A fleet of caiques, known as the Levant Fishing Patrol, operated out of the port of Famagusta, Cyprus, to conduct such work, and also to complement the SOE airdrops to Greece with surface ship supply runs. Responsible for running this fleet was a character in his fifties known as 'Skipper' Pool who, earlier in the war, had won a DSO for evacuating some 200 Allied servicemen hiding in the mountains following the fall of Crete. Although Turkey was neutral it was generally the case that as long as the Allies kept their activities relatively quiet the Turkish secret police were, for the most part, content enough to look the other way. However, this is not to say that Turkey made things straightforward for the Allies, or any side for that matter, and she exercised her prerogative to be consistently unpredictable sufficiently to keep SOE on its toes. Nonetheless, as the war progressed and the German armies retreated towards the Carpathians, the influence the Allies could bring to bear increased, and by early 1944 Turkey's neutrality certainly favoured the Allied cause.[50]

Recruited by the 'Apostles' before the fall of Crete, Gherassimos, a pre-war smuggler, who went by the codename of 'Odysseus', played a significant role in supporting SOE's Aegean caique work. Having first come to prominence during his time at SOE's sabotage school on Suda Island off Crete, he set about establishing a network of safe havens for caiques across the Aegean. In the aftermath of the fall of Crete SOE temporarily lost contact with him, but managed to re-establish it within a few months. Having made his way up to Smyrna, Odysseus sailed from the port in early November 1941 for the Greek mainland, and successfully supplied Prometheus with replacement W/T codes that had been lost in the evacuation. As a result the much celebrated W/T 'Set 333' came on air on 20 November and was to stay in contact with SOE Cairo until Prometheus II and his W/T operator were captured in a RDF operation by the Germans in February 1943.[51]

It was not only the SOE who had a base in Smyrna for MI9, whose official remit was to evacuate escaped prisoners of war, were also, not surprisingly, well represented. Caique traffic on the return trip to Greece would invariably head for a covert harbour established on the coast of Thessaly north of Skopelos. However, quite where the delineation of duties between SOE and MI9 started and finished was not always that clear to either party, although field agents from both worked well together regardless. Both organizations would also rub shoulders habitually with the SBS and the Greek Sacred Squadron, who both plied their violent trade around the Aegean islands, the former raiding north of Leros and the latter operating south of Leros. By this stage the Levant Schooner Flotilla, which ferried the raiding forces between the islands, was overtly collecting its supplies from the port of Bodrum (ancient Harlicanassus and hometown of Herodotus), and using Turkey's coast-line as secure anchorages for its base ships without undue concern from neutral Turkey.

The SOE base, which was run by Alan Paton, was some fifty miles west of and two hours away from Smyrna, at the port of Egrilar on the Chesme peninsula. A shadow of its pre-war self, Egrilar was none-theless a cheerful enough bay, with its waterfront bars and brothels blasting forth their loud music. The ubiquitous caique offered the Allied secret and clandestine organizations a degree of anonymity as they went about their business. However, these local schooners were also converted regularly by Germans into patrol boats, so one could never be too careful. Accordingly SOE spent a good deal of time, effort and money in endeavouring to corner the market and deny the caiques to the Germans, by encouraging their Greek captains to sail out of German-controlled waters and instead harbour in British-held ports. A further cause for extreme caution was that Smyrna, like Istanbul and Ankara, was also a hotbed for Intelligence agencies of all persuasions. Beside those of the Allies and the neutral countries, one could be sure that the *Abwehr*, responsible for German military intelligence and counter-intelligence, and the *Sicherheitsdienst* (SD), the SS's Security Service, would both be in the vicinity.[52]

On 9 November 1944, his tour of duty complete, Wand-Tetley sailed out of Smyrna by caique and returned to Cairo, where for the next month he was an SOE conducting officer with East Mediterranean Group. Most junior SOE officers were required to take their turn at this post whose responsibilities consisted of ensuring that SOE field agents were prepared properly for their mission, received the appropriate briefings, were correctly kitted out, and were despatched on schedule. Finding the work too sedentary for his taste, and envying those that he was despatching into the field, the following month he applied for a more active operational assignment. Interviewed on 6 December by Lieutenant Colonel Oldham, Wand-Tetley made clear that he would, in order of preference, wish to be employed on operations in any theatre, with the SOE, SBS or any other special force. At the time it seemed that there might be an opportunity in Australia, and he was considered with several other volunteers, but this possibility would not transpire.[53]

Greek Liberation
Meanwhile in Greece a party of several Russians, headed by Colonel Grigori Popov, had arrived unannounced at the Neraidha airstrip from Bari at the end of July, breaking an earlier agreement with the Allies that they would not send a mission to Greece. Since SOE Cairo had imposed sanctions upon ELAS and was not delivering the andartes any supplies, Siantos hoped that the Russian party might be more forthcoming. This was not to be the case, and the Russian party eventually departed having proved to be somewhat of a disappointment to PEEA and ELAS. By August Siantos realized that he had reached an impasse and that, if he and the communists were to remain influential and take any credit for the imminent liberation of Greece, it would be wise for him to ensure that they had representation within Papandreou's Government of National Unity, and to ensure that ELAS took an active part in NOAH'S ARK. It was at this stage, at the end of August and following a fortnight's visit from Barker-Benfield, that Hammond handed over command of the AMM to Edmonds and flew out of the Neraidha airstrip to the SOM at Bari.[54]

Greek liberation was to come finally in mid-October 1944, in Operation MANNA, although the last German soldiers would not leave Macedonia until 1 November and the islands would for the most part remain in German hands for several more months. At a signed agreement at Caserta on 26 September Zervas and Sarafis, the two andarte generals, placed the forces of EDES and ELAS under Papandreou's Government of National Unity and thus under command of the Allied liberation forces of Lieutenant General Sir Ronald Scobie. Under the terms of the agreement drawn up by 'Jumbo' Wilson, the andarte groups were allowed to retain areas of influence, but the aim of the AMM finally had been achieved. As the Germans withdrew, so British light forces were landed in southern Greece and advanced north, but the andartes expended as much energy in settling old scores with their political rivals, the former in Prevesa, and the latter throughout the Peloponnese where they clashed with the Security Battalions. Kalamata, Gargaliani and Meligala in the Peloponnese suffered particularly, and in the process much innocent civilian blood was also spilt.

As the Allied liberation army under Scobie entered and secured Greece, so the remaining AMM agents, whose various missions across the country amounted to some eighty British officers and some 400 men, were free to leave the country, their work done. Commensurate with this reduction, Colonel Louis Franck, with SOE experience in Washington where he had been chief liaison officer with OSS, and in West Africa, assumed command of SOM from Stawell. Between 1941 and 1944, it has been estimated that some 25,000 casualties were inflicted upon the enemy, some 150 trains damaged or destroyed, and 250 ships sunk or damaged, while during the widespread sabotage of 1943 as a result of ANIMALS, some thirteen Italian Divisions were retained in Greece and after the Italian capitulation the Germans kept some six divisions. The most significant acts of sabotage in the Peloponnese were the two successive attacks upon Koutsopodhi (Argos) airfield and the demolition of the Kaki Scala bridges. Thus the work orchestrated by SOE had not been insignificant.[55]

The Greek Government and Scobie's 23 Armoured Brigade were in Athens by 18 October. In a change from previous form, it seems that EAM/ELAS chose not to capitalize upon the window of opportunity offered by the five-day interval between the German departure from the city and the Greek Government's arrival. In the event Papandreou was able to hoist the Greek flag over the Acropolis unchallenged, an act that preceded a thanksgiving service in Athens Cathedral and several days of victory celebrations.

The communists launched their second concerted effort to seize power in a December revolution, by which time the earlier fleeting moment of opportunity had passed and Papandreou's Government had started to establish itself in Athens. Precipitated by a breakdown in negotiations concerning the demobilization and surrender of andarte groups and their arms, ELAS reconstituted its GHQ in open defiance of the Government's authority. Matters came to a head on 3 December during a demonstration fomented by the KKE in Constitution Square, at which the Greek gendarmerie lost control and fired into the crowd. The communists seized the propaganda initiative and proceeded to march through the city displaying the victims of the shooting for all to see.

That night Papandreou blamed, correctly, the communists for instigating the violence, and matters deteriorated rapidly in what came to be known as the Battle of Athens, which heralded the 'Second Round' of the Greek Civil War. Fighting broke out once again and spread across the country and Zervas was forced to retreat to Corfu. Field Marshal Sir Harold Alexander flew into the city on 11 December with Harold Macmillan and, appalled at the parlous situation, sent for Major General 'Ginger' Hawkesworth from Italy and placed him in charge of ground operations. Churchill and Eden flew into the capital for Christmas, at which stage the Archbishop of Athens, Damaskinos, was appointed Regent until such time as a plebiscite could be held. However, it would be some five weeks before the communist forces admitted defeat, with a truce coming into effect on 15 January 1945 following the Varkiza Conference.[56]

However, this was not to be the end of it, and the 'Third Round' of the Greek Civil War was shortly to commence, for the communists, led once more by Nikos Zachariades following his release from a German concentration camp, had not given up on their vision of incorporating Greece in a Soviet federation of the Balkans. Having exhausted all means at their disposal and failed thus far to bring this about, for the next two years the communists would attempt to disrupt and destroy the state from within, endeavouring to create the conditions under which the Soviet Union might intervene. They succeeded in doing this by the time of the March 1946 elections, at which stage the Soviet Government had made a formal complaint at the first United Nations Security Council about the presence of British troops who had arrived in Athens as part of the Allied Mission for Observing the Greek Elections (AMFOGE). The Soviet Union's clear interest in Greece brought the country sharply back in to focus on the world stage. Greece knew that at the elections it had to choose between the Soviets and the West. It chose the latter and returned the monarchist, right-wing Populist Party with an overall majority of 68 per cent.

Support for the King had increased dramatically following the communist uprising the previous December, and he returned to Athens in late September to a spontaneous and rapturous welcome from his Greek subjects. Not from the communists however, who escalated matters by forming their own 'Democratic Army' under Markos Vaphiades; by the early autumn the civil war had spread from northern Greece to the Peloponnese. The decision by Greece to ally itself to the West was cemented a year later in May 1947, by a reconstruction loan from the United States to Greece of $400 million, thus placing Greece firmly in the Western sphere of influence and signalling a switch in responsibility from Britain to America. The Greek and American governments were compelled to form a Joint General Staff in November 1947 to combat the escalating civil war, with the American Mission for Aid to Greece (AMAG), meanwhile, increasing its provision of military operational advice, equipment and weapons. This allied approach was to prove too much for the communists, but the effects of the civil war would make themselves felt until the summer of 1949 when, following the battles in the Grammos and Vitsi mountains, the guerrilla remnants of the communist 'Democratic Army' were finally forced to make good their escape over the border into Albania.[57]

Notes

1. HS 9/1453/7, Peter Michael Wand-Tetley, 1939–1946.
2. Deakin, *The Myth of an Allied Landing in the Balkans during the Second World War*, (paper in Auty and Clogg).
3. Mackenzie, *The Secret History of SOE: The Special Operations Executive 1940–45*. Ch. 4.
4. Ian Fleming purposefully erred from fact and gave the head of SIS (MI6) the symbol M in his James Bond novels. In fact M was the symbol of SOE's director of operations and training. Commander Ian Fleming RNVR, as he was during the war, was Personal Assistant to the Director of Naval Intelligence (DNI), Admiral John Godfrey. In this role Fleming was instrumental in conceiving and setting up No. 30 Commando (later 30 Assault Unit), an inter-service unit, that advanced with, or in front of, forward troops to secure intelligence documents of importance from seized enemy headquarters. It was a 'composite' of an officer from this unit, and others that he met in the line of his intelligence work, upon whom he based his principal character.
5. Mackenzie, op cit, Ch. 5.
6. Foot, *An Outline History of the Special Operations Executive 1940–46*. Ch. 1.
7. Ibid, Chs. 2 & 3.
8. Quoted in Sweet-Escott, *Baker Street Irregular*. Ch. 3.
9. Ranfurly, *To War with Whitaker: The Wartime Diaries of the Countess of Ranfurly 1939–45*. Ch. 4.
10. Sweet-Escott, op cit.
11. Mackenzie, op cit, Ch. 21.
12. Moss, *Ill Met by Moonlight*.
13. HS 7/150, SOE activities in Greece 1940–1942 (Chs. 1–6) by Maj. Ian Pirie. Ch 2.
14. Ibid, Ch. 5.
15. Mackenzie, op cit, Ch. 18.
16. Ibid, Ch. 7.
17. Myers, *Greek Entanglement*. Ch. 1.
18. Ibid.
19. Ibid, Ch. 2.
20. Ibid.
21. Ibid, Ch. 4.
22. Clogg, *Pearls from Swine: the Foreign Office papers, SOE and the Greek Resistance*, (paper in Auty and Clogg).
23. Woodhouse, *Apple of Discord: A Survey of Recent Greek Politics in their International Setting*. Ch. 2.
24. Ibid, Ch. 3.

25. Myers, op cit, Ch. 14.
26. Hammond, *Venture into Greece: With the Guerillas 1943–44*. Ch. 4.
27. Mackenzie, op cit, Ch. 18.
28. Hammond, op cit, Ch. 3.
29. Sweet-Escott, op cit, (paper in Auty and Clogg)
30. Wand-Tetley personal papers. HS 5/699, Peloponnese: Area 5 Peloponnese; personnel M-W; (Report by Capt. Wand-Tetley) 1944–1945.
31. Lieutenant W. Arthur Hubbard, a New Zealand SOE officer.
32. Although the concept and genesis of 'Hearts and Minds' operations is often attributed to General Sir Gerald Templer in the Malayan Emergency, it is evident that the concept, in one form or another, has long existed.
33. Time Pencils, or 'Delay Firing Device No.10' to give the correct nomenclature, was an SOE invention. They were 5 inches long and 0.03 inches in diameter. When a lead-covered acid ampoule was broken, the acid would eat through a copper wire which would then release a spring-loaded firing pin which in turn would hit a percussion cap. The thickness of copper wire used in the Time Pencil would determine the delay, ordinarily between ten minutes and several hours.
34. '808', or PE-808, is plastic explosives. Invented by the British just prior to the war, it is a stable, shockproof, waterproof putty-like explosive that is easily shaped and moulded. Consisting of Research Department Explosive (RDX) – cyclotrimethylene-tritramine – mixed with plasticizing oil, it does, however, have the drawback of giving the handler a severe headache.
35. HS 5/698, Peloponnese: Area 5 Peloponnese; personnel A-K; Report by Capt. Fraser; SOE Activities in the Peloponnese 1943–44 by Capt. Fraser, 1944.
36. Ibid.
37. The 'trusted and ruthless lieutenant' in question is probably the andarte officer operating under the codename 'Orion', whom Wand-Tetley and Reid met with at Platania in August 1943.
38. Woodhouse, op cit, *Summer 1943: the Critical Months*, (paper in Auty and Clogg).
39. Myers, op cit, *The Andarte Delegation to Cairo: August 1943*, (paper in Auty and Clogg).
40. Clogg, op cit (paper in Auty and Clogg).
41. Woodhouse, op cit, Ch. 3.
42. Ibid.
43. Woodhouse, op cit, (paper in Auty and Clogg).
44. Sweet-Escott, op cit, Ch. 7.
45. Woodhouse, op cit, Ch. 4.
46. Hammond, op cit, Ch. 9.
47. Woodhouse, op cit, Ch. 5.
48. Beevor, *Recollections and Reflections 1940–45*. Ch. 4.
49. HS 9/1453/7, Peter Michael Wand-Tetley, 1939–1946.
50. Sweet-Escott, op cit, Ch. 3.
51. Mackenzie, op cit, Ch. 7.
52. Sweet-Escott, op cit, Ch. 7.
53. HS 9/1453/7, Peter Michael Wand-Tetley, 1939–1946.
54. Hammond, op cit, Ch. 9.
55. Myers, op cit, Retrospect.
56. Clive, *A Greek Experience, 1943–1948*. Ch. 5.
57. Ibid, Ch. 7.2

Chapter 5

Paratrooper

7th (Light Infantry) Parachute Battalion

Following Wand-Tetley's interview with Lieutenant Colonel Oldham in Cairo on 6 December 1944, in which he requested a further field assignment, events moved rapidly and in a direction that he could not have foreseen. His request for further work in the field with SOE or special forces was accepted and, having handed over his duties as Conducting Officer to Lieutenant Shenow, he packed and prepared to leave Cairo for London. Arriving back in England on 7 January 1945 he was placed on the pool strength of SOE London pending an anticipated assignment to Asia and Force 136, SOE's cover name in the Far East, which in the previous month had moved its headquarters from Meerut, India to Kandy, Ceylon. Retrospective authority was granted by HQ SOM, Bari on 11 January for Wand-Tetley, along with Lieutenant H. Sisley, a Sapper, and Lieutenant P. G. LeBosquet, Reconnaissance Corps, to be posted from Force 133 (SOE Cairo) to MO1(SP), the War Office cover name for SOE London. The posting order noted that the movement had actually already taken place and that all three officers had been struck off the strength of Force 133 with effect from 24 December 1944.[1]

Now back in London, Wand-Tetley was subjected to a routine security check by SOE, which was undertaken habitually for Baker Street by an in-house MI5 team. In a minute dated 24 January 1945 MI5 advised SOE: 'our only information concerning Wand-Tetley is that when he was at Cambridge in 1939–40 [sic][2] he was a member of a communist cell there. He has not come to notice since.' This, of course, changed everything. That Wand-Tetley was never communist-orientated and, as had been evident throughout his life, was by political persuasion otherwise inclined, counted for little at the time. Understandably, SOE could not afford to take any chances.

Throughout the 1930s Cambridge University had developed a certain notoriety as a spawning ground for communism. For SOE to try and distinguish between those students who were serious ideologues

164

and those who had merely flirted with or intellectually explored the doctrine, as Wand-Tetley had, would have been impossible to ascertain. Although he was too perceptive a thinker to be seduced by communism, Wand-Tetley had clearly been too inquisitive for his own good and, as he clearly understood, his earlier curiosity would now cost him his position as an SOE agent. Nor did the fact, learnt earlier the same month, that in addition to his MC he had now been Mentioned in Despatches for gallantry in the field – for which SOE Cairo had recommended him the previous August at the time that he deployed to Smyrna – make the bitter pill of disappointment any easier to swallow.

Within the week Wand-Tetley had been informed that, given the adverse trace, it was now no longer possible for SOE to employ him and that he would have to be posted back to the Army. On 22 February he was struck off the strength of SOE London and given a posting order to 7th Battalion the Gloucestershire Regiment, but within a fortnight he had managed to change the transfer order to a regiment more suited to his experience, the Parachute Regiment. Where one door had closed another had now opened and, furthermore, with the war in Europe now drawing to a close, he would be deployed to the Far East as he had hoped.[3]

On 7 March 1945 he was formally transferred from the Wiltshire Regiment, which had nominally remained his parent regiment throughout his service with special forces, to the Parachute Regiment, which at that stage was part of the Army Air Corps. He would remain with his new regiment for the remainder of the war. On transfer he retained his seniority and rank of captain and was re-granted parachute pay at four shillings per day. By the end of March he had learnt that he was to be assigned as second-in-command to a company within 7th (Light Infantry) Parachute Battalion.[4]

The 7th (LI) Parachute Battalion had been formed from 10th Battalion The Somerset Light Infantry in November 1942, a time when British airborne forces were undergoing rapid expansion. Initially one of the three battalions within 3 Parachute Brigade of 1st Airborne Division, in April 1943 the brigade and its three battalions were assigned to form the nucleus of a new, second airborne division, designated 6th Airborne Division, the orders for the formation of which were issued on 2 May. Besides 3 Parachute Brigade, the new division would also contain two new brigades, 5 Parachute Brigade and 6 Airlanding Brigade. The division was given its motto 'Go To It' by the newly-appointed GOC, Major General Richard Gale, who had previously commanded 1 Parachute Brigade. In late May he took the decision to transfer 7th (LI) Parachute Battalion, which would be commanded by Lieutenant Colonel Geoffrey Pine-Coffin for most of the war, to the nascent 5 Parachute Brigade. Formed on 1 July, 5 Parachute Brigade, under its commander,

Brigadier Nigel Poett of the Durham Light Infantry, also took under command 12th (Yorkshire) Parachute Battalion and 13th (Lancashire) Parachute Battalion, both of which had similarly been converted to the parachute role from line infantry battalions of the Green Howards and the South Lancashire Regiment respectively.[5]

Wand-Tetley was due to join a parachute battalion which, in its relatively short existence, had won impressive military laurels and one in which, but for his own distinguished military service, he would undoubtedly have experienced difficulty in being accepted by his fellow paratroopers. After a year of hard training 7th (LI) Parachute Battalion, as part of 5 Parachute Brigade, had taken to the battlefield in Operation OVERLORD on 6 June 1944. The D Day Normandy beach landings were preceded by Allied airborne landings, and 6th Airborne Division's task was to secure the left flank of the British assault and thus the eastern flank of the entire Allied invasion force.

In OVERLORD the Allies staged the greatest amphibious landing in history, between the Cherbourg Peninsula and the estuary of the River Orne, with the First US Army on the right and the Second British Army on the left. The British plan called for Second Army's XXX Corps to assault on the right with its I Corps on the left. However, prior to the beach landings it was imperative that the British first secured their left flank, on the River Orne and Caen Canal against possible German counterattack; this task was given to 6th Airborne Division under command of I Corps. Five Parachute Brigade's specific task was to capture intact the two key bridges over the River Orne (Horsa Bridge) at Ranville and the Caen Canal (Pegasus Bridge) at Benouville, with 7th (LI) Parachute Battalion reinforcing the gliderborne troops of the 2nd Battalion The Oxfordshire & Buckinghamshire Light Infantry at the two bridges. Meanwhile 3 Parachute Brigade was to silence the Merville coastal gun battery at Franceville Plage that threatened the Allied invasion fleet, and to destroy the River Dives bridges. The divisional area having been secured and the open ground of German anti-glider defences cleared, 6 Airlanding Brigade would come in by glider to take its part in holding the Allied flank against counterattack.[6]

In the subsequent breakout from Normandy and the advance to the River Seine, 7th (LI) Parachute Battalion, as part of 5 Parachute Brigade of 6th Airborne Division, played a significant part. In early September, after three months of hard fighting and with its task in Normandy completed, the battalion returned with its brigade and division to England. Later that same month the 1st Airborne Division was despatched to Arnhem. For its part, 6th Airborne Division returned to north-west Europe in December 1944. In the Ardennes in January 1945 it played its part in halting the German counterattacks in the Battle of the Bulge. Forced to operate in deep snow and bitterly cold, wintry conditions, this was the most extreme weather the soldiers of 7th (LI) Parachute Battalion had yet experienced. Having returned briefly to Wiltshire to prepare for the invasion of Germany, in March 1945 the battalion took to the skies with 6th Airborne Division. Operation VARSITY, the airborne assault to secure the north bank of the Rhine at Wesel, formed a key component of Operation PLUNDER, the British Second Army's amphibious crossing of the Rhine and invasion of Germany. VARSITY was a resounding success and 7th (LI) Parachute Battalion then played its part in the subsequent advance to the Baltic.[7]

In the closing days of the war in Europe events had moved rapidly. By 25 April the Red Army had encircled Berlin, and by 30 April Soviet troops had raised their flag over the Reichstag building, the day that Hitler committed suicide in his *Führerbunker* under the Reich Chancellery garden. The Soviets met fierce resistance but Berlin surrendered on 2 May, the same day that 6th Airborne Division had reached Wismar. However, this was not the last of the fighting, for the last pocket of German resistance went on fighting in Czechoslovakia, only surrendering on 11 May, despite Germany having surrendered unconditionally to the Allies on 7 May. At a ceremony in Berlin on 8 May the war in Europe was declared officially at an end, the day being declared 'VE Day'. With the fighting over, 6th Airborne Division and its units returned to their bases around Salisbury Plain. It was thus a battle-hardened 7th (LI) Parachute Battalion that Wand-Tetley was about to join.

Wand-Tetley had no trouble in empathizing with the Parachute Regiment ethos. Indeed, the regiment shared the same Army commando heritage that he himself had adopted so readily. At the start of the war Britain had no airborne forces, but Churchill had been deeply impressed by Germany's airborne campaigns in Scandinavia and the Low Countries, particularly the capture of the powerful Belgian fort of Eben Emael near Liège and the bridges over the Albert Canal by combined glider and *Fallschirmjäger* troops in the spring of 1940. Accordingly, in a minute to General Sir Hastings Ismay, head of the Military Wing of the War Cabinet Secretariat, he ordered that Britain should develop its own capability.[8]

This minute followed hot on the heels of the two that Churchill had sent earlier in June in which he had called for the formation of a Commando force. Initially the General Staff took the pragmatic approach of combining the two requirements. Of the twelve commando units designated for establishment, it was decided that No. 2 Commando would be raised from the outset as a Parachute Commando. Notwithstanding its parachute role, No. 2 Commando was initially governed by the same criteria as the other Commando units. However, its men were paid extra parachute pay of four shillings a day for officers

167

and two shillings a day for other ranks, which came into effect once the first three parachute jumps had been completed.[9]

The RAF was made responsible for the parachute training at RAF Ringway. Named the Central Landing School (CLS), it was placed under command of the First World War flying ace, Squadron Leader Louis Strange DSO MC DFC and Bar. Strange, educated at St Edward's School, Oxford, had joined the Royal Flying Corps and risen to the rank of lieutenant colonel. Major John Rock, a Sapper, was sent to assist him and they were allocated some twenty-five Parachute Jumping Instructors (PJIs), all of whom were volunteers from the APTC and the RAF. Tatton Hall Park, five miles south-east of Ringway, was selected as the parachute-dropping zone.

On 9 July 1940, troops from No. 2 Commando reported to Ringway as the first parachute students. In the early days a student's first two parachute jumps would be made using the 'pull-off' method from a converted Whitley bomber. The parachutist would position himself in the rear-gunner's turret, the back of which had been removed and, holding on to a bar to steady himself, would pull his rip-cord so that the canopy would deploy fully in the slipstream before he let go of the bar and was pulled off the back of the aircraft. The next six jumps made by a student would be by jumping through a hole cut in the Whitley's floor. The first method was meant to build confidence, but most found it 'extremely alarming' and soon it was discontinued. The second method had its own risks, for if the jumper did not align himself correctly as he jumped he would invariably bang his face against the side, a painful and often bloody experience known as 'ringing the bell'. If the parachutist was fortunate enough to be using a Bombay transport aircraft in training then he would be able to jump out of a side door, but it would not be until the arrival in England of the US Dakota in mid-1942 that paratroopers would be able habitually to use a side door on exiting.[10]

At the beginning of October the CLS was redesignated the Central Landing Establishment (CLE) to recognize an expansion in its role, which now included a Glider Training Squadron (GTS) and a new Development Unit (DU). Glider and parachute-training techniques continued to be developed, and parachutists now made their first two jumps from a barrage balloon. In November No. 2 Commando was renamed 11th Special Air Service Battalion (not to be confused with *the* SAS formed later by Stirling in North Africa), later redesignated as 1st Parachute Battalion, and by the end of 1940 its 500 soldiers had for the most part all been parachute trained.[11]

Keen to test its new airborne capability, in early 1941 the War Office conceived a plan to disrupt water supplies to the southern Italian ports that served German and Italian troops campaigning in North Africa and Albania by blowing up the Tragino Aqueduct. Operation COLOSSUS, as it was named, was an ambitious plan in which men of 11th SAS Battalion were successful in blowing up the aqueduct, but all the paratroopers were rounded up as they attempted to make their way across mountainous terrain to the coast for their rendezvous with the submarine HMS *Triumph*.[12]

Meanwhile the CLE at Ringway, renamed the Airborne Forces Establishment (AFE), stepped up its training to keep pace with the required throughput. Next, an airborne divisional headquarters was approved, and by the end of October Major General Frederick 'Boy' Browning assumed his appointment as GOC 1st Airborne Division. Given the rapid expansion of parachute battalions, it was no longer practical to fill their ranks from individual volunteers, and it was decided therefore to convert entire line infantry battalions to the parachute role.[13]

By the beginning of 1942 Browning was conscious that the fledgling airborne forces should be provided with an opportunity to prove their worth. Although the Telecommunications Research Establishment (TRE) had a good understanding of the German acquisition radar, *Freya*, they knew little about the narrow-beam radar, *Würzburg*, which was used to vector *Luftwaffe* nightfighters onto RAF bombers. It was imperative that TRE acquire the components of a *Würzburg* radar if they were to counter the problem. The target selected for the raid was a radar site on a clifftop at Bruneval, just north of le Havre. Having examined the captured radar components, the scientists at TRE were able subsequently to defeat the *Würzburg* by using 'window' – strips of tinfoil to confuse the radar. In Operation BITING, as the raid was codenamed, the paratroopers had just won the Parachute Regiment's first battle honour, 'Bruneval'.[14]

With the airborne capability developing apace, in the summer of 1942 Browning decided that the airborne forces should have their own distinctive beret and specific emblem. Although rumour often has it that Daphne du Maurier, the novelist and wife of Browning, chose the maroon beret on the basis that the hero of *Frenchman's Creek*, which was being filmed at the time, wore a maroon beret, the decision was in fact put to the Chief of the Imperial General Staff. General Sir Alan Brooke, unable to decide, asked the opinion of the soldier who had been asked to try on the different coloured berets; he favoured the maroon one, and so the matter was settled. For the airborne emblem, Browning chose the mythical warrior Bellerophon riding his winged steed Pegasus, who in Greek mythology was famous for slaying the fire-breathing monster Chimaera, and was the first recorded instance of an airborne warrior.

Furthermore, it was recognized that the parachute battalions, which in February 1942 had been placed under the newly formed Army Air Corps, should have their own, specific parent regiment. The Parachute Regiment was therefore formed officially on 1 August 1942 and, along with the Glider Pilot Regiment, placed under the auspices of the Army Air Corps. At this stage the Army Air Corps cap-badge was still worn by all ranks, but in May 1943 the Parachute Regiment adopted one of its own, a parachute supported by two wings with, above it, the royal lion and king's crown (the 'dog and basket').

Destination: the Far East

Three months after the remnants of 1st Airborne Division had made their weary way back to England from Arnhem, the 6th Airborne Division returned to the European theatre and, as related earlier, fought hard until the end of the war there. Having returned to their Bulford barracks on Salisbury Plain, Wand-Tetley now had the chance of meeting the highly respected CO of 7th (LI) Parachute Battalion, Pine-Coffin, known affectionately as 'Timber Casket' or 'Wooden Box' by the battalion, and of getting to know his fellow officers and men. Those in the battalion were distinguished easily from men in other parachute battalions, for they wore a distinctive green diamond backing behind their winged cap-badge, a legacy of their Light Infantry heritage, and marched at the Light Infantry rate of 140 paces to the minute. Pine-Coffin, whom Wand-Tetley would come to know very well in the next year, was a tall, lean and tough officer, but he possessed a very genuine interest in the welfare of his men. Considerate by nature, he had a humorous twinkle in his eye and was quick to see the funny side of events.

The battalion and the rest of the soldiers of 6th Airborne Division were now contemplating what the future might hold in store for them. With the war in Europe over, the deliberations of the Prime Minister and the military planners were very firmly focused upon defeating the Japanese in the Far East. Hitherto Wand-Tetley had been engaged in the war against Axis forces in North Africa and in the Mediterranean theatre, while the battalion's operational experience had been gained in Europe. Thus the majority of the men had only a passing knowledge of the war with Japan. The course of the war in the Far East now became a major topic of conversation in the mess as Wand-Tetley and his fellow officers endeavoured to bring themselves up to speed with events there as quickly as possible. Nor did they need any encouragement to pin back their ears at the regularly held brigade and battalion intelligence briefings.

The attack on Pearl Harbor on 7 December 1941 had, of course, been one of the defining moments of the Second World War, and was the catalyst for drawing America into the war. Given America's opposition to both Japan's war with China and her designs on South East Asia's rich oil reserves and natural resources, Japan knew that war with America was almost certainly inevitable. Japan was negotiating a settlement

170

with the US – the Hull-Nomura talks – until the US demanded an immediate withdrawal of all Japanese forces from mainland Asia. These demands were unacceptable to Japan, which then launched a pre-emptive strike against the US Pacific Fleet at its Pearl Harbor base in Hawaii in an effort to neutralize the only force capable of opposing her seizure of South East Asia.

The response was immediate; America declared war on Japan and on 11 December Germany declared war on America. With this vast new theatre in Asia and the Pacific, the war now became truly global. Hitler was delighted with Japan's actions, believing that with such an ally Germany could not possibly lose the war. From the British perspective, with America now in the war, Churchill, on the other hand, believed the Allies would prevail.

Simultaneously with the attack on Pearl Harbor, Japan invaded American, British and Dutch colonies in South East Asia. Within just six months Japan enjoyed a series of victories which saw her capture the British colonies of Hong Kong, Malaya, Singapore and Burma, drive American forces from the Philippines, and secure the Dutch East Indies, before suffering a defeat by the US fleet off the Pacific island of Midway. Nevertheless, by June 1942 Japan had secured the entire region and had taken control of the area's natural resources of oil, rubber and raw materials.

In the second half of 1942 the Allied ground forces defeated the Japanese on Guadalcanal and in eastern New Guinea. Superior US air power forced the Japanese to withdraw from Guadalcanal and invest their forces in the upper Solomons. By the end of 1943 they had been defeated comprehensively in both theatres and the Americans and their allies had gained the initiative.

The American offensive, Operation GALVANIC on 10 November 1943, aimed at the Gilbert Islands, heralded a drive right across the central Pacific. In large part this success was down to two key factors: first the adoption by the US of an island-hopping policy to bypass and isolate key Japanese defences; and, second, the commissioning in 1943 of an enormous tonnage of warships into the US Navy, equal to the size of the entire Japanese fleet of 1941. By the end of 1943 the Americans had gained the upper hand in New Guinea and went on to land at Aitape and Hollandia in April 1944.

By January 1944 the Americans had experienced success in the Marshall Islands in the western Pacific and this allowed the navy to launch a devastating attack on Japanese shipping at its anchorage at Truk in the Caroline Islands in February 1944. As a result the Japanese fleet was forced to retire to Singapore, providing free rein to the US Navy throughout the western Pacific. American forces landed in the

Marianas in June 1944, with the campaign completed effectively by the end of the month.

For the British, the Japanese conquest of Burma between December 1941 and May 1942 had to be reversed. In particular, the Americans were keen to see the overland route to China reopened. Two offensives in 1942–43 were launched by the British, one into the Arakan and one across the border by the Chindits, but little in real terms was achieved. In 1943 the British sought again to re-establish the overland route to the Chinese Nationalists. This precipitated the Japanese 'March on Delhi' into north-east India to secure the border towns of Imphal and Kohima.

The Japanese failed to capture both towns, the siege of Kohima being broken and Imphal being relieved the same month on 22 June 1944 by Allied forces from Kohima. The British undertook the main Allied offensive in northern Burma, the capture of Ramree Island in the Arakan in December 1944, heralding the capture of a number of strategic targets. Meiktila was taken in March and Rangoon was entered unopposed in May, the Japanese having withdrawn into Siam (now Thailand).

After the 1937–38 invasion of China, the Japanese had adopted a largely defensive posture, realizing that they faced a war that could not be won. This followed a particularly brutal occupation phase. The most infamous of episodes was 'the Rape of Nanking', in which 50,000 Japanese troops looted and burned the city and surrounding towns, massacring in the region of 100,000 to 300,000 Chinese civilians and raping some 20,000 women and girls before murdering them. Many were buried alive or used for live bayonet practice. However, between 1938 and 1944 an undeclared truce existed in many areas. Because the Chinese felt that Japanese defeat was inevitable, both the Nationalists and Communists chose to spare their strength for a later resumption of civil war.

However, the United States looked to China for full assistance, and also wished to use Chinese airfields from which to bomb the Japanese homeland. The USAAF raid against Formosa (now Taiwan), launched from within China, precipitated a Japanese offensive, *Ichi-Go*, which secured lines of communications from Korea to Malaya. Nonetheless, the spring of 1945 saw a general drawdown of Japanese forces in southern China in readiness for a move to Manchuria.[15]

American victory at the Marianas in June 1944 had left the Japanese without an effective carrier fleet to maintain her defensive commitments. By taking the Philippines the Americans could cut Japan's lines of communications and achieve as much as an invasion of the home islands. Thus landings on Formosa were set aside in favour of landings on the Philippines, and accordingly the Philippine island of Leyte was invaded in October. The ensuing naval battle, fought over 450,000 square miles, saw the Japanese comprehensively defeated by the American fleet and the Imperial Navy relegated to coastguard status.

The Japanese continued to fight on after the Allies had liberated Europe, and Americans would see some of the toughest fighting yet in the Pacific. In January American forces landed on the main Philippine island of Luzon but, in the face of fierce Japanese resistance, it was a month before they were able to liberate the capital, Manila. In February, an assault on Iwo Jima was launched. Again it took a month of fierce fighting to subdue the Japanese.

With Iwo Jima captured US fighters could now reach mainland Japan and, from March, B-29 bombers and Mustang fighters began to deploy to the island. At this time the Americans began to bomb Japan using low-level incendiary attacks by night and the effect on the Japanese wooden cities was devastating, but the Japanese determination to continue fighting did not let up. On 1 April the Americans launched an offensive on Okinawa, supported by 1,500 ships including the British Pacific Fleet. However, with fanatical resistance and *kamikaze* attacks against Allied shipping, the Japanese did not surrender until 17 June.

The Allies planned next for the final assault on the Japanese home islands, which was anticipated to be extremely costly. Allied plans included an airborne operation, and Major General Eric Bols was told to prepare 6th Airborne Division for operations in South East Asia. It was intended that the division would form part of the British Liberation Army, although divisional banter had it that BLA stood for 'Burma Looms Ahead'. The 7th (LI) Parachute Battalion set about training in earnest for the deployment, and the eventuality seemed all the more likely when Pine-Coffin informed his battalion that their GOC had flown with two divisional staff officers and the Commander of 5 Parachute Brigade, Nigel Poett, to Ceylon (now Sri Lanka) to meet the Supreme Allied Commander, Admiral Lord Louis Mountbatten. At the same time a number of advance parties from across the division were despatched to India and attached to infantry units there to learn from their expertise in jungle warfare.

Having arrived in Ceylon, Bols and Poett were met and taken by 'Boy' Browning, now a lieutenant general and Mountbatten's Chief of Staff, to Kandy, the location of HQ South East Asia Command (SEAC), the initials of which were said by some American wags to mean 'Save England's Asian Colonies'. Mountbatten briefed Bols and Poett that 5 Parachute Brigade would take part in a forthcoming offensive to recapture the Malayan Peninsula, codenamed Operation ZIPPER. The brigade's part in the plan would be to conduct a seaborne landing on the Morib Beaches on Malaya's western coast and, having established a beachhead, then link up with the British Fourteenth Army advancing from Burma south through the Malayan peninsula. Subsequently,

5 Parachute Brigade would move back to Rangoon, from where they would launch an airborne operation to capture the causeway linking mainland Malaya with Singapore. However, during further planning it became clear that the remainder of 6th Airborne Division would not be required, and so the GOC and his two staff officers departed to England, leaving behind Poett who subsequently moved to Bombay (now Mumbai) to await the arrival of 5 Parachute Brigade.

Wand-Tetley embarked with 7th (LI) Parachute Battalion on 19 July. Besides the other two parachute units, 12th (Yorkshire) Parachute Battalion and 13th (Lancashire) Parachute Battalion, the 5 Parachute Brigade Group deployed also with its supporting arms, including 22nd Independent Parachute Company (the brigade's pathfinders), 4 Airlanding Anti-Tank Battery RA, a detachment of 2 Forward Observation Unit RA, 3 Airborne Squadron RE, and 225th Parachute Field Ambulance. Having arrived in Bombay, the brigade immediately set about acclimatizing and preparing for ZIPPER.

However, on 6 August the first atomic bomb was dropped on Hiroshima, killing 78,000 outright, followed by a second on Nagasaki on 9 August, killing 35,000 in the initial blast. The first US forces reached Japan on 28 August and, on 2 September, the formal surrender of Japan was accepted aboard the USS *Missouri* in Tokyo Bay. This was followed in Singapore on 12 September by the formal surrender of Japanese forces in South East Asia. Poett was later able to brief his brigade that on 26 July Allied leaders meeting at Potsdam had presented an ultimatum to Japan to surrender unconditionally or suffer 'prompt and utter destruction', but the Japanese had rejected the demand. The war thus came to a sudden end and, not surprisingly, the men of 7th (LI) Parachute Battalion were delighted. Wand-Tetley and his fellow officers had been anticipating a long and bloody war in the Far East, including the invasion of Japan, with anticipated casualty estimates far in excess of the numbers killed in Nagasaki and Hiroshima. However, although the war in the Far East was over, the situation was far from stable and British troops would find themselves drawn increasingly into counter-insurgency operations as various factions vied for control over the Asian colonies.

In an endeavour to stabilize the political and military vacuum that the Japanese surrender had created and, in particular, to ensure that Communists did not assume power, it was decided that the first phase of ZIPPER should go ahead. Thus 7th (LI) Parachute Battalion embarked with the rest of 5 Parachute Brigade on the P&O liner SS *Chitral*, and on 9 September set sail for Malaya. Having arrived off the Morib Beaches on 17 September, Wand-Tetley and the men of 7th (LI) and 12th (Yorkshire) Parachute Battalions transferred to landing craft and then waded ashore for 500 yards through chest-deep water and knee-deep mud. Having marched a short distance inland the two battalions, which were the only units of the brigade to disembark that day, settled down for an uncomfortable night of heavy rain in a rubber plantation. It was intended that the brigade would advance upon the capital city, Kuala Lumpur, the following day to counter any attempt by the Communists to take control. However, that night Poett received a signal confirming that the capital city was already in British hands, and that the two battalions should therefore return to the beaches to re-embark and sail with the brigade for Singapore.

Having arrived in Singapore on 21 September, 5 Parachute Brigade would remain there for the best part of the next three months. Shortly after disembarking Wand-Tetley and the men of 7th (LI) Parachute Battalion heard from their CO that their mission would be to help impose law and order in the city. This news followed a visit that Poett had made to Lieutenant General Sir Miles Dempsey, now C-in-C Allied Land Forces SEAC. The C-in-C was an old friend of the brigade from his time as Commander of Second Army during the Normandy landings and, with the Under Secretary of State for War Mr J. Lawson, paid a formal visit to the battalion and spoke to the troops the following week. Another visitor to the battalion was General Sir William Slim, who inspected the battalion the following month. The situation in Singapore was chaotic, for during the Japanese occupation the police force had been all but dismantled. Therefore, the brigade immediately set about restoring order and rebuilding the police force, and within three months it had accomplished this to a degree that allowed it to hand over the role to a Malay Volunteer Force.

In early December 5 Parachute Brigade was despatched to Batavia (now Jakarta), the capital of Java, which at the time was part of the Dutch East Indies (now Indonesia). However, before departing, 7th (LI) Parachute Battalion were visited in their barracks by Field Marshal Lord Alanbrooke, and before sailing Lord Louis Mountbatten was piped aboard HMS *Emma* to address the troops and explain to them the reason for their move. When the brigade arrived, Java was in a state of anarchy. When the Japanese had invaded in 1942 they had brushed aside the Dutch colonial forces, quickly occupied the country and incarcerated its Dutch colonialists, an act not entirely unpopular with the native Indonesians, for the Dutch regime had been distinctly unpopular. When Japan surrendered in August 1945 its forces in Java ignored the Dutch and handed over a good number of their weapons to the Indonesians before leaving the towns and moving inland to concentration areas to await the arrival of the Allies. This was against the instructions issued by Mountbatten, who had made it clear that the Japanese forces should stay where they were with their weapons and maintain order until the Allies arrived.[16]

With the Dutch still incarcerated, the Indonesian politician, Dr Sukarno, seized the opportunity to declare independence for his country and proclaim himself President. He was supported by a number of other nationalist politicians and by significant numbers of militant supporters, now armed with Japanese weapons. The various militant bands immediately moved into the towns vacated by the Japanese and set about settling old scores, indulging in armed robbery, terrorising the population, and fighting amongst themselves for ascendancy. On only one matter were the Indonesians generally united: the desire to rid themselves of their pre-war colonial masters. With no Dutch troops available in the East Indies, and with thousands of European and Allied prisoners of war at the mercy of bandits, the British Army was obliged to step in and restore law and order pending the eventual arrival of the Dutch, whose responsibility it would then be to address the future of the country.[17]

When 5 Parachute Brigade disembarked in Batavia the city was already in British hands in the guise of 23rd Indian Division. Poett's brigade was almost immediately called upon to take part in Operation POUNCE, a divisional clearance of the capital city. This entailed internal security operations, including the dispersal of riots by day and conducting street patrols at night, while all the time being under threat of sniper fire. Seventh (LI) Parachute Battalion was accommodated in Tanah Tingai Barracks. On 28 December, Wand-Tetley was selected by Pine-Coffin to assume the appointment of Adjutant, this being the key post for a captain in the unit, and one in which he would have the ear of his CO and be responsible for maintaining discipline in the battalion. With the extra responsibility came the entitlement to draw Adjutant's additional pay.[18]

Once Batavia had been stabilized and a sense of normality restored, Poett approached the divisional commander, Major General D. C. Hawthorn, and asked whether 5 Parachute Brigade might now be redeployed to a more challenging task better suited to its expertise and one that offered a greater degree of autonomy. Hawthorn considered the request favourably and despatched the brigade, with supporting arms in the shape of A Squadron 11th Cavalry (Prince Albert Victor's Own), equipped with Honey light tanks, and 6 Indian Field Battery Royal Indian Artillery, to the key port of Semarang, situated on the northern coast between Batavia and Surabaya. Before his departure, Poett was approached by a Dutch delegation and, separately, by an Indonesian named Sjahrir who claimed to be Dr Sukarno's nominated Prime Minister. Both requested that he take them with him to help reestablish Semarang's governance and administration. Poett politely but firmly refused both parties, stating that his brigade would be more than capable of undertaking its mission without such assistance.

176

Five Parachute Brigade's deployment from Batavia to Semarang was completed over 9 to 10 January 1946. It arrived to find that the town had suffered in a similar fashion to Batavia at the hands of heavily armed Indonesian militants and bandits, who seemed as content to terrorize the local population through murder and robbery as they were to attack British troops. Poett's brigade relieved 49 Indian Infantry Brigade, under Brigadier de Burgh Morris, which had just completed a major operation to secure Semarang, in order to enable the evacuation of significant numbers of Allied prisoners of war and British and Dutch internees, of whom there were some 20,000. Throughout the evacuation, in which the POWs and internees were moved from their camps at Ambarawa, Banjobiroe and Magelang to Semarang and thence to Batavia by ship and aircraft, fighting had persisted against militant Indonesians who had done all they could to disrupt the operation and had managed to cut power, water and food supplies to the town.

De Burgh Morris had been assisted in his task by a battalion of Japanese troops under the command of Major Kido. This Japanese battalion had been in Semarang at the end of the war, and initially had handed over many of their weapons to the Indonesians in line with a direction from the Japanese High Command. However, when the more extreme Indonesian militants started to ransack the town, and following an incident in which the bandits executed some eighty-five Japanese prisoners, Kido undertook to recover his weapons from the bandits and re-establish control of Semarang. This was the situation when the first Allied troops, 3rd Battalion 10th Princess Mary's Own Gurkha Rifles, arrived in mid-October at Semarang's port. The Gurkha battalion arrived in landing craft from HMS *Glenroy*. Initially unaware of each other's presence, the British and Japanese, operating from opposite ends of the town, set about clearing Semarang of its Indonesian militants. Meeting in the middle of the town, there was a brief clash between British and Japanese forces until they realized that their aims were similar, at which time Kido placed himself at the disposal of the CO of the Gurkhas, Lieutenant Colonel Dick Edwards.

Thus the erstwhile enemies found themselves fighting alongside one another, there being little doubt that the single Gurkha battalion would have had difficulty in containing the anarchic situation without the assistance of the Japanese battalion. A composite brigade, under Brigadier Richard Bethell, Commander Royal Artillery (CRA) 23rd Indian Division, arrived shortly thereafter to relieve Edwards and begin the task of evacuating some 11,000 Allied prisoners of war and civilian internees. Kido's battalion had continued to operate under the British, with the composite CRA Brigade and from mid-December under 49 Indian Infantry Brigade.[19]

Thus Poett found himself in the unusual position of having a Japanese battalion placed under his command when he arrived at Semarang in January to relieve 49 Indian Infantry Brigade. Upon disembarking, Wand-Tetley found the town to be a relatively modern port, with predominantly new buildings. Most were still in relatively good condition, except for those that had suffered at the hands of militant bandits and looters and some in the Bodjong district which, two months previously, had been on the receiving end of RAF bombers. Before the war the town had been a thriving hub and had handled the majority of central Java's exports. The residential suburbs were inland, on higher ground to the south some three miles from the town and port. Farther inland still, another two miles to the south-east, was Gombel Hill, which dominated Semarang and its approaches for several miles around. Besides its sea port, the town was served by an airport some three miles to the west, which could handle planes of at least Dakota size. The town's population numbered some 225,000: the majority were made up of some 185,000 Indonesians, with about 40,000 Chinese, and approximately 5,000 Dutch. The Dutch had held the majority of key administrative positions prior to the war and were viewed by the Indonesians with disdain. However, the Chinese fared worst, for during the occupation it was they who suffered most at the hands of the Japanese, and after the armistice they were subsequently victimized by Indonesians who accused them of collaborating with the British. For its electricity and water supply the population relied upon Oengaran, about fifteen miles inland, while for food it relied upon supplies from the hinterland, for there was very limited agriculture close to the town.

It was clear to Poett that he would have to hold the vital ground of Gombel Hill and the airport, through which his brigade would be re-supplied and the remaining Allied prisoners of war would be evacuated. Having conducted an appreciation of the defensive positions in the area he established a twelve-mile perimeter around the town, using a canal to the eastern side of town as one boundary which included Gombel Hill, and a canal on the western side as the other boundary. Given that the perimeter was too long to man in its entirety he established company bases, with platoon outstations, on the principal routes in and out of town. A company base was also established at the airport, and platoons and detachments covered all other key bases such as the port, the railway station and principal public buildings. A vigorous patrol programme was established to police the areas in between the numerous bases. Major Kido and his battalion were given the task of holding the vital ground, Gombel Hill. The Japanese troops were perceived by Poett to be indispensable but, owing to the harsh treatment meted out by them during their occupation, they were less than popular with the town's citizens. Thus the Gombel Hill task presented a pragmatic solution as to how best to employ Kido's troops for, although the role was vital, it was well away from the town.

When Pine-Coffin returned from Poett's Orders Group, Wand-Tetley learned that 7th (LI) Parachute Battalion's task would be to secure the main residential area to the south of town. The battalion would also provide the brigade reserve, should any other sector need reinforcing at short notice. The residential area contained the HQ of RAPWI (Recovered Allied Prisoners of War and Internees). This organization's HQ and camps, whose role, with the Red Cross, was the provision of humanitarian relief and medical help to POWs and internees, would require particularly close protection. With the Japanese battalion on Gombel Hill on the eastern boundary, the 12th (Yorkshire) Parachute Battalion was given the task of defending the western boundary and the airport, and 13th (Lancashire) Parachute Battalion the town centre and docks. The three parachute battalions and the Japanese set up a patrol programme that covered not only the town, but an area outside their perimeter to a distance of 2,000 yards. The patrols made sure to visit all the local villages or 'kampongs' within the area, not only to reassure the locals but also to prevent the militants from basing themselves there. The brigade settled quickly to its task of securing and rebuilding Semarang. However, it was clear that the militants were not going to give up without a fight and the various factions, none of which appeared to be controlled centrally, made it clear that they intended to expel the British and dispose of both the Dutch and Chinese afterwards.

With patrols from the three parachute battalions and the Japanese providing security and keeping the extremists out of Semarang, Poett set the remainder of 5 Parachute Brigade to the business of re-imposing law and order and re-establishing vital services within the town itself. The brigade was assisted in the task of civil administration by the Allied Military Administration Civil Affairs Bureau (AMACAB), which was established on 15 January and led by a Dutchman, Dr Angenent, an experienced pre-war civil administrator. He was supported in his role by the commander of RAPWI, Major Kenneth Milne of the King's Royal Rifle Corps, who acted as principal military liaison officer to Poett. AMACAB was arranged in four branches, dealing with law and order, engineering, health, and food. Each branch head worked closely with an appointed officer of 5 Parachute Brigade, who would advise and bring the resources of the brigade to bear as required. The vast majority of the civil population were keen to return to a peaceful existence and to have the opportunity of rebuilding their lives and businesses, and it was imperative that the brigade quickly restore their confidence. This was not helped in the early days by a rumour put about by the militants that 5 Parachute Brigade, in its entirety, were violent convicts who had been released from prison on the condition that they become parachutists! However, as the town's citizens found that they could once again walk the streets without being murdered or robbed, and as improvements were introduced, with food, water and electricity being restored, the British soldiers were gradually accepted.

The task of policing Semarang was given to 2 Observation Unit RA, under Major John Bamford, assisted by 4 Airlanding Anti-Tank Battery RA and 6 Indian Field Battery RIA. A curfew between 2230 hours and 0430 hours was imposed, and Bamford and his Gunners immediately set about rebuilding the town's police force, which had been broken up during the Japanese occupation. Bamford put out the word for pre-war policemen and fresh volunteers to step forward and man the new police force. Co-ordinated by a central police HQ and organized within four divisions, new police posts were set up across the town. The divisions were commanded by British officers assisted by Gunners, but the constabulary was found entirely from the local population, two of the divisions being Indonesian, and one each being Dutch and Chinese. Each night British troops would patrol the streets by jeep, enforcing the curfew and visiting all the police posts. The new force was provided with uniforms, and regular pay and rations meant that the constabulary were soon imbued with high morale and a sense of *esprit de corps*. Crime was reduced dramatically, public confidence in the police was quickly established, and before long the town's population was once again reporting incidents to their local police post for investigation.

The restoration of essential services to Semarang, including power and water, fell largely to 3 Airborne Squadron RE, under Major Peter Moore. In this he was assisted ably by local citizens who had worked before the war as engineers. As a priority, the Sappers and their ever-increasing team of citizen helpers set about repairing damaged water-points and constructing new ones. The main power station and its electricity substations also received their attention; these were repaired and new generators installed. The town's gasworks and refrigeration plant were brought back into service. The roads, railways and docks, all of which had been damaged in Allied bombing raids, were next in line to receive attention. Roads were resurfaced, railway culverts and bridges and four locomotives were repaired, and two dry docks and their adjacent warehouses were repaired and put back into service. The Sappers also built two sawmills, and ensured that any buildings rendered unsafe by bombing were demolished safely. Meanwhile, the brigade headquarters Signal Section took control of Semarang's telephone system and its two exchanges and ensured that it was maintained effectively while 225th Parachute Field Ambulance, under Lieutenant Colonel John Watts, organized medical facilities throughout the town, and the brigade's RASC detachment organized the distribution of food.

Meanwhile, 7th (LI) Parachute Battalion, in common with the other two parachute battalions, held and secured their section of perimeter against militant infiltration, maintained their patrols, and conducted a number of cordon and search operations. The militants wore a variety of uniforms and were armed with a miscellany of weapons, including Dutch and Japanese rifles, British Bren guns, mortars, and a few 75mm and 105mm light artillery guns. Initially, their mortar and artillery fire was extremely inaccurate, but it improved over time and the Japanese battalion on Gombel Hill became the principal recipient of such fire. Accordingly, 2 Forward Observation Unit RA was given the task of countering this threat. Having established a series of observation posts on high ground to take sound bearings, the unit called in counter-battery fire from 6 Indian Field Battery RIA and the 4.2-inch mortar troop of 4 Airlanding Anti-Tank Battery RA. Such counter-battery fire, brought down quickly upon the enemy positions, proved to be most effective.

The militants also made use of the numerous kampongs in which to hide and from which they would sally forth on their nefarious activities. In the early days the parachute battalions would move in close to their target, engage any bandits with small-arms fire, and subsequently burn the kampong to the ground. Even if only searching for weapons and hides, a good deal of damage to property might occur. It became clear quickly that the villagers suffered unnecessarily in such operations, and although such tactics might be suited to conventional war they were somewhat heavy-handed for counter-insurgency operations and did little to win over the hearts and minds of the villagers. Accordingly, such cordon and search operations were dropped in favour of a more subtle and ultimately more effective intelligence-based system, run by the brigade and battalion intelligence sections, that enabled the militants and their arms caches to be targeted more precisely with less risk of collateral damage. Besides, the militants soon realized that they were no match for the British paratroopers or, for that matter, Major Kido's Japanese troops and, if they perceived there was any danger that they might be cornered, adopted the tactic of changing quickly into a set of civilian clothes that they kept handy and then hiding amongst the villagers. Only when the militants were stiffened by the presence of renegade Japanese troops who had gone over to the other side would they stand and fight it out with the paratroopers.[20]

At the beginning of February 1946 the C-in-C Allied Land Forces SEAC visited 5 Parachute Brigade in Semarang and toured the battalion positions. Dempsey was evidently impressed by what he saw, and asked the brigade commander to pass on his congratulations and thanks to all commanding officers and their units. During his visit he also informed Poett that he had been selected as Director of Plans at the War Office and would be flying back to London shortly to take up his new appointment. For Poett this meant that he would have to leave the brigade he had formed and the comrades with whom he had experienced so much, the Normandy invasion, the Rhine Crossing, the advance to the Baltic, and their more recent deployment to the Far East. He received a warm and heartfelt farewell from the brigade, and consoled himself with the fact that he would be leaving on a high and, with the war over, a posting in England was probably long overdue. He handed over command of 5 Parachute Brigade to Brigadier Ken Darling on 16 February. Darling was very well known to and very much respected by the brigade, for he had been the previous CO of 12th (Yorkshire) Parachute Battalion, which he had commanded from the time of the Rhine crossing.

Events continued to move rapidly for, within a fortnight of Darling assuming command of 5 Parachute Brigade, Wand-Tetley was informed by his CO, Pine-Coffin, that the brigade would be relieved in mid-March by T Regiment Group of the Royal Netherlands Army. In many respects this was very welcome news, but the officers were also conscious that they only had two weeks to prepare for the arrival of the Dutch formation. However, it was understood that there would at least be time for a measured, two-month handover of duties. Darling had briefed his commanding officers that a good deal of tact and diplomacy would be needed to reassure the locals, for none of the Indonesians were likely to take kindly to the news that the British were to be replaced by the Dutch. A smooth handover was essential if all the hard work in rebuilding Semarang was not to unravel. The British thus spent a good deal of time and effort in reassuring the local communities and ethnic leaders that the Dutch formation would be more than capable of maintaining law and order and of protecting the town's citizens from militant extremists. It was also stressed that the Dutch would remain under British command until the official handover of responsibility on 'flag day', which was due to be 15 May, and that it was in nobody's interest to allow the town to revert to its previous anarchic condition.[21]

Echoing the direction of their brigade commander, Pine-Coffin and his officers also stressed to the men of 7th (LI) Parachute Battalion the importance of maintaining good relations with the Dutch troops throughout the extended handover period, for any friction would almost certainly be exploited by those with a different political agenda. They need not have worried though, for when the Dutch troops under Colonel van Langen arrived in mid-March, the paratroopers found them to be very professional in their approach. Many of them had served previously alongside British and American forces, or had served in the Dutch Resistance movement. The handover proceeded well, and the paratroopers ensured that all they had learnt in Semarang was

182

passed on to the Dutch troops. For the best part of the first month all the Dutch units had attached to them a small British liaison party consisting of officers and NCOs. It was soon realized that the Dutch troops were not as well equipped or trained as the British in terms of machine gunners, mortarmen and signallers, and so the paratroopers took the time to train their counterparts in these skills. Initially also lacking in artillery support, this was addressed by the arrival of a Dutch field-gun battery. A good quantity of logistic and maintenance stores were also handed over. In the second month the Dutch units were gradually given greater autonomy, although the paratroopers were always at hand should advice or assistance be required.

The arrival of the Dutch created a watershed, allowing the brigade commander the opportunity to evacuate Major Kido, his battalion and all Japanese civilians from Semarang. They departed on 23 March via the evacuation staging camp at Galang Island. On leaving, Kido presented his sword to Darling as a sign of respect, and sent a signal to all ranks of 5 Parachute Brigade expressing his warmest appreciation and thanks.

The presence of the Dutch T Regiment Group allowed 5 Parachute Brigade to celebrate the first anniversary of the Rhine crossing in style with a parade. The men of 7th (LI) Parachute Battalion had not done any square-bashing for some time and so, as Adjutant, Wand-Tetley and the Regimental Sergeant Major had their work cut out to bring the men up to standard with very limited rehearsal time. Nonetheless the men rose to the challenge admirably and on 24 March, with the Dutch troops manning the defensive positions around the town, 5 Parachute Brigade in its entirety with all its supporting arms paraded through the centre of Semarang. The salute was taken by Lieutenant General Sir Montagu Stopford, Allied Commander Netherlands East Indies. While the parachute battalions marched past, A Squadron 11th Cavalry (Prince Albert Victor's Own) tracked past in their Honey light tanks, and 6 Indian Field Battery RIA drove past towing their field guns.[22]

Ever since first hearing the news in late February that they were to be relieved by Dutch troops, Wand-Tetley and his fellow officers had discussed their future options. It soon became apparent that 5 Parachute Brigade was likely to leave Semarang to join the remainder of 6th Airborne Division in Palestine. However many of those in 7th (LI) Parachute Battalion had enlisted specifically because of the war, and so they now debated the pros and cons of staying in the Army. Although the battalion had deployed to the Far East while the war was still underway, following the Japanese surrender it had been engaged in what was essentially a post-war counter-insurgency operation.

Wand-Tetley discussed his options with Pine-Coffin, who stressed to his Adjutant that with his distinguished war service and natural talent as a soldier, he should have no problem in carving out a worthwhile career for himself if he decided to stay. However, his CO also pointed out that the battalion's imminent departure from Semarang would be a natural watershed, and that if he did wish to leave then he would allow him to do so before he became caught up in the battalion's move to Palestine. Having considered the matter, Wand-Tetley decided that although he had had what in those days was called a 'good war', and had the prospect of a bright future in the Army ahead of him, with the war now over he would return to civilian life. He bade farewell to his battalion on 3 April and left Java, proceeding on Class A Release to the UK, which he reached on 16 May.

Five Parachute Brigade duly handed over to the Dutch T Regiment Group and left Java on 15 May. Having stopped over in Malaya for a short while, the brigade moved on to Singapore and in July set sail for Palestine, which it reached on 7 August, to rejoin 6th Airborne Division. The brigade's tour of duty in Java had been extremely successful. They had provided security to Semarang and set the town back on its feet, while their impartial and fair approach had won the hearts and minds of the town's ethnic minority communities. This significant achievement was something of which all those in 5 Parachute Brigade could be justifiably proud.

However, such conditions proved to be only fleeting for, despite the end of the war, peace did not come easily to Indonesia and the Far East. In Japan it transpired that America was extremely successful at rebuilding and setting the conditions for Japan's post-war recovery. However, elsewhere in Asia, the end of the war signalled the start of decolonization, a general decline of empire, and a good deal of bloodshed in the process. Indonesia finally achieved independence from the Netherlands after a four-year guerrilla war. In 1947 Britain granted independence to India and Pakistan and in 1948 to Burma (now Myanmar) and Ceylon. Malaya eventually achieved independence, but not before the British had fought and won a protracted counter-insurgency campaign against communist forces. The United States honoured its commitment to grant the Philippines independence on the proviso that it could retain a military presence there. However, France was desperate to retain its colonies in Indochina, leading it into a costly war with Vietnam that would also later see America embroiled, but for Cold War rather than colonial considerations.

Notes

1. HS 9/1453/7, Peter Michael Wand-Tetley, 1939–46.
2. Wand-Tetley was in fact at Cambridge in 1938–9 (not 1939–40). He enlisted for initial military training on 19 October 1939.
3. HS 9/1453/7, Peter Michael Wand-Tetley, 1939–46.

4. Army Service Record (Army Form B199A) of P. M. Wand-Tetley.

5. Otway, *The Second World War 1939–1945, Army: Airborne Forces*. Chs. 9 & 12.

6. Gale, *With the 6th Airborne Division in Normandy*. Ch. 6.

7. Crookenden, *Battle of the Bulge 1944*. Chs 1 & 14.

8. NA Kew, CAB 120/262, Churchill to War Office, 22 June 1940.

9. Otway, op cit, Ch. 3.

10. Ibid.

11. Ibid.

12. War Office. *By Air to Battle: The Official Account of the British 1st and 6th Airborne Divisions*. Ch. 4.

13. Otway, op cit, Ch. 6.

14. War Office. *By Air to Battle: The Official Account of the British 1st and 6th Airborne Divisions*, op cit, Ch. 4.

15. Nationalist weakness and incompetence in the face of the *Ichi-Go* offensives served to underpin a shift in public opinion that eventually would see the Communists come to power in 1949.

16. NA Kew, WO 203/6011, 5 Parachute Brigade: report on activities in Semarang, Jan-May 1946.

17. Ibid.

18. Army Service Record (Army Form B199A) of P. M. Wand-Tetley.

19. NA Kew, WO 203/6011, op cit.

20. Ibid.

21. Ibid.

22. Ibid.

Chapter 6

Colonial Service

Nigeria

On arriving back in England Wand-Tetley returned first to his parents' house in Kensington, west London, and then went on four months' Release Leave. He had no particular plans for his future and for the next few months lived a carefree existence, relaxing in the company of a girlfriend who was the barmaid at the pub he favoured, and greatly enjoying the general sense of freedom that came in the aftermath of the war. In September his Army leave and salary came to an end, and although he had savings these would not last indefinitely. Furthermore, after a number of months in London the constant round of parties had started to pall somewhat. During daylight hours he increasingly found himself at a loose end, so he started to think seriously about a career and his future.[1]

Having mulled over a number of options, he decided to apply for a job in the Colonial Administrative Service. His decision to follow such a career would involve him in the period of the breakup of the old British Empire. After the war what Prime Minister Harold Macmillan was later to describe as a 'wind of change' was blowing, and would engage Wand-Tetley and his fellow colonial officers in assisting the newly independent Commonwealth countries in establishing themselves as self-governing countries. It happened that, around this time, Dick Greswell, a friend later discovered to be a distant cousin on his mother's side, returned from Nigeria. He reported very favourably on his experiences working abroad, for he had enjoyed his travels immensely and had evidently also been impressed by the local girls from the far north of that country, whom he described as especially alluring. There was nothing that Greswell said that caused Wand-Tetley to have second thoughts about his chosen career path and so in 1947 he set sail for West Africa.[2] Wand-Tetley recalls:

> Shortly after being demobilized I applied for a job in colonial administration, not because I had any idea of what it entailed, but

186

because life at home was boring and such work seemed suited to my qualifications, which were nil. The evening before my interview I met an agreeable fellow called Dick Greswell, who said that I should insist that my preference was for Northern Nigeria. So I did, and a few weeks later I was on an Elder Dempster boat, final destination Minna.[3]

Wand-Tetley brought with him to Africa his young bride Joan (née Engelbach), an artist employed in the film industry, whom he had married in England the previous year. Joan's family, of French lineage, had emigrated from Alsace to England at the end of the eighteenth century. Joan had been born in Egypt, the daughter of the celebrated Egyptologist and Chief Keeper of the Cairo Museum, Reginald (Rex) Engelbach who, among many archaeological achievements, orchestrated the opening of Tutankhamun's tomb by the British archaeologist Howard Carter. It appeared to their relatives that the two newlyweds had relatively little in common but they assumed that it was a case of opposites attracting.

Upon arriving in Lagos, then the capital, they travelled up-country to Minna, in the Northern Region, by train. Here Wand-Tetley was to spend his first four years as an Assistant District Officer (ADO). Minna was in Niger Province, and was surrounded by rolling savannah broken by thick forests. Wide expanses separated the many tribes, some of which had yet to see white men. Wand-Tetley got to know Minna's surrounding country well, for he, like all junior officers, was expected to spend a good deal of each month touring the province by foot, horse or kit-car.

Wand-Tetley had to familiarize himself quickly with a civil service hierarchy of authority and an approach different to that of the Army. Sir Frederick Lugard, instrumental in forging the fledgling country at the beginning of the twentieth century, had established a system of Residents, each aided by an Assistant Resident, to oversee the provinces (later to be called states), with Senior District Officers (SDOs), DOs and ADOs overseeing the provincial districts. However, the whole system of governance relied upon 'Indirect Rule' whereby, where practical, the Native Authorities and their indigenous institutions were kept in place to administer in accordance with local custom. The British administrators provided a supervisory and advisory role to the Native Authorities, and established a coherent and systematic method of raising revenues. Such an approach was in fact a pragmatic and economic expediency given the British skeleton staffs and the enormous tracts of land they had to oversee. In the Muslim north of Nigeria the British governed through the emirs, a number of whose emirates made up a province, in a benign form of colonialism headed by a predominantly Oxbridge-educated administrative service.

Wand-Tetley found that a colleague who had worked with him in the SOE had, by chance, also found his way out to Nigeria and was now his senior officer. Wand-Tetley:

> My first Resident was Max Backhouse, who was something of a terror, especially when drunk, but we had wartime experience in common and I got on well with him. A newly arrived ADO was traditionally greeted in the North with the words, 'The Hausa for horse is *doki*. Get one and then I don't want to see your face for three weeks'. I can't claim mine was quite like that, but it was the general idea. The purpose was to acquaint us with the people, the country, the lingua franca (this was *Gwari* country), so we held meetings with village heads and their councils, inspected records, looked at crops, received petitions, listened to complaints and wrote reports, which occasionally caused the Resident or DO to prick up his experienced ears and descend wrathfully on some erring district head.[4]

However, despite all this and the best of intentions, a fair degree of frustration evidently was experienced in everyday work, particularly with regards to the lack of funding. As in the Army, a good sense of humour was necessary to see one through such irritations. Wand-Tetley:

> Otherwise it was all a bit aimless, since there was no money available for development or to satisfy any petition that involved expenditure. I incautiously supported a petition for a road to a village, and was ordered to go out and supervise its construction by voluntary labour. This I did until all ten miles of the route had been cleared, and I accompanied the first lorry on its perilous journey. Needless to say, it did not survive the first rains.[5]

As for all colonial officers across the British Empire there were a good many service examinations that one was expected to pass if one were to climb the slippery pole of advancement. The subjects included Law, Colonial Regulations, General Orders and Financial Instructions. These provided the policy and basis of colonial rule, but an officer needed to be able to harness effectively the Native Authorities which provided the essential administrative backbone of a district. In Northern Nigeria learning the official language was pivotal to this and so, having passed his examination in Lower Standard Hausa, Wand-Tetley progressed and later passed his Higher Standard Hausa.[6]

After four years in charge of Divisions in Niger Province in the north, Wand-Tetley was posted to the Government Headquarters in Lagos, where he worked on various subjects, especially lands administration and new constitutional arrangements. Lagos was a far cry from the somewhat rustic environs of Minna, and the capital enjoyed a cosmopolitan and sophisticated social scene. Joan had sailed back to England in 1950 to have their son, Charles, and subsequently joined her husband in Lagos. They asked Max Backhouse to be godfather. Unfortunately, with a young child it was difficult for Joan to partake fully in the hectic social whirl of Lagos life into which Wand-Tetley had thrown himself so wholeheartedly. Wand-Tetley entered into an intense affair with a young married Nigerian barrister who had been educated in England and called to the Bar in London. This affair not only caused Joan great distress but was too public for the susceptibilities of the Government hierarchy. It was therefore decided by the Government to post Wand-Tetley to Wukari, a punishment station in the north, where he would be less likely to cause waves. Joan and Charles went with him but, for a marriage already weakening, the Lagos episode was a fatal blow. Also, Joan's health was not coping well with the Nigerian climate, and she heeded her doctor's advice to return to the UK. When Wand-Tetley returned on leave to England they agreed to part.[7]

Thus it was that Wand-Tetley found himself in Wukari, Benue Province. Many would have referred to this as 'Middle Belt' rather than the true north, but here was a fascinating glimpse of the old, disappearing Africa, where neither Islam nor Christianity had made an undue impact. The Resident, Cedric 'Foxy' Cole, resided a hundred miles to the west as the crow flies at Makurdy, and was more often than not preoccupied with the Tiv people, particularly in building for them a council chamber at Gboko sixty miles to the south. Some of the northerners thought that the Tiv, a warlike tribe with a particularly belligerent reputation and with faces scarred by tribal markings, were cannibals, but this was not true. However, if one felt so inclined one only had to travel 200 miles north-east of Wukari to Nigeria's border with the French Cameroons to find such a people, the Komo Vomni, of the Alantika mountains. As late as 1961 they ate a tax collector, followed by the police sergeant and six constables who came looking for him.[8]

This was not the only example of 'old ways' dying hard. Not far from Ikot Ekpene, between Port Harcourt and Calabar in the east, the Ibibio tribe traditionally were of the leopard cult. Similarly to lycanthropy (the werewolf legend), the people believed they could turn at will into leopards. Between 1945 and 1948, when Wand-Tetley was first in Nigeria, there were 196 proven or suspected leopard-men murders in the forests of Abak, and ninety-six men were convicted, of which seventy-seven were hung and the remainder acquitted through lack of evidence. It transpired that behind the leopard-men murders was a secret ju-ju society called the 'Idiong', whose ceremonies included ritual consumption of human organs and the feeding of ju-ju shrines with human blood.[9]

Although Wukari was a quiet backwater, it had the compensation that one was left largely to one's own devices. Indeed, for many this was perceived as a distinct advantage, and some conspired actively to maintain their autonomy. Wand-Tetley:

> After four years in Lagos, I was posted to Wukari, as the only white face; the doctor was a Northern Yoruba from Offa. It was a delightful spot and life was leisurely and uneventful, the Jukun being a peaceful tribe who only wished to be left alone to pursue their rituals. Here another famous anecdote was allegedly born – that of a predecessor who, on being advised by telegram of a Resident's intended visit during the rains, replied, 'No bridge at Mile 108', so the visit was cancelled. When the Resident did come in the dry season, he checked mile 108. Sure enough there was no bridge, and never had been.[10]

Furthermore, given the long distances and the difficult communications within the country, amusing misunderstandings would also occur. Wand-Tetley:

> We all know the tale of Freddy Parsons, excellent post-war teacher of Hausa at LSE, but pre-war Zaria ADO. Touring officers had to be especially alert to locusts, and to report their location and breeding cycle. If near the railway, telegrams were sent up line station to station by the laborious and unreliable *rororo* and *rarara* versions of Morse, kept as short as possible. Freddy reported, LOCUSTS FOUND NEAR BIRNIN GWARI COPULATING. The reply, when it arrived the following day, was short and to the point, STOP COPULATING KILL LOCUSTS.[11]

Wand-Tetley had now been promoted to District Officer, and although the autonomy he enjoyed in the provinces undoubtedly had its plus side he found the pace of life too slow and eventually became bored. He made his feelings known to his superiors. As a result in 1958 he was posted to Northern Region Headquarters, Kaduna, where he assisted in setting up a new Ministry to deal with civil service affairs and acted as head of it until replaced by a Nigerian under the localization programme.

Kaduna had been selected well as Nigeria's northern capital. The Queen and Prince Philip had visited the city in 1956, and a great durbar with some 10,000 participants had been held in their honour. The Native Authorities from the north, dressed in robes of pure white or powder blue, turned up from far and wide. For their part, the Colonial Service officers were resplendent in their 'tropical whites', many with war medals upon their chests, the rank of the officer identifiable by the size of the oak leaves on the high collar gorget patches, with the more senior sporting the largest oak leaves. With self-government came a change in the design of the 'tropical whites' to accommodate Muslim leaders who wished to adopt the uniform; the jackets were lengthened to just above the knee and a stylish astrakhan side-cap replaced the Victorian helmet.[12]

It was in Kaduna that Wand-Tetley met and married, in 1960, the vivacious young lady, Felicia 'Flick' (née Bloxham) who had recently arrived from England to assume her appointment with the Government of Northern Nigeria through the Crown Agents. The two of them made an excellent match, and this time the marriage would last, for they both had a good deal in common. Flick thoroughly enjoyed Africa, and was also from an Army family. Her grandfather, Victor, had fought in the Boer War with an irregular mounted infantry regiment rejoicing in the title of Kitchener's Horse, and in the First World War had re-enlisted to fight with the South Wales Borderers, with whom he had won an MC in Mesopotamia and been Mentioned in Despatches. Her father, Charles, had followed in his father's military footsteps and had been wounded badly at Mons as an 'Old Contemptible' in the BEF of 1914, distinguished himself as a Bisley rifle marksman and been honoured with an MBE in an impressively long career that spanned both world wars.

Flick had gone out to Nigeria because she had wanted a change from working in London. She had already considered a post with an oil company in Qatar, but her sister Rosemary and her husband Allen Scott were at that time in Port Harcourt, in the east of Nigeria, and when the Crown Agents advertized the post in Nigeria, albeit the north, Flick thought, 'why not?' Allen Scott had gone out to Libya in 1954 with Barclays Bank DCO, but had moved from Tripoli to Nigeria in 1957 and would remain in the country for twenty-seven years. Not surprisingly, Wand-Tetley was asked to be a godfather to Rosemary's son Michael, when he was born in Ijebu Igbo in 1961. Flick had already picked up the honours of being a godmother to Rosemary's first child, Sally-Anne, born in Port Harcourt three years earlier; her third child, Caroline, was born in the less exotic climes of Surrey when the Scotts were back home in England on a long leave. Thus the two sisters, Flick and Rosemary, would both come to know this corner of West Africa very well. Indeed, Rosemary would later be decorated with the MBE for her valuable services to the Nigeria-Britain Association.

While in Kaduna Wand-Tetley would occasionally engage in shooting guinea fowl and 'bush-fowl' (francolin), aided by his pointer, Flanagan. However, he spent more time managing a rifle club, persuading the British Army regiment that was posted there to lend him the rifles and their ranges. This was a relatively low-key affair, but it proved to be a pleasant distraction and allowed him once again to pursue his passion for shooting and also to socialize with the armed forces.

When Wand-Tetley had first arrived in Nigeria it was generally perceived that some twenty-five years was the time frame to independence. However, this was not to be. Nigeria achieved internal self-government in 1959, and independence in 1960. After independence Wand-Tetley stayed on for a further four years. He did so, in common with some of his fellow expatriate Northern Nigerian officers, because senior politicians and Native Authority officers had known and worked with them as ADOs and DOs over the years, and they trusted them. For his many years of service he was awarded an OBE in 1962, although the investiture for this would take place in Nairobi in 1965, for by that stage he had moved to Kenya. On balance he thoroughly enjoyed his time in Nigeria. Nonetheless, Wand-Tetley, like many of his fellow colonial officers in Nigeria, harboured mixed feelings about the degree of success achieved during the relatively rapid British withdrawal, as they perceived it, and the transition to Nigerian self-rule. Wand-Tetley:

> My last five years were spent in Kaduna establishments, where new ministers were NA [Native Authorities] councillors or officials with whom we had worked closely in earlier days, and who, we earnestly hoped, would carry on in a similar tradition. In the end most of us left sadly but without regret, with no sense of achievement but also a feeling that we had done our best and had little to be ashamed of.[13]

Wand-Tetley and Flick flew out of Nigeria from Kano in 1964.

Kenya

The early sixties saw a spate of British colonies in Africa achieve independence, and time finally ran out for expatriate colonial administrative officers. However, new opportunities arose for them to use their expertise as advisers within various organizations to assist the fledgling Commonwealth countries. One such organization was the Department of Technical Cooperation (later the Ministry of Overseas Development), and in 1964 Wand-Tetley was appointed by this body as Adviser on Civil Service Administration to the East African Common Services Organization (EACSO), Nairobi, which operated a range of public services on behalf of the Governments of Kenya, Tanzania and Uganda. He assisted in the negotiations which led to the Treaty of East African Cooperation and the formation of the East African Community (EAC) in 1967, and in the same year accepted a ten-year appointment with the Corps of Specialists of the Ministry of Overseas Development.[14]

Wand-Tetley and Flick arrived in Kenya six months after the country had achieved independence. Jomo Kenyatta was proving to be a promising Head of State, although the Mau Mau rebellion, or 'The Emergency', was still a fresh and raw memory for many. Kenyatta urged all, regardless of race or tribe, to contribute to the economic growth of the newly independent Kenya through personal effort and group cooperation, in a doctrine that he termed *Harambee* ('all pull together'). He achieved political stability and maintained essentially capitalist, pro-Western policies, and a reasonably prosperous mixed economy, and encouraged foreign, state and private investment in agriculture, industry and services in which tourism was a key element. However, despite progressive education and health policies, significant tribal divisions and rural poverty remained, as did corruption. Nonetheless, relations between the EAC countries were good and the advantages to the three neighbours in combining the general services, particularly communications, were obvious and, much to Wand-Tetley's satisfaction, work went ahead with enthusiasm.

As in Nigeria, Flick had a full time job in Kenya. She worked in the British High Commission, which only six months after independence was expected to establish good relations with the newly independent Kenyan Government and deal with the varying needs of British subjects who either had left or wanted to leave a Kenya now subject to African rule. Life in Kenya was distinctly different to that in northern Nigeria, where there had been no white settler community. In Kenya the expatriates who had settled there to put down roots and make it their home had done their best to ensure that the country, and particularly Nairobi, catered to their own enduring lifestyle requirements as well as those of the Africans and Asians who had also settled there.[15]

Soon after arriving Wand-Tetley joined the Kenya Rifle Club and, as a member of the Kenya Team, shot at Bisley in 1968. Also in the team was Dave Drummond who, as a member of special forces, had played a leading role in pioneering covert operations against the Mau Mau rebellion. Wand-Tetley took up game-fishing off the coast at Mnarani Club on Kilifi Creek, and in his final year in the country, 1968, made a record catch of a tuna. Advisers and experts involved in setting up EACSO were entertained and especially given an opportunity to meet Ugandans, Kenyans and Tanzanians who had to make this union of the three states work. Most welcome were Nigerian friends, many, like the Wand-Tetleys themselves, helping the new Kenya Government to adjust to self-government. The Nigerian High Commissioner for East Africa at the time, Ade Martins, was in fact an old friend and fellow government officer from Nigeria.[16]

Tanzania

In 1968 the administrative headquarters of the East African Community moved from Nairobi to Arusha, in northern Tanzania, a town which up until this time had been known primarily as a safari centre and a 'pit stop' for the East African Safari Rally. Wand-Tetley moved south with the EAC. He was one of the few expatriates to do so, although a large number of senior Kenyan and Ugandan EAC officials made the journey south over Kenya's border to swell the population of Arusha.[17]

The Republic of Tanzania had been formed four years prior to Wand-Tetley's arrival, when Tanganyika united with the island of Zanzibar. Tanganyika itself had achieved independence in 1961 with not one life lost in the process. Julius Nyerere led the country in an often controversial and staunchly socialist manner. He would nonetheless establish for himself a reputation as one of Africa's most respected politicians, and was known throughout Tanzania as *Mwalimu* (teacher).

Nyrere's national policy of *ujamaa na kujitegemea* (socialism and self-reliance) was inspired by his studies of Karl Marx, his observations of the Chinese communist system, and his reading of the Bible. This policy was embodied in his Arusha Declaration of 1967. Central to his philosophy was the formation of the *ujamaa* (familyhood) villages, the intention being that these would be self-reliant collective farms, with people compulsorily resettled if necessary and all united by the single language of Kiswahili. Other tenets of his policy included nationalization of the economy, the redistribution of wealth through taxation, a universal primary school system and a public health service. The economic policies were not destined to succeed, although there is no doubt that a great sense of national unity was created despite there being some 130 tribes within the country, when much of the rest of Africa would remain beset by tribal problems and rivalry.

Arusha is Tanzania's safari centre for good reason, for the game parks between the town and Lake Victoria are arguably the finest anywhere in Africa. With an interest in the great outdoors, the Wand-Tetleys could not have been better located. They lived just out of town at Tengeru, in the shadow of Mount Meru. In the distance to the east they could see Mount Kilimanjaro, rising thousands of feet above the town of Moshi and the surrounding forests and plains. Much closer to home and almost 'back-garden' was the attractive forest-fringed Lake Duluti where at the weekends Wand-Tetley would often fish for tilapia, followed by a leisurely stroll with Flick.[18]

Seychelles and St Kitts-Nevis-Anguilla

In 1969 Wand-Tetley's appointment with the EAC ended. His work on Africa's continent was at an end, and his future was destined to be on islands. From late 1969 to mid 1970 he carried out two short assignments, first as Salaries Review Commissioner in Seychelles, and then as Chairman, Civil Service Review Commission, in the state of St Kitts-Nevis-Anguilla.[19]

Wand-Tetley was based in the Secretariat Building in the capital, Victoria, on the largest of the islands, Mahé. Seychelles was administered by the Governor, Sir Bruce Greatbatch, appointed by London's Foreign and Commonwealth Office, supported by a legislative and executive Governing Council. In the early 1960s two local political parties had emerged. The Seychelles Democratic Party (SDP), led by James 'Jimmy' Mancham, which sought continued integration with the United Kingdom, and the Seychelles People's United Party (SPUP) led by France-Albert René, which sought full independence. By the end of 1969 Wand-Tetley had completed his Salaries Review and, all too quickly for him and Flick, they departed these idyllic islands. They then went from Mahé to Mauritius for a short period, again to advise on the structure and cost of the civil service.

In early 1970 Wand-Tetley flew to St Kitts-Nevis-Anguilla. Prior to their arrival the three islands of St Christopher (St Kitts), Nevis and Anguilla (SNA) had been in the international news headlines. As Britain divested itself of its empire, part of the process involved this colony becoming, in 1967, an internally self-governing Associated State, with Britain retaining responsibility for defence and foreign affairs. This represented a significant step towards full independence.

However, Anguilla felt it would benefit little from such an arrangement and rebelled, refused to accept rule from St Kitts, evicted the Royal St Kitts Police Force who were on the island, and threatened to declare unilateral independence from Britain. An 'interim agreement' proved effective until early 1969, but later that same year Britain's Under-Secretary of State for Foreign and Commonwealth Affairs was expelled. Britain's reaction was swift. Two frigates, along with some 300 paratroopers, followed by a squad of Royal Engineers and a team of fifty London Metropolitan Police officers, were despatched to restore order. At the time Wand-Tetley arrived in SNA the political argument was still in full spate and British troops were still on Anguilla. Furthermore, in 1970, the Nevis Reformation Party was formed, and it similarly called for separation for Nevis from St Kitts. Wand-Tetley would depart SNA in mid-1970 with the dispute still unresolved.

Seychelles (once more)

23 July 1972. It had been an early start for Wand-Tetley, but the thirty-two-foot *La Mouette*, a charter boat from Bob and Monique Barker's Game Fish Club, was now five miles off Beau Vallon Bay and trawling along the likely line of a confluence of two currents. Also aboard were Charlie Marzochi and Graham France. They were after marlin.

Immortalized by Ernest Hemingway in *The Old Man and the Sea*, winning the Pulitzer Prize but to his disappointment never landing one of the giant fish himself, marlin are the fish most coveted by big-game fishermen. Weighing up to 900kg and up to 4.6 metres of supercharged muscle in length, they are the biggest, fastest, most dangerous game fish in the ocean. Impressive predators, that in short bursts can reach 97 km/h, marlin can swallow fish the length of a man's arm in a single gulp, and thrill big-game fishermen with their spectacular leaps from the sea in their endeavours to dislodge hooks.

Without warning Wand-Tetley's lure was violently struck, and the line started being stripped from his reel with the speed and power of a massive torpedo. As the powerful fish hurtled through the water on its first great run Wand-Tetley knew that this was a very large one indeed, almost certainly a billfish, but was it a marlin? This was answered when the heavyweight leapt from the water. The seasoned skipper had never seen a marlin of this size. The boat was a hive of activity, with Bob shouting instructions to Charlie at the wheel to manoeuvre the vessel so as to match the powerful runs of the giant fish. Wand-Tetley settled himself for a long, hard fight, and knew that one mistake on his part would result in the fish of a lifetime breaking the line or slipping the hook and escaping. The fight ended an exhausting three hours and twenty minutes later when he finally brought the marlin to the gaff. When it was brought ashore to be weighed the rope on the Yacht Club scales snapped, so he took it instead to the United Concrete weighbridge under the official supervision of Gerard Compty. The 528lb black marlin was a new Seychelles record for a billfish caught on rod and line. Wand-Tetley was quoted in the following day's paper:

> Though I was on the rod we couldn't have had a better team, which is what matters against a fish that size. As skipper, Bob watched the fish's every movement and relayed information to Charlie whose boat-handling was superb. It really made all the difference. And for three hours Graham did anything that was needed, not least in keeping me well supplied with cold beer![20]

In terms of promoting tourism and big-game fishing in the Seychelles, this was a coup for Wand-Tetley. His catch came a month after a Dutch visitor had landed a 330lb blue marlin. He was to write, in 1974, *Sport Fishing in Seychelles*, a small booklet distributed free by the Tourism Department of the Seychelles Government, to inform anglers what Seychelles had to offer in terms of sport fishing. However, his immediate thoughts at the time of his record catch focused upon what else might be prowling the ocean off the shores of Seychelles. Wand-Tetley:

The question that now has to be answered is: if marlin like this can be caught practically on Beau Vallon beach, what lies out in the deep water on the edge of the shelf?[21]

Wand-Tetley had returned to Seychelles in June 1970 as Secretary to the Chief Minister, later Prime Minister Sir James Mancham, in which capacity he was responsible at the official level for an impressive and extremely wide-ranging portfolio that included development planning and co-ordination, town and country planning, tourism, trade and industry, immigration, and public relations, and for conducting negotiations with hotel and other developers.[22]

Two personalities in Seychelles came to dominate Wand-Tetley's working and personal life. One was Mancham, educated in England and called to the Bar of the Middle Temple. A bon vivant with a tremendous *joie de vivre*, with whom he worked very closely and developed a firm friendship, Mancham wrote of him, 'I was lucky to have as my Secretary, Peter Wand-Tetley, a civil servant of high integrity and competence and total dedication'.[23]

The other was the Governor of Seychelles, Sir Bruce Greatbatch, who had been British Deputy High Commissioner in Nairobi and prior to that a fellow officer of Wand-Tetley in Northern Nigeria. It was said of Sir Bruce, 'for anyone wanting to understand how, on the ground, the transition to independence from imperial power took place few could be more rewarding to study than Greatbatch.'[24]

Wand-Tetley's work took him to most of the islands, and also provided the opportunity to help receive and entertain numerous visitors to the country including, in 1972, the Queen and the Duke of Edinburgh and, in the previous year, Princess Margaret and Lord Snowdon. Others included Archbishop Makarios of Cyprus, who came to Mahé to visit the house at Sans Souci to which he had been sent in exile by the British Government, and international stars such as Bing Crosby. With Wand-Tetley's portfolio including environment and wildlife conservation, he also enjoyed the company of such luminaries as the famous naturalist Sir Peter Scott and the world-renowned ornithologist Dr. Roger Peterson. Lars Lindblad, who had helped to develop environmentally sensitive tours on his cruise ship, the *Lindblad Explorer*, also provided invaluable advice and was another very welcome visitor, as was the President of the World Wildlife Fund at the time, Prince Bernhard of the Netherlands.[25]

Travel for Wand-Tetley was not confined to the islands, for in the work of closer integration with East Africa he was the government officer selected to accompany Mancham and his party of Seychelles leaders on an official visit to Kenya. With Dr Mungai, Minister for Foreign Affairs, and other Kenyan ministers, they worked upon policies to improve trade relations and create a tourist scheme that would benefit both countries. Next the Seychelles party flew down to Mombasa to meet Jomo Kenyatta at State House. The visit proved to be a great success and the relationship between the two countries flourished as a result.[26]

In 1974, when Mancham was visiting London, the British Government informed him, much to his great disappointment, that Seychelles was to be granted full independence. As a result elections were held in which Mancham's SDP won thirteen of the fifteen Assembly seats over René's SPUP. Accordingly, Mancham was sworn in as Prime Minister of a self-governing coalition government in 1975, and the following year, upon full independence, he became President of the Republic of Seychelles, with René as his Prime Minister.

It was while he was in Seychelles that Wand-Tetley and his brother John, a successful doctor, heard of the tragic death of their youngest brother Nigel. Having joined the Royal Navy in 1942, Nigel's last day of service was in 1969 in the Roaring Forties as he raced his trimaran *Victress* in the *Sunday Times* Single-handed Non-stop Race Round the World. Tragically, *Victress* broke up in a gale and sank north of the Azores after sailing over 27,000 miles, just 1,100 miles from home, and having crossed her outward track to complete the circumnavigation in 179 days.[27] It is likely he would have made it home in record time to claim the *Sunday Times* £5,000 prize had it not been that he was pushing *Victress* so hard after hearing radio reports that Donald Crowhurst was contesting his lead keenly. In fact, the delusional and paranoid Crowhurst had throughout the race fooled the world that he was in contention, yet he had never left the Atlantic, in an infamous voyage that Sir Francis Chichester has called 'the sea drama of the century.'[28]

Having been rescued from the wreck of the *Victress*, Nigel had been planning a second attempt to sail single-handed around the world in his new trimaran *Miss Vicky*. However, suffering from increasing financial difficulties he had become increasingly depressed and, in February 1972, had been found dead, hanging from a tree in a wood near Dover, after having been reported missing by his second wife Evelyn.

Caribbean

In 1975 when his assignment in the Seychelles came to an end, Wand-Tetley was appointed Regional Advisor on Civil Service Administration and attached to the British Development Division in the Caribbean, headed by his old friend Sir Bruce Greatbatch. Based in the Division's headquarters in Barbados, he worked on a wide range of administrative and political problems, re-organized the British aid scheme for scholarship and training in the Caribbean, and assisted in the planning and administration of development aid for tourism. This work necessitated regular and constant visits to British Associated States and Dependencies across the West Indies. However, this seemingly ideal existence was to come to an end in 1978 upon completion of his ten-year appointment with the Corps of Specialists of the Ministry of Overseas Development.[29]

Social life on Barbados itself was somewhat limited by the frequent absences arising from work and the requirement to visit the other islands. Nonetheless, the Wand-Tetleys spent most free Sundays on a quiet beach with their old friend Sir Bruce Greatbatch. When he commenced his work in the Caribbean Wand-Tetley was fifty-five, the normal retirement age for many expatriates abroad, so he had been aware from the outset that this would be his last assignment. His three fascinating years spent in the islands during this pivotal period, when many were in the process of gaining full independence, and during which time he was able to make a genuine contribution to facilitating the process, passed all too quickly as far as he was concerned.

Home from the Hill
When in 1978 his time was up in the Caribbean, Wand-Tetley retired with Flick to Jersey, where his mother Cécile lived, to map out their next move. He and Flick enjoyed exploring Jersey and getting to know the island over that first summer but, as the autumn days began to shorten, not unnaturally they sought warmer climes in which to over-winter. Their old friend Jimmy Mancham, now deposed President of Seychelles, came to their rescue and offered them the loan of a house in Majorca for six months. Mancham had been ousted in June 1977 by his Prime Minister, René, in an armed *coup d'état* while he was out of the country attending a Commonwealth Heads of Government Conference in the United Kingdom on the occasion of the Queen's Silver Jubilee.

When Cécile died in January 1980, Wand-Tetley inherited his mother's house in Jersey and it seemed that life on islands was confirmed. Finding himself at somewhat of a loose end in retirement, compounded by the relatively limited lifestyle often to be found on small islands, Wand-Tetley sought something to keep himself occupied. He found it in the shape of a Jersey firm of advocates, which offered him employment as a legal clerk. He found the work stimulating and just what was required in semi-retirement, for dealing with company matters on a 'tax haven' island such as Jersey proved extremely interesting.[30]

In the summer of 1981 Wand-Tetley returned with Flick to Greece on a battlefield tour of his old wartime stamping ground, the Peloponnese, staying and travelling with a Nigerian friend who had a house in Athens. He had already made an earlier trip there some years before while on leave from Kenya and had met up with his old wartime comrade-in-arms from his Peloponnese mission, George Photiades. They were particularly keen to visit the beach at Neochori, near Zakharo, where Wand-Tetley had swum out to sink the submarine. When they arrived they heard from the villagers that the wreck, which had been lying in shallow waters since the war, had only been moved the year before. In attempting to discuss the war with the Greek men of his generation, Wand-Tetley found them particularly reticent. It became clear that this was on account of the painful memories such conversation evoked with regard to the civil war that had pitted Greek against Greek.[31]

It was while he was in Jersey, in 1983, that Wand-Tetley heard from his son Charles the good news that he was now a grandfather, for Charles' wife, Jackie, had given birth to a healthy son, Michael, who was to be followed by a younger brother, Peter, three years later. In 1987 Wand-Tetley moved from Jersey with Flick to a small village in Wiltshire where he was to see out the remainder of his days. He commented upon the move in a letter to a wartime SOE comrade, Nicholas Hammond, 'My wife is inclined to regard Jersey as just another overseas posting, so the days of my humble employment in a lawyer's office are numbered and repatriation to geriatric horticulture looks inevitable.' Although Wand-Tetley may have had initial misgivings about the move to the mainland these were fairly quickly dispelled.[32]

2 June 2002: despite deteriorating health, Wand-Tetley was in particularly fine form that Sunday. There was much to celebrate. In recognition of the Queen's Golden Jubilee a Bank Holiday weekend had been granted. It was a glorious summer's day in England, the author and his wife were hosting a small lunch party in the garden of their Army married quarter in Hampshire, and all took great pleasure in toasting the Queen's health. Relaxed by the champagne, Wand-Tetley was happy to reminisce about his wartime service. His colonial service also cropped up in discussion, for it was a Nigeria reunion of sorts. It was in Port Harcourt that the author first met his future wife, Debby (née Watson-Jones), an Oxford University zoological graduate and medical graduate, now a doctor specializing in tropical medical research. Besides the Wand-Tetleys, the other guests were the author's elder sister, Sally-Anne, and her husband, Simon Sheard. Having been born in Port Harcourt, Sally-Anne had many years later also cemented her romantic intentions at the Polo Club there with Simon, who had subsequently become a Surgeon Commander in the Royal Navy. And the author and his wife, Debby, were now actively hunting for a home in East Africa.

Over lunch there was therefore much to reminisce upon and discuss, and Wand-Tetley was very happily at the centre of things. Thereafter his health gradually deteriorated and he died in Wiltshire on 16 March 2003, aged eighty-three, but that glorious summer's day will remain as an enduring memory of Wand-Tetley, as he laughed and reflected upon a life lived to the very full.

Notes

1. Notes and Interview 2008/09, Felicia Wand-Tetley with author.
2. Ibid.
3. Peter Wand-Tetley – personal papers. Also quoted in, Clark, *Was it only Yesterday? The Last Generation of Nigeria's Turawa*, Ch. 26.
4. Ibid.
5. Ibid.
6. Notes and Interview 2008/09, Felicia Wand-Tetley with author.
7. Ibid.
8. Clark, op cit, Ch. 11.
9. Huxley, *Four Guineas: A Journey through West Africa*. Ch. 4: see also: Leonard, *The Lower Niger and its Tribes* and Talbot, *Tribes of the Niger Delta: Their Religions and Customs*.
10. Peter Wand-Tetley – personal papers. Also quoted in Clark, op cit, Ch. 26.
11. Ibid.
12. Clark, op cit, Ch. 21.
13. Peter Wand-Tetley – personal papers. Also quoted in Clark, op cit, Ch. 26.
14. Peter Wand-Tetley – personal papers (personal history).
15. Notes and Interview 2008/09, Felicia Wand-Tetley with author.
16. Ibid.
17. Peter Wand-Tetley – personal papers (personal history).
18. Notes and Interview 2008/09, Felicia Wand-Tetley with author.
19. Peter Wand-Tetley – personal papers (personal history).
20. *Seychelles Bulletin*, 24 July 1972.
21. Ibid.
22. Peter Wand-Tetley – personal papers (personal history).
23. Mancham, *Paradise Raped*. Ch. 7.
24. Quoted in *The Times* 15 August 1989, Obituary, Sir Bruce Greatbatch.
25. Notes and Interview 2008/09, Felicia Wand-Tetley with author.
26. Mancham, op cit, passim.
27. See Tetley, Nigel. *Trimaran Solo: 'Victress' Round the World*.
28. See Tomalin and Hall, *The Strange Voyage of Donald Crowhurst*.
29. Peter Wand-Tetley – personal papers (personal history).
30. Ibid.
31. Ibid.
32. Ibid.

Glossary, Abbreviations and Acronyms

AAA	[Greek] Liberation Struggle Leadership (*Apeleftherosis Agon Arkhigia*)
Abwehr	German military intelligence and counter-intelligence service
ADO	Assistant District Officer
AFE	Airborne Forces Establishment
AFHQ	Allied Force Headquarters
AI	Air Intelligence
AI(10)	RAF cover name for SOE
ALC	see LCA
ALO	Allied Liaison Officer
AMACAB	Allied Military Administration Civil Affairs Bureau
AMAG	American Mission for Aid to Greece
AMFOGE	Allied Mission for Observing the Greek Elections
AMM	Allied Military Mission
APTC	Army Physical Training Corps (now Royal Army Physical Training Corps)
BEF	British Expeditionary Force
BLA	British Liberation Army [South East Asia]
BLO	British Liaison Officer
BMM	British Military Mission
C	symbol for head of SIS/MI6
Caique	Greek trading and fishing schooners, often fitted with diesel engines
C-in-C	Commander-in-Chief
CBTC	Commando Basic Training Centre
CCO	Chief Combined Operations
CD	symbol for executive head of SOE
CLE	Central Landing Establishment
CLS	Central Landing School
CMWTC	Commando Mountain Warfare Training Camp
CO	Commanding Officer
COHQ	Combined Operations Headquarters
COTDC	Combined Operations Training Development Centre
CIGS	Chief of the Imperial General Staff

CRA	Commander Royal Artillery
CTC	Combined Training Centre
Section D	MI6 sabotage section, and precursor to SOE
DCO	Dominion & Commonwealth Overseas [Barclays Bank]
DCO	Director Combined Operations
DO	District Officer
DFC	Distinguished Flying Cross
DMI	Director/Directorate of Military Intelligence
DMO	Director of Military Operations
DNI	Director/Directorate of Naval Intelligence
DU	Development Unit
DZ	Dropping Zone (for parachute operations)
EAC	East African Community
EAM	[Greek] National Liberation Front (*Ethniko Apeleftherotiko Metopo*)
EACSO	East African Common Services Organisation
EDES	[Greek] National Democratic Greek League (*Ethnikos Dimokratikos Syndesmos*)
EH	Elektra House, and precursor to SOE London
EKKA	[Greek]) National and Social Liberation (*Ethniki kai Koinoniki Apeleftherosis*)
ELAS	National Popular Liberation Army (*Ethnikos Laikos Apeleftherotikos Stratos*)
EOEA	National Bands of Greek Guerillas
EOM	National Organisation of Magnetes
Fallschirmjäger	German term for paratrooper; literally 'parachute-hunter'
Flak	anti-aircraft fire (from the German *fliegerabwehrkanone*)
FO	Foreign Office
Force 133	SOE Cairo cover name, from Nov 1943
Freya	German acquisition (long-range) radar
GC & CS	Government Code and Cipher School (at Bletchley Park)
Gestapo	Nazi secret state police (*Geheime Staatspolizei*)
GHQ	General Headquarters – [Middle East]
GOC	General Officer Commanding
G(R)	General Staff (Research) – [formerly MI(R) and precursor to SOE Cairo]
G (RF)	General Staff (Raiding Forces) – [branch of GHQ Middle East]
GSO1	General Staff Officer Grade 1 – [i.e. lieutenant colonel rank]
GS(R)	General Staff (Research) – [branch of War Office]
GTS	Glider Training Squadron
HAC	Honourable Artillery Company
HQ	Headquarters
ISRB	Inter-Services Research Bureau (SOE cover name)
ISTDC	Inter-Services Training and Development Centre
KKE	Communist Party of Greece (*Kommounistiko Komma Elladas*)
LCA	Landing Craft, Assault
LCM	Landing Craft, Motor
LCS	London Controlling Section (a.k.a. the deception service)
LRDG	Long Range Desert Group
LZ	Landing Zone (for glider operations)
M	symbol for director of operations and training of SOE

ME 102	Military Establishment 102 (SOE STS, Mount Carmel, Haifa)
MEW	Minister/Ministry of Economic Warfare
MI	Military Intelligence
MI5	Security Service
MI6	Secret Intelligence Service
MI9	Escape Service
MI(R)	Military Intelligence (Research), and precursor to SOE London
MLC	see LCM
MNBDO	Mobile Naval Base Defence Organization
MO	Military Operations – (branch of the War Office)
MO1(SP)	Military Operations 1 (Special Projects) (War Office cover name for SOE)
MO4	formerly D Section, and precursor to SOE Cairo
MTB	Motor Torpedo Boat
NA	Native Authorities
NID	Naval Intelligence Department
NID(Q)	Admiralty cover name for SOE
OCTU	Officer Cadet Training Unit
OSS	Office of Strategic Services [USA equivalent to SOE]
PAO	[Greek] Pan-Hellenic Liberation Organization (*Panelliniki Apeleftherotiki Organosis*)
PEEA	[Greek] Political Committee of Greek Resistance/or National Resistance
PIAT	Projector Infantry Anti-Tank
PJI	Parachute Jumping Instructor
POW	Prisoner of War
PTS	Parachute Training School
PWE	Political Warfare Executive
RA	Royal Artillery
RAF	Royal Air Force
RAPWI	Recovered Allied Prisoners of War and Internees
RASC	Royal Army Service Corps
(R)DF	(radio) direction finding
RE	Royal Engineers
RGS	Royal Geographical Society
RHA	Royal Horse Artillery
RIA	Royal Indian Artillery
Rip-cord	Manual device for deploying parachute canopy
RSR	Raiding Support Regiment
RSS	Radio Security Service
RTU	Returned to Unit
SAS	Special Air Service
SBS	Special Boat Section/Squadron/Service
SD	German Nazi Security Service (*Sicherheitsdienst*)
SDO	Senior District Officer
SDP	Seychelles Democratic Party
SEAC	South East Asia Command
SIG	Special Interrogation Group
SIS	Secret Intelligence Service [MI6]
SMLE	Short Magazine Lee-Enfield (rifle)

SO	Symbol of ministerial head of SOE
SO	Special Operations
SOE	Special Operations Executive
SOM	Special Operations Mediterranean
SPUP	Seychelles People's United Party
SS	Special Service (British, as in Special Service Battalion)
SS	German Nazi military force, with the mission of protecting Hitler and protecting the Reich (*Shutzstaffel*)
SSR	Special Service Regiment
Static Line	Strap or cord linking parachute to aircraft, allowing automatic canopy opening
Stick	A group of paratroopers due to drop in a single aircraft run over a DZ
STS	Special Training School (SOE)
TEWTS	Tactical Exercises Without Troops
TRE	Telecommunications Research Establishment
USAAF	US Army Air Forces
VE Day	Victory in Europe Day
VP	Vulnerable Point
WD	War Department
W/T	Wireless Telegraphy
Würzburg	German narrow-beam gun-laying radar
YVE	[Greek] Defenders of Northern Greece (*Yperaaspistasi Voreiou Ellados*)

Bibliography

Almonds Windmill, L., *Gentleman Jim. The Wartime Story of a Founder of the SAS and Special Forces* (Constable & Robinson, 2002)
——, *A British Achilles. The Story of George, 2nd Earl Jellicoe* (Pen & Sword, 2005)
Amery, J., *Sons of the Eagle. A study in Guerrilla War* (Macmillan, 1948)
Antill, P., *Crete 1941. Germany's Lightening Airborne Assault* (Osprey Publishing, 2005)
Asher, M., *Get Rommel. The Secret British Mission to Kill Hitler's Greatest General* (Weidenfeld & Nicolson, 2004)
——, *The Regiment. The Real Story of the SAS: The First Fifty Years* (Viking, 2007)
Atherton, L., *SOE Operations in Africa and the Middle East. A Guide to the Records in the Public Record Office* (PRO Publications, 1998)
——, *SOE Operations in the Balkans. A Guide to the Records in the Public Record Office* (PRO Publications, 1998)
Auty, P. and Clogg, R., (eds.) *British Policy towards Wartime Resistance in Yugoslavia and Greece* (London University Press/Methuen, 1975)
Baerentzen, L., (ed). *British Reports on Greece 1943–44* (Museum Tusculanum Press, 1982)
Barker, E., *British Policy in South-East Europe in the Second World War* (Macmillan, 1976)
Bailey, R., *The Wildest Province. SOE in the Land of the Eagle* (Jonathan Cape, 2008)
Beckett, I. F. W., *Territorials. A Century of Service* (DRA Publishing, 2008)
Beevor, A., *Crete. The Battle and the Resistance* (John Murray Publishers, 1992)
Beevor, J. G., *SOE. Recollections and Reflections 1940–45* (Bodley Head Ltd, 1981)
Bradford, R. and Dillon, M., *Rogue Warrior of the SAS. Lt Col 'Paddy' Blair Mayne* (John Murray, 1987)
Buckingham, W. F., *Paras. The Birth of British Airborne Forces from Churchill's Raiders to 1st Parachute Brigade* (Tempus, 2005)
——, *The Creation and Development of British Airborne Forces 1941–1945* (MLRS Books, 2006)
Buckley, C., *Greece and Crete 1941* (HMSO, 1952)
Buckmaster, M., *Specially Employed* (Batchworth Press, 1952)
Byrne, J. V., *The General Salutes a Soldier. With the SAS and Commandos in World War Two* (London, 1986)
Chappell, M., *Army Commandos 1940–45* (Osprey Publishing, 1996)
Chrichton Stuart, M., *G Patrol* (William Kimber & Co Ltd, 1958)

Churchill, W., *The Second World War. Volumes 2 and 3* (Cassell, 1950)

Clark, T., (ed.) *Was it only Yesterday? The Last Generation of Nigeria's Turawa* (BECM Press, 2002)

Clive, N., *A Greek Experience 1943–1948* (Michael Russell, 1985)

Connor, K., *Ghost Force. The Secret History of the SAS* (London, 1998)

——, *Ghosts. An Illustrated Story of the SAS* (London, 1998)

Cookridge, E. H., *Inside SOE* (Arthur Barker, 1966)

Cooper, A., *Cairo in the War 1939–1945* (Hamish Hamilton, 1989)

Cooper, J., *One of the Originals. The Story of a Founder Member of the SAS* (Pan, 1991)

Courtney, G. B,. *SBS in World War Two. The Story of the Original Special Boat Section of the Army Commandos* (Robert Hale, 1983)

Close, R., *In Action with the SAS. A Soldier's Odyssey from Dunkirk to Berlin* (Pen & Sword, 1994)

Cowles, V., *The Phantom Major. The Story of David Stirling and the SAS Regiment* (Collins, 1958)

Croix, Philip de Ste., (ed.) *Airborne Operations* (Salamander Books Ltd, 1978)

Crookenden, N., *Drop Zone Normandy* (Ian Allen Ltd, 1976)

——, *Airborne at War* (Ian Allen Ltd, 1978)

——, *Battle of the Bulge 1944* (Ian Allen Ltd, 1980)

Curtis, H., *A Pedigree of The Tathams of County Durham* (Privately Published, 1927)

Dalton, H., *The Fateful Years. Memoirs 1931–1945* (Muller, 1957)

Davidson, B., *Special Operations Europe. Scenes from the Anti-Nazi War* (Gollancz, 1980)

Deakin, F. W. D., *The Embattled Mountain* (Oxford OUP, 1971)

De Gramont, S., *The Story of the Niger River. The Strong Brown God* (Hart Davis, 1975)

Derbyshire, J. D. and Derbyshire I., *Political Systems of the World* (Helicon, 1996)

Dugan, S., *Commando. The Elite Fighting Forces of the Second World War* (Macmillan, 2001)

Dunning, J., *It had to be tough* (Pentland Press, 2000)

Durnford-Slater, J., *Commando* (William Kimber & Co Ltd, 1953)

Ferguson, Gregor. *The Paras. British Airborne Forces 1940–84* (Osprey, 1984)

Fileding, X., *Hide and Seek* (Secker & Warburg, 1954)

Foot, M. R. D., *An Outline History of the Special Operations Executive 1940–46* (BBC Books, 1984)

Fowler, W., *SAS. Behind Enemy Lines. Covert Operations 1941–2005* (Collins, 2005)

Gale, R., *With the 6th Airborne Division in Normandy* (Sampson Low, Marston & Co. 1948)

——, *Call to Arms. An Autobiography* (Hutchinson & Co, 1968)

Garnett, D. *The Secret History of PWE 1939–45. The Political Warfare Executive 1939–45* (St Ermins, 2002)

Gibson, T., *Famous Regiments. The Wiltshire Regiment* (Leo Cooper, 1969)

Greenacre, J., *Churchill's Spearhead. The Development of Britain's Airborne Capability During the Second World War II* (Pen & Sword, 2010)

Hammond, N., *Venture into Greece. With the Guerillas 1943–44* (William Kimber, 1983)

Hamson, D., *We Fell Among Greeks* (Jonathan Cape, 1946)

Harclerode, P., *Go To It! The Illustrated History of The 6th Airborne Division* (Bloomsbury, 1990)

——, *Para! Fifty Years of the Parachute Regiment* (Cassell, 1992)

Harling, W. F., (ed.) *Marlborough College. The Corps 1860–1960* (Marlborough College, 1960)

Harrison, D. I., *These Men are Dangerous. The SAS at War* (Cassell, 1957)

Hastings, S., *The Drums of Memory. An Autobiography* (Pen & Sword, 1994)

Hinsley, F. H., *British Intelligence in the Second World War. Its Influence on Strategy and Operations* (HMSO, 1984)

Hoare, M., *The Seychelles Affair* (Bantam Press, 1986)

Hoe, A., *David Stirling. The Authorised Biography of the Creator of the SAS* (Little Brown, 1992)

Howarth, P., (ed.) *Special Operations* (Routledge & Kegan Paul, 1955)

Howarth, P., *Undercover. The Men and Women of the Special Operations Executive* (Routledge & Kegan Paul, 1980)

Huxley, E., *Four Guineas. A Journey through West Africa* (Chatto & Windus, 1954)

——, *Nine Faces of Kenya* (Harper Collins, 1990)

Jackson, R., *The Secret Squadrons. Special Duty Units of the RAF and USAAF in the Second World War* (Robson Books, 1983)

James, M., [Pleydell, M.,] *Born of the Desert. With the SAS in North Africa* (Collins 1945)

Johnson, R. F., *Regimental Fire! The Honourable Artillery Company in World War II, 1939–1945* (Williams Lea & Co., 1958)

Jones, T., *SAS Zero Hour. The Secret Origins of the Special Air Service* (Greenhill, 2006)

Jordan, B., *Conquest Without Victory* (Hodder & Stoughton, 1969)

Kelly, S., *The Hunt for Zerzura. The Lost Oasis and the Desert War* (Butler & Tanner, 2002)

Kennedy Shaw, W. B., *Long Range Desert Group. The Story of its Work in Libya 1940–1943* (Collins 1945)

Kemp, A., *The SAS at War 1941–1945.* (Penguin, 1991)

Kenrick, N. C. E., *The Story of The Wiltshire Regiment (Duke of Edinburgh's)* (Gale & Polden, 1963)

Keyes, E., *Geoffrey Keyes VC* (George Newnes Ltd, 1956)

Ladd, J. D., *SAS Operations. More than Daring* (Robert Hale, 1986)

Langley, M., *Anders Lassen VC MC of the SAS* (New English Library, 1988)

Lee, C., *Seychelles. Political Castaways* (Elm Tree, 1976)

Leeper, Sir Reginald., *When Greek meets Greek* (London, 1950)

Leonard, A. G., *The Lower Niger and its Tribes* (Macmillan, 1906)

Lewes, J., *Jock Lewes. Co-founder of the SAS* (Pen & Sword, 2000)

Lloyd Owen, D., *The Desert My Dwelling Place* (Cassell, 1957)

——, *Providence Their Guide. The Long Range Desert Group 1940–45* (Harrap, 1980)

Lodwick, J., *The Filibusters* (Methuen & Co Ltd, 1947)

Lovat, The Lord. *March Past* (Weidenfeld & Nicolson, 1978)

Macdonald, C., *The Lost Battle. Crete 1941* (Papermac, 1995)

Mackenzie, W. J. M., *First Athenian Memories* (Cassell, 1931)

——, *The Secret History of SOE. The Special Operations Executive 1940–45* (St Ermin's Press, 2000)

Maclean, F., *Eastern Approaches* (Jonathan Cape, 1949)

Maine, I., *Aldershot. A Military Town* (Tempus Publishing, 2002)

Mancham, J. R., *Paradise Raped. Life, Love and Power in the Seychelles* (Methuen, 1983)

Marks, L., *Between Silk and Cyanide. A Codemaker's War 1941–1945* (Harper Collins, 1998)

Marrinan, P., *Colonel Paddy. The Man Who Dared* (Ulster Press, 1960)

Mather, C., *When the Grass Stops Growing. A War Memoire* (Pen & Sword, 1997)

Messenger, C., *The Commandos 1940–46* (William Kimber & Co Ltd, 1985)

——, *The Middle East Commandos* (Michael Joseph Ltd, 1949)

Michel, H., *The Shadow of War. Resistance in Europe 1939–1945* (André Deutsch, 1972)

Montgomery, B. L. *The Memoirs of Field Marshal The Viscount Montgomery of Alamein* (Collins, 1958)

Moorehead, A., *African Trilogy. The Desert War 1940–1943* (Hamish Hamilton, 1944)

Moreman, T., *British Commandos 1940–46* (Osprey Publishing, 2006).

Mortimer, G., *Stirling's Men. The Inside History of the SAS in World War II* (Cassell, 2005)

Morgan, M., *Sting of the Scorpion. The Inside Story of the Long Range Desert Group* (Sutton, 2000)

Morris, E., *Guerrillas in Uniform. Churchill's Private Armies in the Middle East and the War Against Japan 1940–1945* (Hutchinson, 1989)

Moss, W. S., *Ill Met by Moonlight* (Harrap, 1950)

Mulgan, J., *Report on Experience* (Oxford, 1947)

Myers, E. C. W., *Greek Entanglement* (Hart Davis, 1955)

Neillands, R., *The Raiders. Army Commandos 1940–46* (Weidenfeld & Nicolson, 1989)

Newnham, M., *Prelude to Glory. The Story of the Creation of Britain's Parachute Army* (Sampson Low, Marston & Co, 1947)

Norton, G. G., *Famous Regiments. The Red Devils. The Story of the British Airborne Forces* (Leo Cooper, 1971)

Oldfield, E. A. L., *History of the Army Physical Training Corps* (Gale & Polden, 1955)

Otway, T. B. H., *The Second World War 1939–1945, Army. Airborne Forces* (The War Office, 1951)

Pine-Coffin, R. G., *The Tale of Two Bridges* (Petworth. Pine-Coffin, 2003)

Pitt, B., *The Crucible of War. Western Desert 1941* (Jonathan Cape, 1980)

——, *The Crucible of War. Year of Alamein 1942* (Jonathan Cape, 1980)

——, *Special Boat Squadron. The Story of the SBS in the Mediterranean* (Century, 1983)

Peniakoff, V., *Popski's Private Army* (Oxford University Press, 1991)

Poett, N., *Pure Poett. The Autobiography of General Sir Nigel Poett* (Leo Cooper, 1991)

Psychoundaki G., *The Cretan Runner* (Faber, 1978)

Ranfurly, Countess., *To War with Whitaker. The Wartime Diaries of the Countess of Ranfurly 1939–45* (Heinemann, 1994)

Reynolds, D., *Paras. An Illustrated History of Britain's Airborne Forces* (Sutton, 1998)

Richards, B., *Secret Flotillas* (HMSO, 1976)

Rootham, J., *Miss Fire* (Chatto & Windus, 1946)

Ross, H., *Paddy Mayne. Lt Col Blair 'Paddy' Mayne, 1 SAS Regiment* (Sutton Publishing Ltd, 2003)

Sadleir, R., *Tanzania. Journey to Republic* (Radcliffe Press, 1999)

Sarafis, M., (ed.) *Greece. From Resistance to Civil War* (Russell Press, 1980)

Saunders, H. St. G., *The Green Beret. The Story of the Commandos 1940–1945* (Michael Joseph Ltd, 1949).

——, *The Red Beret. The Story of the Parachute Regiment at War 1940–45* (Michael Joseph, 1950)

Seymour, W., *British Special Forces* (Sidgwick & Jackson, 1985)

Shortt, J. G., *The Special Air Service* (Osprey Publishing, 1981)

Stafford, D., *Britain and European Resistance 1940–1945. A Survey of the SOE with Documents* (Macmillan, 1980/83)

——, *Secret Agent. The True Story of the SOE* (BBC Books, 2000)

Stevens, G., *The Originals. The Secret History of the Birth of the SAS in their Own Words* (London, 2005)

Stewart, I. McD. G., *The Struggle for Crete, 20 May–1 June 1941* (OUP 1966)

Strawson, J., *A History of the SAS Regiment* (Guild Publishing Ltd, 1985)

Sutherland, D., *He Who Dares. Recollections of Service in the SAS, SBS and MI5* (Leo Cooper, 1998)

Sweet-Escott, B., *Greece. A Political and Economic Survey* (Royal Institute of International Affairs, 1954)

——, *Baker Street Irregular* (Methuen, 1965)

Sykes, C., *Evelyn Waugh* (Collins, 1975)

Talbot, P. A., *Tribes of the Niger Delta. Their Religions and Customs* (Sheldon, 1932)

Tatham, F. S., *A Memoire* (Privately Published, 1934)

——, (ed.) *In Memoriam. Sub-Lieutenant W. Tatham RN, And Second-Lieutenant E. V. Tatham* (Privately Published, 1916)

Tetley, N., *Trimaran Solo. 'Victress' Round the World* (Nautical Publishing Co, 1970)

Thesiger, W., *A Life of My Choice* (London, 1987)

Thompson, J., *War Behind Enemy Lines* (Sidgwick & Jackson, 1998)

——, *The Parachute Regiment at War 1940–1982. Ready for Anything* (Weidenfeld & Nicolson, 1989)

Timpson, A., with Gibson-Watt, A., *In Rommel's Backyard. A Memoir of the Long Range Desert Group* (Barnsley, 2000)

Tomalin, N. and Hall, R., *The Strange Voyage of Donald Crowhurst* (Hodder & Stoughton, 1970)

Turner, D., *Aston House, Station 12, SOE's Secret Centre* (Sutton Publishing, 2006)

Warner, P., *The Special Air Service* (Kimber & Co Ltd, 1971)

——, *The Secret Forces of World War II* (Granada, 1985)

Waugh, E., Davie, M. (ed.) *The Diaries of Evelyn Waugh* (Weidenfeld &Nicholson, 1976)

Waugh, E., Amory, M. (ed.) *The Letters of Evelyn Waugh* (Weidenfeld & Nicholson, 1980)

West, N., *Secret War. The Story of SOE* (Hodder & Stoughton, 1992)

Wilkinson, Sir Peter, and Astley, J. B., *Gubbins and SOE* (Leo Cooper, 1993)

Wilson, Field Marshal, the Lord. *Eight Years Overseas 1939–1947* (London, 1956)

Woodhouse, C. M., *Apple of Discord. A Survey of Recent Greek Politics in their International Setting* (Hutchinson, 1948)

——, *European Resistance Movements* (Permagon Press, 1960)

——, *The Struggle for Greece 1941–49* (Hart Davis MacGibbon, 1976)

——, *Something Ventured* (Granada, 1982)

Wynter, H. W., *Special Forces in the Desert War 1940–1943* (PRO War Histories, 2002)

Young, P., *Commando* (Macdonald & Co, 1970)

——, *Storm from the Sea* (Greenhill Books, 1989)

War Office, *By Air to Battle. The Official Account of the British 1st and 6th Airborne Divisions* (HMSO, 1945)

Articles

Clogg, R., 'Pearls from Swine'. *The Foreign Office Papers, SOE and the Greek Resistance*, (paper in Auty, P. and Clogg, R.)

Deakin, F. W. D., *The Myth of an Allied Landing in the Balkans during the Second World War*, (paper in Auty, P. and Clogg, R.)

Myers, E. C. W., *The Andarte Delegation to Cairo: August 1943.* (paper in Auty, P. and Clogg, R.)

Sweet-Escott, B., *SOE in the Balkans*, (paper in Auty, P. and Clogg, R.)

Woodhouse., C. M., *Summer 1943. The Critical Months*, (paper in Auty, P. and Clogg, R.)

Booklets, Newspapers

Wand-Tetley, P. M., *Sport Fishing in Seychelles*, (Seychelles Tourism Department, 1974)

Seychelles Weekly

National Archives, Kew

Cabinet Office Papers

CAB 44/151, history of Long Range Desert Group, Jun 1940-Mar 1943

CAB 44/152, history of Commandos and Special Service Troops in the Middle East and North Africa, Jan 1941-Apr 1943

CAB 106/3, history of Combined Operations Organisation, 1940–1945

CAB 120/414, Combined Operations, Jun 1940-Nov 1943

CAB 120/262, Airborne Forces, Jun 1940-Nov 1946

War Office Papers

WO 166/1462, WO 166/6964, WO 175/307, WO 169/9462, WO 170/918, WO 170/4832, war diary 12th (HAC) Regiment RHA

WO 365/77, WO 365/152, WO 365/163, WO 365/193, WO 365/195, WO 365/196, war diary OCTUs, strength and situation reports

WO 95/1415, WO 95/2243, WO 95/2165, war diary 1st Battalion The Wiltshire Regiment, Aug 1914-May 1919

WO 166/9015, WO 167/844, WO 167/845, 169/5072, 169/10307, 169/16331, 170/1489, WO 171/5289, WO 174/37, war diary 2nd Battalion The Wiltshire Regiment, 1939–1946

WO 193/384, Independent Companies (memorandum dated 13 Jun 1940), Jun–Dec 1940

WO 260/3, irregular operations by Independent Companies, Apr 1940

WO 260/32, Special Infantry and Independent Companies, Apr–May 1940

DEFE 2/4, war diary Combined Operations HQ (Col Dudley Account, 30 Oct 1942), 1942

DEFE 2/45, war diary No. 4 Special Service Battalion, Nov 1940–Feb 1941

WO 218/152, war diary No. 3 Special Service Battalion, Nov 1940–Feb 1941

WO 201/717, personal papers Commander's (Lt Col Laycock) Layforce, 24 Jun–15 Jul 1941

WO 218/166, war diary HQ 'Z' Force (later Layforce), Jan–Jul 1941

WO 218/168, war diary Layforce 'A' Battalion (No. 7 Commando), Jan–May 1941

WO 218/169, war diary Layforce 'B' Battalion (No. 8 Commando), May–Jun 1941

WO 218/170, war diary Layforce 'B' Battalion (No. 8 Commando), Jan–Mar 1941

WO 218/171, war diary Layforce 'C' Battalion (No. 11 Commando), Mar–Oct 1941

WO 218/172, war diary Layforce 'D' Battalion (No. 52 (ME) Commando/'A' Battalion (No. 7 Commando)), Dec 1940–Jun 1941

WO 218/158, war diary Middle East Commando Depot, Jan–Dec 1941

WO 218/159, war diary Middle East Commando Depot/Middle East Commando, Jan–Jun 1942

WO 218/160, war diary Middle East Commando 'A' Sqn, May–Jun 1942

WO 218/161, war diary Middle East Commando 'B' Sqn, Apr–May 1942

WO 218/149, war diary 1 Special Service Regiment, Jul–Oct 1942

WO 218/150, war diary 1 Special Service Regiment 'A' Sqn, Aug–Oct 1942

WO 218/151, war diary 1 Special Service Regiment 'B' Sqn, Jun–Oct 1942

WO 218/96, war diary 1 SAS, Oct–Dec 1942

WO 218/97, war diary 1 SAS, Jan–Apr 1943

WO 218/106, M Detachment 1 SAS, Feb 1943

WO 218/173, operational reports, L Detachment SAS Brigade, Jul 1942

WO 201/721, brief history, L Detachment SAS Brigade and 1 SAS Regiment 1941–1942

WO 201/743, operation instruction, Raiding Forces GHQ, Sep–Oct 1942   .

WO 201/747, battle file SAS, Oct–Nov 1942

WO 201/752, appointment of Commander Raiding Forces, Oct–Nov 1942

WO 201/773, future policy of SAS, formation of Squadron in PAIC, Nov 1942–Apr 1943

WO 201/785, history L Detachment SAS Brigade, May–Jun 1943

WO 204/8857, political and economic intelligence, Peloponnese, 1943–1944

WO 204/8879, political, economic and general information, Peloponnese, 1944

WO 373/46, combatant gallantry awards (P. M. Wand-Tetley, MC citation)

WO 203/6011, 5 Parachute Brigade, report on activities in Semarang, Jan–May 1946

WO 203/2410, 5 Parachute Brigade, airborne formations, Dec 1945–Mar 1946

WO 203/2587, 5 Parachute Brigade, organisation and movement, Nov 1945–Jun 1946

WO 203/2661, 5 Parachute Brigade, operation reports, Nov 1945–Apr 1946

WO 203/6356, 5 Parachute Brigade, operation instructions, Jan–Mar 1946

WO 203/6357, 5 Parachute Brigade, operation situation reports, Feb–Apr 1946

WO 171/1239, war diary 7th Parachute (LI) Battalion, Jan–Dec 1944

WO 172/7684, war diary 7th Parachute (LI) Regiment, Jul–Dec 1945

WO 223/18, story of 7th Battalion (LI) Parachute Regiment, 1943–44

WO 172/7685, war diary 12th Parachute Regiment, Jul–Dec 1945

WO 172/7686, war diary 13th Parachute Regiment, Sep–Dec 1945

Foreign Office Papers

FO 286/1169, political situation in Peloponnese, 1945

FO 286/1181, Peloponnese, political and general situation, 1946

Prime Minister's Papers

PREM 2/159, honours lists and papers 1965, (PM Wand-Tetley's OBE citation)

SOE Papers

HS 5/546, signals to and from field

HS 5/227, review of Force 133 Activities in Greece 1944 by Lt Col Dolbey, report on Greece by Brig. Woodhouse 1944–1945

HS 5/278, Peloponnese, political aspects, 1943–1944

HS 5/626, Peloponnese, main and local resistance groups, 1944–1945

HS 5/637, Peloponnese, general reports on activities, 1943–1945

HS 5/698, Peloponnese, Area 5 Peloponnese; personnel A-K, report by Capt. Fraser, SOE Activities in the Peloponnese 1943–44 by Capt. Fraser, 1944

HS 5/699, Peloponnese, Area 5 Peloponnese; personnel M-W, report by Lt Col McMullen, report by Maj. Reid and George Photiades, report by Yannopoulos, report by Capt. Wand-Tetley, 1944–1945

HS 7/150, SOE activities in Greece 1940–1942 (Ch. 1–6) by Maj. Ian Pirie

HS 7/152, Inside Greece, a review by Brig. Myers, report on SOE Activities in Greece and Aegean Islands by Lt Col Dolbey, 1943–1945

HS 7/153, report on SOE Activities in Greece and Aegean Islands by Lt Col Dolbey (continued), appendices V–XIII, 1945

HS 9/1453/7, Peter Michael Wand-Tetley, 1939–1946

HS 9/1243/8, William Frederick Reid, 1939–1946

HS 9/70/3, Maxwell Vaughan Backhouse, 1939–1946

Personnel Files
Army Service Record (Army Form B199A) of Wand-Tetley, P. M.

London Gazette
ZJ1/1234/1235/1236 (*London Gazette*), notice of OBE award to Wand-Tetley, P. M.

Imperial War Museum Archives, London
Imperial War Museum, photographs

National Army Museum Archives, London
Middle East Commando Historical Research Group (MECHRG) papers
MECHRG document No. 67108, Young, G. A. D. and Rose, S. M., 1 Apr 1983

Marlborough College Archives
Archive notes compiled by Rogers, Dr. T., (archivist, Marlborough College)
The Marlburian, Aug 1935 (shooting), and Nov 1936 (fencing)
Marlborough College Photograph Album V, sports and prefects 1930–1937

Downing College Archives, Cambridge University
Archive notes compiled by Thompson, K., (archivist, Downing College)
Downing College, Cambridge, Wand-Tetley, P. M., Tutorial File, Ref. No. DCAT/1/2/2060
The Griffin (student magazine), Michaelmas 1938; Lent 1939

Honourable Artillery Company Archives, London
Archive notes compiled by Taylor, J., (archivist, HAC)

Wiltshire Regiment Archives (at The Rifles Museum), Salisbury
Transcripts, history and war diary 1st Battalion The Wiltshire Regiment, 1914 to 1919

Transcripts, history and war diary 2nd Battalion The Wiltshire Regiment, 1939 to
  1946
The Journal of The Wiltshire Regiment, 1933–1935

Royal Army Physical Training Corps Museum Archives, Aldershot

Archive notes compiled by Kelly, R., curator, Royal Army Physical Training Corps
  Museum, Aldershot

Correspondence

Carter (née Tatham), A., letter to the author, dated 30 Mar 2009
Wand-Tetley, P. M., letter to his great-niece Sheard, H., dated 7 Jun 2000

Index

Military ranks given are those finally achieved, where known.

216

220

INDEX OF OPERATIONAL CODENAMES